THE
DUNDEE
WHALERS

THE DUNDEE WHALERS

1750–1914

Norman Watson

TUCKWELL PRESS

First published in Great Britain in 2003 by
Tuckwell Press Ltd
The Mill House
Phantassie
East Linton
East Lothian, Scotland

ISBN 1 86232 207 4

British Library Cataloguing-in-Publication Data

A catalogue record of this book is available
on request from the British Library

Typeset by Hewer Text Ltd, Edinburgh
Printed and bound by The Cromwell Press, Trowbridge, Wiltshire

Contents

Illustrations

Maps and Tables

Acknowledgements

Many institutions, members of the public, colleagues and friends helped with this work. Among them, I am indebted to the archivists and librarians of Broughty Castle Museum, Dundee Museum and Art Galleries, Dundee City Archives, the University of Dundee Archives, Perth Museum and Art Galleries, Montrose Museum and the National Libraries of Scotland. I should especially like to thank Eileen Moran, Deirdre Sweeney and the staff of the Local Studies department, Dundee Central Libraries for their guidance, and my colleagues at D. C. Thomson & Co Ltd for support when most required. Among members of the public who showed a keen interest in the work and who contributed useful information were Captain Austin Murray, Isobel Walker and James W. Barrie. Friends who generously offered support included Ian Hendry, David Torrie and Laurence Patton. Careful help with the preparation of the text was cheerfully given by Shirley E. Blair and indexing was completed by Linda Caston, whom I must also thank for her patient tolerance of authorship. No history of Dundee whaling would have been possible without the notes compiled by the late John Ingram and the research carried out by David Henderson of Dundee Museums.

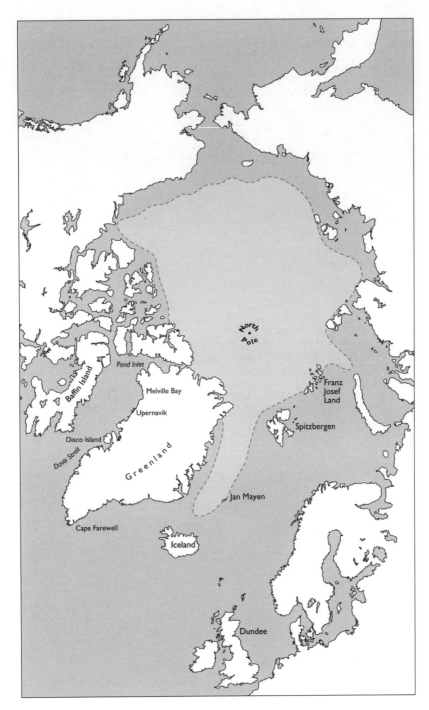

Map 1. The Arctic

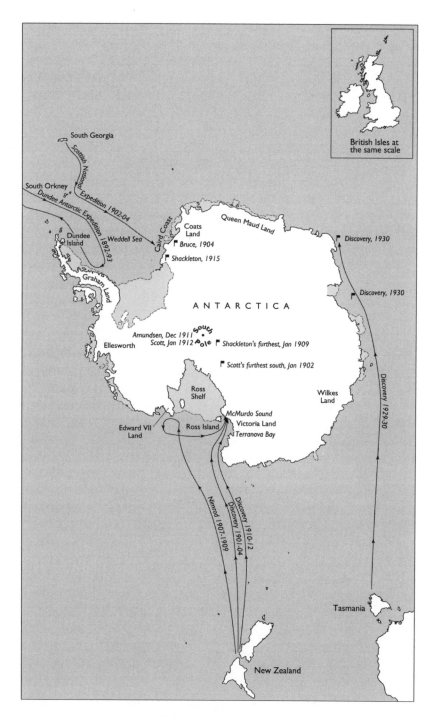

Map 2. The Antarctic

Introduction

The wrecks of 40 Dundee whalers lie beneath the ice of the Arctic whaling grounds. Almost without exception the stout, wooden-hulled ships of the town met their fate crushed by converging floes, swelling the number of vessels that had 'left their bones in the battlefield of Melville Bay'.

The rugged, hard-muscled Dundee crews who launched the city's whaling interests 250 years ago in 1753 lived with the ever-present prospect of danger, deprivation and death. A harpooned whale could upset a flimsy whaleboat, dumping men into freezing water that killed them in seconds, but the greatest fear was being imprisoned in ice. Ships 'beset' offered only a terrible ordeal, leaving sailors stranded in an unknown land with few skills essential for survival. Many men lost limbs from frostbite or faced the 'death monster' scurvy. James McIntosh of the *Chieftain* watched four comrades drinking seawater in his stranded open boat and die one by one, insane. Left to his loneliness, he ate his hat and survived, but had both frostbitten legs removed on his return to Dundee. Journals written by numbed fingers tell of the barely living taking off the clothes of those who dropped dead in front of them. After one Newfoundland disaster 25 bodies lay in a frozen mass and had to be cut apart and thawed before being placed in coffins.

Captains and crews took themselves to these limits of human endurance in order to reap the enormous profits of the catch. Arctic whaling was a means to acquire wealth, and for the participants it was often as profitable as it was dangerous, a journey of exhilaration, a life of adventure and of hard-earned success. Whaling anticipated the wealth of the North Sea era of oil and gas and of industrial plastics. Whale oil lit up British cities and rural lamps, lubricated the Industrial Revolution, provided the soap to wash off factory grime and eventually smoothed the process of jute production in Dundee. At the Dundee quayside whalebone changed hands for up to £3000 a ton as the expanding Victorian middle classes demanded waist-tightening undergarments. So the men who signed articles in the whale company offices around Dundee's docks could earn more in an Arctic season than in years in the jute mills. Everyone from the captain to the ship's apprentice received a share of the catch. Owners and crew were ever willing to speculate to accumulate.

Whaling today is socially, morally and ethically unacceptable to many people. It remains an emotion-charged subject engendering debate among conservationists, scientists, biologists and governments. Some whale populations remain fragile after indiscriminate hunting, now outlawed by the International Whaling Commission through a moratorium agreed by all but a handful of nations. In the eighteenth and nineteenth centuries, however, whale hunting was viewed as a strategically important industry and it involved hundreds of ships, thousands of men, and innumerable jobs in ports on both sides of the Atlantic. In charting the history of a fleet which participated in Arctic whaling longer than any other, we can perhaps place ourselves dispassionately back in time and not judge the past by today's standards.

The chief quarry of the Dundee whalers was *Balaena mysticetus*, the Greenland Right whale, so called to distinguish it from the wrong one to catch. It was 'right' in that it was slow-moving, easy to hunt and floated when it was dead. This docile giant possessed a fortune in its cavernous upper jaw – overlapping plates of springy, tough baleen which was valued like a currency as demand grew for corsets and other flexible products. No other whale had such a mass of 'bone', making the Right whale a prime commercial target. Its heavy layer of fat, or blubber, was another valuable commodity when boiled to oil.

Right whales, however, could be found only on their migratory routes in largely uncharted Arctic waters. Ocean currents and polar winds meant masters needed navigational expertise, seamanship and leadership qualities to get them beyond mountainous seas to the whaling grounds, and once there, with lances sharpened in anticipation, to penetrate the pounding pack ice in pursuit of their brutal calling. Ships failed to return almost every year. Many were helplessly imprisoned. One Dundee whaler, the *Advice*, lost 59 men out of 69 in 1837. But the *Advice* made another 22 trips to the Arctic before being lost after 74 years' service. Her story is typical of the fortitude and depths of courage shown by the whale men of Dundee.

At first the Dutch were the dominant whalers, but their navy's defeat by the British in 1797, led by Admiral Duncan of Dundee, meant that large numbers of their ships were seized and they quickly lost their status as industry leaders to English ships from London and Hull. Boosted by a Government cash bounty, the Scottish whaling industry had been launched with a single ship out of Leith in 1750. Three years later the first whaler from Dundee sailed for the hitherto unvisited whaling grounds – a 'strongly-built' former merchantman appropriately named *Dundee*. Around 80 vessels eventually followed in her wake from the port, and by the end of Dundee's participation in pelagic whaling over 160 years later, the Greenland whale was almost extinct and seal numbers were seriously depleted.

Thanks to whaling journals, bounty returns and the first history of the industry by William Scoresby Jnr in 1820, we know a great deal about the whaling practices established in the trade's early years. Ships bought and fitted out for whaling represented a considerable investment to the partnerships of merchants, bankers, shipowners, physicians, lawyers and gentry who usually made up their shareholders. An average whaler was said to cost as much as New Lanark mills in 1786. A second-hand Colonial-built ship cost £3000 in 1810, and almost the same again to convert and equip for whaling. By 1860 the average cost for a new Dundee-built steam whaler was £12,000. Paradoxically, whale ships did not catch whales, but acted as transporters to get the men to the fishery and to return the catch.

The Dundee whalers were dispatched to Arctic waters every spring with the cheers of vast crowds speeding them on their way with oranges, red herrings and pennies thrown shore to ship for luck by well-wishers. Emotional farewells were said, the ships' horns sounded and the crews lined stern rails to give three final cheers as the fleet nosed out of Victoria Dock and masters set their compasses northwards. With them, inevitably, went boy stowaways hoping to avoid life as 'half-timers' in the city's jute mills.

When a whale was sighted from the ship's crow's nest, whaleboats were bundled into the water for a pursuit which might take several hours of back-breaking rowing as the quarry was stealthily approached, harpooned, then 'played' like an angler's fish until exhausted, when it was finished off with lances. It was as exciting as it was dangerous. Dead whales were lashed to the ship's side prior to the whaling processes of flensing and making off, which would see blubber stripped from skin and packed in barrels for the return journey, when the ships were scrubbed clean by men deep in thought calculating their bonus. Only when Dundee's portside boiling yards had converted the raw products would bonus money be paid to the men – and depending on the success or otherwise of the voyage they might be in debt or they might have made a small fortune. Dundee, in common with other ports, showed cyclical patterns of profit and loss.

While Right whales had only nature to protect them, whalers came under threat from Royal Navy press-gangs and from enemy privateers. Journals report crews fleeing ashore to avoid conscription, and whaling companies applied to Government for protection passes for 'essential' crew, such as harpooners and boat-steerers, but men were seized regardless. Heavily armed privateers viewed whale ships as easy prey and more than one Dundee whaler sailed with her crew armed to the teeth. In the whaling grounds, however, time stood still. There was no post office in Davis Strait and no communication with Scotland for eight months or more. In 1873 a Dundee captain found that the Danish community of Upernavik had received no European news for nearly 12 months, 'so that the finding of Livingstone, the death of Napoleon, and the abdication of the King of Spain' were all news to the governor.

Huge numbers of whales were taken in the decades after 1800 and many thousands of seals were also slaughtered for their skins and oil. Yet catching whales and escaping ice remained a hazardous and dangerous enterprise, a risky business both for its financial backers and for the masters and crews who annually faced severe Arctic conditions. Losses reached a peak in 1830 when, of the 91 British ships in Davis Strait, 19 were lost and 21 returned to port 'clean'. Then, in the saddest episode in Dundee's whaling history, over 70 men were lost from two vessels in 1836, leaving 'one hundred fatherless children' in the town. The toll of such losses and paucity of whales acted as a turning-point in British Arctic whaling. From a peak of over 160 vessels in 1815, barely 30 sailed in 1830. Yields dropped, companies failed, boiling yards closed and men were paid off. London abandoned whaling in 1835 and Leith in 1840. The once-mighty Aberdeen fleet was cut to three vessels by 1839. Dundee was not immune from the recession. Three whaling companies were put up for sale and their ships placed on the market.

Just when it looked as if the trade in Dundee faced extinction, a timely restoration of fortunes returned to the port through the innovative decision to introduce steam power to the fleet. Steam propulsion offered many advantages. It provided speed to the fishery, ice-breaking capabilities in the whaling grounds, and safety in being able to press forward or to cautiously retreat. With the wooden-hulled steam fleet hastily constructed in the town by Alexander Stephen & Co, Dundee had stolen an advantage on Peterhead and other whaling centres which had tried and failed with iron hulls. The timely advance of auxiliary steam was matched by the coincidental discovery that preliminary processes in Dundee's vigorously expanding jute industry could be smoothed by the application of whale oil. The jute industry, boosted by orders for coarse cloth during the American Civil War – when, ironically, the Stephen-built *Shenandoah* mauled the Yankee whaling fleet – guaranteed a doorstep market for the whale oil brought to port.

These factors stimulated quayside prices for oil and acted to motivate owners to construct bigger and better vessels to stalk the Right whale. Dundee pursued steam power relentlessly and soon boasted the most powerful whaling fleet in the world. Steam power also encouraged her whaling masters to push towards new horizons in the Arctic, and what did not change was that the hunt for profit meant ships could be tempted to dally too long in unknown, unexplored seas. Thus whaling remained as risky a venture as it had always been. The deadliest enemies remained freezing fog and crushing ice and, ironically, more Dundee whalers went to the bottom in the 'safe' era of steam than in the age of sail.

Hidden from history until now is the industry's support for polar exploration. Sir Ernest Shackleton used the port's *Nimrod* and *Aurora*, while Captain Robert Falcon Scott was reliant on the city's shipbuilding skills for *Discovery* in 1901 and the whaler *Terra Nova* for his ill-fated expedition in 1910. Dundee whaling ships searched for Franklin in 1850, were used on the Greely relief expedition in 1882, on the Baldwin-Ziegler expedition in 1901, provided a supply ship for Peary in 1910, sailed with Sir Douglas Mawson in 1911 and were used by the American explorer Admiral Byrd in 1934. American, Danish, Swedish and Norwegian governments rewarded Dundee's masters. Amundsen and Nansen sought their advice before historic treks to the polar regions.

The town built more exploration ships than any other, provided the ships of conveyance for the world's greatest explorers, and was the port they turned to first for relief and rescue – exploits that were followed avidly all around the world. Dundee also represented a body of expert seafaring knowledge. The port's ice-men contributed significantly to the surveying of remote regions at the ends of the earth. They sailed to uncharted seas, mapped coastlines, sounded harbours, observed weather systems and changing topography,

wrote reports for eminent geographical societies, and offered the
world the first glimpse of regions hitherto unknown or unexplored.
Moreover, the Dundee whaling fleet expanded our knowledge of the
Arctic's inhabitants. They met, befriended and bartered with remote
and nomadic communities of Inuit who had no previous experience
of Europeans – including the so-called Arctic Highlanders who tried
to wipe the 'white' off the Dundee men's skins. As time passed, and
ships began to overwinter in the area, the native Greenlanders
brought their own expertise to the whaling ships by providing
guides and hunters – and joined in football games with the Scots
in temperatures of minus 40°C. Eventually Eskimos visited Scotland
aboard whale ships and became familiar sights in fur skins in the
unlikely setting of Juteopolis.

Arctic whaling fell away as Right whales were hunted to the verge
of extinction for quick returns in conditions that became increasingly
arduous. Catches diminished in quantity and quality and ships lost
were not replaced. Diversification attempts – longer voyages, ex-
ploitation of new areas, overwintering and especially Dundee's
historic Antarctic expedition of 1892 – all proved fruitless in terms
of the traditional whaling practices the port employed. Ironically, as
the Dundee trade declined through over-fishing, the Norwegians
created a lucrative industry on Scotland's doorstep, while, at the
same time, pioneering the Antarctic factory ships that eventually
took the industry to new levels of slaughter. One by one Dundee's
once-majestic fleet – over 80 ships in 160 years of participation – had
been lost or sold on.

This is their adventure story: the exploits of the tough, resilient,
resourceful men who served the whaling trade with grim cheeriness
in the face of the ever-present prospect of shipwreck, scurvy and
starvation; the rise, supremacy and inevitable decline of an industry
which stands out in history as a unique symbol of the enterprise and
initiative of what has been called the 'first generation' of Scottish
capitalists.

ONE

Northward Ho!

The Courier for April 30, 1912 painted a bleak picture for Dundee's whaling industry as its wooden-hulled fleet, which had left port newly painted to the cheers of vast crowds, returned beggarly and empty from the Arctic hunting grounds – or in whaler parlance, 'clean'. Its headline asked, 'Will the Port Lose an Ancient as Well as Romantic and Picturesque Industry?' Viewed from the vantage point of the twenty-first century, whaling would scarcely be considered ethically and socially acceptable, far less picturesque and romantic. Effectively outlawed by the International Whaling Commission, with global compliance scrutinised by conservationist and environmentalist organisations, all but an ostracised handful of countries insist on protection for whales. For 150 years, however, whaling provided Dundee mariners with a life of adventure in the most sterile, inhospitable and remote regions on earth.

Today's vibrant university city retains strong emotional ties to the trade that froze 40 of its ships in the destructive 'whalers' graveyard' known as Melville Bay. Journals written by numbed fingers in this frozen world bear witness to the conflicting problem of catching whales and escaping ice. Maps of the Arctic are dotted with the names of Dundee masters and ships. City street names evoke memories of the long-gone trade. The research ship *Discovery* remains a striking symbol of the era, while Broughty Castle museum tells the story of the ice-scored ships which sailed through minefields of fast-moving ice floes, immense icebergs and ghostly fogs in pursuit of the Right whale.

Nature was the whale's only defence and she pushed whaling captains and crews to the limits of human endurance. Insufferable cold and chilling polar winds gnawed at their bones. Starvation, frostbite and the 'death monster' scurvy permeated each voyage. The frail wooden ships, too, paid a high price for their boldness in northern latitudes. Almost every year a ship failed to return, squeezed and sunk under the ice pack pressure. The Dundee-built *Aurora*'s action-packed calling saw her icebound in 1882, rescue

American explorers in 1884, be twice given up for lost in 1886, feature in a 'scurvy' court case, lose seven whaleboats in a storm and search for lost Swedish explorers, all in 1893, spend a month in pack ice in 1895, collide with another Dundee whaler in 1908 and be reported sunk with the loss of 187 men after hitting an iceberg in 1910. Yet the *Aurora* turned up again and again. In 1911 she steamed 30,000 miles in southern oceans on Douglas Mawson's expedition and was then battered in a long imprisonment by ice during Shackleton's heroic Antarctic adventure in 1914–16. She was last seen in 1917 somewhere between Australia and Chile . . .

Throughout its history, commercial whaling was a business that called for equal measures of experience and luck, a trade as much a risk for its entrepreneurial backers as it was for the famous band of whaling captains who penetrated distant and unexplored northern seas. Each master could expect to be wrecked at least once in his career. An estimated one in 17 voyages ended in disaster. Life expectancy was not good. Yet always central to a port's commitment to whaling were the economic advantages to be gained from the sale of blubber and bone. This is why whiskered, formidable captains sailed and then steamed out of Dundee's Georgian and Victorian docks and steered northward ho, towards the highest latitudes known to man. Their quarry was the whale – or 'fish' – but also seals, polar bears and walrus. They took them in astonishing numbers, turning the Arctic ice red with blood.

Whaling was launched as a commercial concern around 1500, apocryphally after a storm in the Bay of Biscay washed a dead whale ashore. The story goes that it was found that its flesh dripped oil, its dark red meat could be eaten and that its huge bones could be turned into a range of goods, including tools and handles. By then, in fact, many circumpolar communities already had vast knowledge of whales, and had established shore-based practices for killing them for subsistence consumption and sustainability. This experience has been largely ignored in whaling histories and it is generally accepted that the Basque fishermen of the region between France and Spain established the pelagic industry by developing the skills to catch whales and by pursuing them far into the Atlantic Ocean. As whales became harder to find, the Basques followed the quarry as far as the coast of Iceland and the southern extremity of Greenland. By 1600 their mariners had reached the seas around Spitzbergen and the southern reaches of Davis Strait, the dangerous waters between Arctic Canada and

West Greenland. Here, in 1978, underwater archaeologists discovered three sixteenth-century Basque galleons.

British merchants, meanwhile, were more concerned with practical matters of money. By the 1500s mariners were searching the little-known and unexplored Arctic seas in attempts to discover a shorter and faster shipping lane to the Orient by a northern route between the Atlantic and the Pacific – the fabled North-West Passage. Little was known of the pack ice or what lay north of the southern tip of Greenland when, in 1553, the first of a long series of British expeditions set out to search for the new route over the top of the world. It was a goal not viewed as a matter of national prestige – 'pole bagging' – as it was 350 years later, but as one necessary to be first to reach the riches that lay in the so-called Spice Islands of the Pacific. Henry Hudson, who gave his name to Hudson Bay, was then a distinguished sea captain in the service of the Muscovy Company of London, which had been founded in 1554 to trade with Russia. Hudson returned to England from his voyages in search of the North-West Passage in 1608 and 1609 after being turned back by walls of ice at almost 80°N. He reported that he had a seen a 'great store of whales' in the waters between east Greenland and the island of Spitzbergen, now Svalbard, which confirmed an earlier sighting by his fellow captain Jonas Poole. In 1610 two ships, the *Amitie* under Poole and the *Lioness*, captained by the adventurous naval commander Thomas Edge, were dispatched from London to investigate. Off east Greenland they confirmed that one of the whale's main feeding grounds had been discovered: the meeting of the cold waters from the north with warm waters from the south generated the presence of the shrimp-like krill required by whales for feeding. And in 1611 the first purposely-sent whale ship, the 160-ton *Margaret*, under Thomas Edge, had the distinction of founding the modern whaling trade.

The chief quarry for the next 200 years was *Balaena mysticetus*, the Greenland Right whale, so called to distinguish it from the wrong one to catch. It was also 'right' in the sense that it was slow moving and therefore easy to hunt and had the advantage, as far as whale men were concerned, of floating when dead, whereas most whales sank. This whale, also known as the bowhead, was a docile giant, up to 65 feet long and weighing up to 100 tons or more. Its tail alone could be 30 feet across and its tongue weigh over a ton. In the cold Arctic waters it swam ponderously on the surface with its awesome mouth open, and its food was caught in the long slabs of its 'whalebone'. This was not actually bone, but a soft, springy tooth substitute called baleen that hung from its upper jaw in overlapping plates and acted as a filter for its intake of krill from the large mouthfuls of water taken in and expelled. No other whale had such a mass of baleen, making the Right whale a prime commercial target. Its cavernous mouth could yield a ton of this valuable bone and, as the years passed, fashions changed and whales grew scarce, 'whalebone' rose in price to £3000 per ton on Dundee's wharves. While the Right whale's flesh was not used, its heavy layer of fat, or blubber, the thickest of all whales at between 12 and 18 inches, was another valuable commodity and could produce as much as 7000 gallons of marketable oil after it was boiled on return to port.

A whaler's catch could be put to profitable use. Washed and dried until tough and flexible, easily twisted when heated, whalebone was used to make carriage springs, walking canes, whips, brushes, brooms, bed bottoms, umbrella ribs, upholstery stuffing and fishing rods, while native Eskimos used it for bows and arrows and harpoons. Most of all, baleen was used for women's hooped skirts and the stiffening in corsets and other tight-laced undergarments where great strength and lightness were required. At times of poor catches or industrial demand, whale oil also enjoyed periods of such value that it was considered a quayside currency. The product of blubber, whale oil was vital to industrialisation. It was used to light candles in homes and was the principal source of street lighting before the introduction of coal gas and petroleum. It was an industrial lubricant, powering lighthouses and illuminating factories. It spawned a huge industry in soap production. Later it was used in the manufacture of margarine, cosmetics, varnishes and paints. Locally, it proved a godsend to the rapidly-expanding Dundee textile industry, lighting the first linen factories and proving to be the perfect softener for raw fibres in jute processing – an innovation which secured Dundee's eventual pre-eminence in the whaling industry. Seal oil, which increasingly became a lucrative commodity as the Right whale was hunted to high Arctic latitudes, was also used for lighting and soap and candle manufacture, while cured sealskins were popular accessories in the fashion trade.

Economic interest stimulated, the race to harvest whales drew several nations, but principally the English and the Dutch. These rival mariners viewed each other with international jealousy – and open hostility. In the first years of the trade London ships, led by Admiral Thomas Edge, carried the greater firepower and fished without fear, later the Dutch arrived with a larger number of vessels and prevented the English reaching the whale-rich bays. As it became apparent that vast profits could be obtained, the Scots saw an opportunity to checkmate their quarrelling North Sea neighbours. Legislation drafted in London to grant the Muscovy Company exclusive rights to whaling proved inadequate to cover Scotland, enabling King James to grant a monopoly to the Scottish East India Trading Company to trade in Greenland. Fearing that the unscrupulous Scots would sell off licences to English interlopers, the London company had no option other than to buy off the Scottish concern – which had little intention of whaling in any case.

The Muscovy Company over-extended itself and had ceased its whaling activities by 1623. In contrast, Dutch whaling expanded exponentially and the whaling town of Smeerenberg was eventually created on a flat shore on the island of Spitzbergen, allowing blubber to be boiled to oil near the fishing grounds. At the height of their participation in the seventeenth century the Dutch had 250 boats and 14,000 men operating out of Spitzbergen. Estimates of their activity suggest they took over 10,000 whales and many thousands of seals during the period extending from 1679 to 1683 alone. But wars in Europe and the gradual decline of stocks brought an end to the slaughter and by the early 1700s Dutch whaling was languishing. Even when the South Sea Company tried to revive English whaling in 1725, by extravagantly fitting out 12 brand-new whale ships, the company in subsequent years reported a string of losses.

By this time explorers had learned enough to rule out the possibility of a commercial sea route to the Pacific by way of the unknown 'North Pole'. As interest in the Arctic subsided among merchants, the British government sensed an opportunity to rejuvenate whaling as a means of reducing expensive American imports of oil for lamp lighting and soap making, and passed legislation to encourage the Greenland trade. Besides, support for whaling widened the Admiralty's pool of experienced seamen and spiked the guns, commercially, of the Dutch. Under this support a 20 shillings (£1) per ton whaling bounty was offered in 1733, paid on the tonnage of ships employed in the trade. Despite the inducement, only two English ships sailed to Greenland that year – and still no Scottish boat embarked on the chase for whales.

The revival of British whaling and the origins of the Scottish industry can be dated precisely to a new Bounty Act in 1749 when the Government subsidy was raised to 40s (£2) per ton on all vessels engaged to a limit of 400 tons, to encourage and foster the industry. This meant that a ship of 400 tons' register would generate £800 in bounty if she complied with the Act's conditions. Moreover, extra payments were made to the vessels that arrived soonest at a British port with a catch. A sum of £500 was paid to the first arrival, £400 to the second, £300 to the third, £200 to the fourth and £100 to the fifth. Thus, the total Government bounty that could be paid to a ship amounted to £1300, which comfortably covered the entire expense of a whaling voyage. The catch, consequently, was all profit. Naturally, the fledgling industry responded to the increased incentive – which also included the advantages of duty-free victuals for Arctic warmth, such as coal, roasted coffee and rum. It proved too good an opportunity to pass up. Advertisements in ports across the country asked for subscriptions from interested parties to become share-holding partners in whaling companies. Merchant ships were hurriedly fitted out for the Arctic and crews recruited around docksides with promises of lucrative bonus money for their signatures. Look to the benefits the Dutch had gained from the trade, they were told.

William Scoresby, son of the famous Arctic master of the same name, recalled in 1820, 'The effect of the bounty of 40s per ton, together with other inducements held out to speculators in the whale-fishery, was such that immediately after the passing of the last act of Parliament, the British whale-fishery began to assume a respectable and hopeful appearance'. He also added for the convenience of Scottish historians, 'The merchants of Scotland began to participate with the English in the year 1750'.

The first whaling ship from Scotland was the *Tryal*, a 333-ton former plantation vessel bought from London by the Edinburgh Whale Fishing Company. The *Tryal* departed Leith in April 1750. It failed to secure any whales and, in whaler parlance, returned 'clean' – although four walrus and £666 bounty helped to ease the disappointment. Scottish ports were not discouraged. Without catching any whales the *Tryal* had comfortably managed to defray fitting out and victualling costs. Encouraged by this situation, and the prospect of the profits any catch would yield, other speculators – initially from Glasgow and Campbeltown with two boats each – followed the example of Leith in 1751. Partly because of the continued landings of imported oil by transatlantic trading schooners, the west-coast initiative was short-lived. As 1752 drew to a close, advertisements in the London press offered the two Campbeltown ships, *Argyll* and *Campbelton*, 'lately arrived from Greenland', for sale 'by the candle'.

Then, in 1753, the first exploratory whaling ship from Dundee rigged her masts and set sail for the hitherto unvisited northern fishing grounds. The *Dundee* was bought from London in February 1753 by a group of Dundee merchants and shipowners who had formed the Dundee Whale Fishing Company at a meeting in the town the previous October. The *Dundee* sailed under Captain William Chiene for the Greenland fishery six months later on April 2. She is recorded in bounty records as 'a strongly-built British' merchantman of 345 tons, which made her larger than the Edinburgh and Aberdeen whalers that year. One of her principal backers and the company's clerk was Sir John Halyburtoun, later Provost of Dundee. Other owner/partners included the current Provost Andrew Wardroper and a former provost, Alexander Robertson. From this we see that the momentum to engage in the trade had considerable civic and mercantile backing.

Chiene appears to have been recruited locally. A John Chiene, 'shipmaster at Crail', who was likely a relative, witnessed some of the *Dundee*'s subsequent bounty returns. William Chiene's crew of 46 was not entirely drawn from the Dundee area, however. As was the custom, the *Dundee* recruited expert personnel from overseas whaling nations. Six foreigners were listed in the *Dundee*'s early crews – all harpooners. Chiene's submission to HM Customs for 1753 revealed that the men completed their task competently. The cargo returned to Dundee that year consisted of '143 casks containing blubber of four whales'. For this William Chiene was awarded £691.5s bounty. Shareholders must have noted with some satisfaction that three of the four Glasgow and Campbeltown whalers had returned clean on their maiden voyages. The *Dundee* duly met with further success in the fishery. She took seven whales in 1754, five in 1755 and four in 1756, the year the Dundee Whale Fishing Company established by local burgesses advertised bone and oil for sale at the town's quayside. It was also in 1756 that a second ship, the *Grandtully*, described as an old English-built vessel of 249 tons, was fitted out in Dundee for the following year's sailing to Greenland. The industry, at last, had a toehold in the town.

Dundee of the 1750s was obviously different from today's modern city. With a population of around 12,000 (Edinburgh had 50,000), which rose to around 30,000 by the end of the eighteenth century, it retained much of its medieval look. Lanes ran higgledy-piggledy through high-storeyed buildings between the ancient harbour and St Mary's Tower and the Town House. Some of these lanes, such as

Couttie's Wynd, survive today and typically feature a bend in their alignment so that cold shore winds would be prevented from reaching the town's densely-populated heart. Burgh council records for the period indicate a civic movement towards modernising the town. In April 1751 work was carried out to pave the Nethergate and mend other streets. In October that year the council debated purchasing the first street lighting and, in a desire to enhance hygiene, organised an improved 'rubbish bin' uplift: 'The Council appoint the town drummer to go through the town ordering ye haill inhabitants upon every Monday and Saturday before twelve o'clock to raik all the dung and nastiness upon the high streets opposite their possession and cause to put the same in little heaps so as it may be carried away'.

Rapid advances in trade had made the town's harbour a busy facility and its merchant classes wealthy. Dean of Guild archives highlight trade with London, Holland, France, Portugal and the Baltic – often cargoes of timber. The shoremaster, the member of council whose duties included harbour affairs, was given authority to improve the harbour in 1751 and to remove any rocks remaining there, 'in the cheapest and best manner'. So many petitions were presented to council for permission to build ships next to the pier that in October 1753, as the pioneering *Dundee* was returning from Greenland, the civic authorities recognised an opportunity to raise revenues and decreed that no-one could construct any vessel without first paying 'four shillings Scots [about 4d Sterling] to the council for each ton of ship to be built'. By the end of the eighteenth century the burgh had grown in size and prosperity and its expanding merchant fleet was importing hundreds of tons of Baltic flax from St Petersburg and Riga for its increasingly important linen manufactories. It had also witnessed a rapid expansion in its professional and commercial classes – merchants, booksellers, printers, lawyers and tradesmen – and the architectural historian Charles McKean has described it then as 'a flourishing alert town of ambitious intelligent people'. Ironically, the whaling industry very nearly did not survive infancy to witness these emerging economic foundations. The *Dundee* narrowly avoided tragedy in 1756 when she sprang a leak and 'was obliged to come off to repair the damage, sooner than she intended'. Her rueful master recorded that 'he would have made an extraordinary good voyage, the fish being in great plenty'.

Ships were not usually purposely built for whaling until the middle of the nineteenth century although, once established as whalers, they were often sold on as such. In the industry's first phase, whalers were mostly second-hand merchantmen purchased from trading ports and converted for their polar role. The *Peggy* of Glasgow, in 1754, is described in bounty records as 'a foreign-built ship, a prize made free'. The *Dundee* and *Grandtully* were 'bought from London'. The going rate for pre-owned 300-ton whalers in 1750 was around £2000. At least the same was required for fitting out each vessel. These costs were normally divided among many subscribers. Shares in each vessel – often 64 in number – were advertised for sale to prospective investors and were bought by partners in stock holdings of eighths, sixteenths, thirty-seconds and so on. Some wealthier merchants became multiple-share subscribers, perhaps owning around 10 shares, but there was clearly a reluctance to invest large amounts in an untested market, and shareholdings of one share, of say £35, were not uncommon. The Aberdeen Whale-Fishing Company in 1754, for example, had 99 subscribers for its 154 shares. Thus the risks were divided. Typical Scottish shareholders were merchants, tradesmen, solicitors, physicians and, of course, shipmasters. Nobility and landed gentry played an important role, as they did with most Scottish economic initiatives, but a fair range of occupations such as brewers, booksellers and bankers were involved. One investor in the Aberdeen Whale-Fishing Company is described as a 'wigmaker' in the company's *Contract of Compartnery*, launched in 1753 with £50 shares.

The broad-based investment structure of Scottish whaling, where a manager acted on behalf of several owners, contrasted with the system adopted in England. There, London led the initial involvement in the trade and its cadre of 40 whalers was called 'the darling sister' to the British fishing fleet. These ships were owned under legislation which determined that single vessels were normally joint ventures operated by small numbers of people. The Bubble Act prohibited large partnerships, hence the frequency of names such as *The Two Brothers* or *Three Sisters* on shipping registers. The English system initially produced a very competitive situation where a great many ships were sent to Greenland and Davis Strait by small groups of investors, with the result that many, just as quickly, went out of business, acting as a brake on further expansion. The Scottish 'company' system, where ship shareholders could spread their investment across several vessels, offset the risk of losses and thereby helped the volatile trade towards stability. A further benefit north of the border was that shareholders were limited only to their individual investment as liability did not extend beyond personal shareholding. The publicly-subscribed Scottish companies held another important advantage – they were located nearer to the fishing grounds.

Dundee's whaler-owning base represented a significant investment by the standard of industrial investment in the mid-eighteenth century. Shareholders ploughed an estimated £10,000 into buying and fitting out Dundee's first two ships for the northern fishery. One alone was worth as much as David Dale's New Lanark Mills in 1786 and the famous Belpet cotton mill in the north of England, which cost £5000 in 1793. Whaling also created ancillary services and made considerable demands on the port. It encouraged shipbuilding, ship repairing, ship chandlering and the recruitment and retention of a large workforce. Substantial buildings were needed for the processing and storage of bone and oil. The merchant classes benefited from Government-regulated victualling which the whalers required each season, such as tobacco, sugar and biscuits – hardly a recommended diet today – and Sanger noted, 'The whale fishery permeated all sectors of local economies and contributed to the growth and diversification of the economic base of each whaling town'. The Bounty Act, along with industrialisation, was a significant factor encouraging this expansion. Only two ships sailed to the Arctic fishery prior to the introduction of the £2 bounty in 1749. By 1756 the fleet had grown to 83 vessels, with Government payments acting to support the trade in poor seasons, and adding jam to speculator returns in the good years. Between 1733 and 1800, £1,975,089 was paid out in subsidy, with over a quarter of a million pounds of this huge sum entering Scotland's maritime communities. This artificial stimulant was gradually reduced after 1790 and finally abolished in 1824, but by then whaling had established itself so significantly that the passing of the bounty was hardly noticed.

Scoresby's *Account of the Arctic Regions*, published in Edinburgh in 1820, suggests that the Scots learned the ropes of whaling expeditiously. 'Their successes in 1753 was 61 and a half whales, and in 1754, 36 whales, of which 18 belonged to the Edinburgh companies,' he recorded. *The Scots Magazine* claimed that in order to encourage the local trade, many loyal ladies of Edinburgh 'got their stays and hoops made of the whalebone' brought home by Leith ships.

SCALE OF SCOTTISH WHALE FISHING, 1750–1760

YEAR	NO. OF SHIPS	TONNAGE	BOUNTIES PAID £
1750	1	333	666
1751	6	1933	3866
1752	10	3137	6274
1753	14	4294	8589
1754	15	4680	9361
1755	16	4964	9929
1756	16	4964	9315
1757	15	4530	8567
1758	15	4499	8271
1759	15	4479	8959
1760	14	4238	8477

Source: HM Customs' bounty records, Scoresby 1820. Jackson 1978, Sanger 1985.

The 1750s ships were fitted out for whaling from Leith, Aberdeen, Glasgow, Campbeltown, Dunbar, Bo'ness and Greenock, with the *Dundee* and the *Grandtully* representing Dundee's fledgling fleet. Indeed, the *Dundee* sailed on Arctic duty every year from 1753 to 1782, though she returned several times – for example in 1760, 1761 and 1762 – without a whale. Other voyages paid handsome dividends to the ship's expectant shareholders. In 1779, 1780 and 1781 she took five, 11 and nine whales respectively. It was certainly a roller-coaster ride for the *Dundee*'s backers during her three decades in the Arctic. The fickle nature of the fisheries, where the reproductive cycle of whales was incapable of replenishing stocks, meant that companies often struggled when catches were poor. In 1764, the shareholders of the Aberdeen Whale-Fishing Company received just £1250 for their entire business, including the whaler *City of Aberdeen*, boiling yards, fishing equipment and stores. The following year the *Dundee* took six whales worth nearly three times that amount. In 30 consecutive seasons between 1753 and 1782, when she was lost, the *Dundee* caught an average of 2.7 whales per voyage and remained the symbol of the town's involvement in the industry in more than name only. The *Grandtully* had a shorter Arctic lifespan, sailing between 1757 and 1762, taking only five fish in six years. She presumably had a less experienced crew or perhaps did not meet the return in revenues hoped for. Bounty payment records indicate that no other Dundee vessel sailed during the 20 years following the

Dundee's introduction to the fleet, indicating that the town's merchants were initially reluctant to invest in the industry that would eventually raise the town's status on the maritime map. In lean years, of which there were several, the protective subsidy kept shareholders, and their ships, afloat.

Wars in Europe, which lasted until the Treaty of Paris in 1763 and affected the supply of seamen, combined with a run of poor Arctic weather and indifferent yields, threatened the continued expansion of the northern whaling fleet. The return of peace brought a resumption of activity, but there was no repeat of the rapid increase in UK-wide fleets of former years. These factors, as well as the start of the struggle for independence in America, and the reduction of Government bounty to 30s per ton, acted to reduce the Scottish whaling presence to 10 ships in 1763 and just five in 1778, from a peak of 16 in 1756. Anstruther, for example, entered the industry with a single vessel in 1757 but withdrew just five years later when its second vessel was lost in ice and its first returned clean. This recession was then reversed. The Scottish whaling fleet grew rapidly after American independence in 1776. Post-revolutionary legislation taxed American oil as foreign and served to protect the British home market from the exports of the whaling fleets of the American eastern seaboard towns of Nantucket and New Bedford. Demand also grew as the Industrial Revolution gripped the country. Whale-oil prices rose sharply and quayside demand for bone increased as the expanding managerial classes swelled the ranks of women wearing corsets. By the end of the 1780s the Scottish fleet had also swollen – from an average of five ships at the start of the decade to 23 in 1790 – with four of the vessels based in Dundee.

THE SCOTTISH WHALING FLEET, 1790

PORT	SHIPS
Leith	5
Aberdeen	4
Dundee	4
Dunbar	3
Montrose	3
Bo'ness	2
Glasgow	2

Source: Scoresby, 1820.

THE DUNDEE WHALING FLEET, 1790

SHIP	MASTER	TONS
Tay	Robert Webster	–
Dundee	William Soutar	264
Rodney	Cornelius Frogett	176
Success	James Sinclair	219

Source: Bounty records.

Together, Dundee's quartet of wooden-hulled ships sailed to Greenland between 1789 and 1792, representing the first significant presence of the whaling industry in the town. The *Tay* was recorded as the third most successful British ship in 1791 with 11 whales. She was captured by privateers in 1799 and her master Robert Webster took over as captain of the *Estridge* of Dundee in 1800. The *Dundee* of 1790 was the second ship of that name to sail from the port, the first being lost in ice in 1782. The *Rodney* was a remarkable little ship of only 165 tons that survived around 40 seasons in its long Arctic career, most of them under her piratical-sounding captain Cornelius Frogett. She was eventually lost in 1810. Little is known about the *Success*, which was sold from Dundee in 1792.

To qualify for bounty, each ship had to apply to HM Customs for a whaling licence for the northern fisheries. In return each had to provide Customs House in Dundee with a certificate that the ship was properly crewed and manned, a signed oath from the master that the ship would, indeed, proceed to the Greenland fishery, and a similar declaration from one of the ship's owners. Additionally, security had to be provided in the event that the ship failed to carry out its promised voyage. The bounty legislation declared and described how the qualifying vessels were to be owned, built and navigated and from which ports they might proceed. Each whaler had to possess the proper number of crew, harpoons, lines, stores and provisions and must have sailed 'unless in case of unavoidable necessity by April 10, and unless a certain specific success is obtained must remain within the limits of the Greenland seas until August 10'. The regulations also required vessels to carry at least one apprentice aged between 12 and 20 for every 50 tons of ship weight – partly to secure the industry's future, partly to establish a surplus of trained seamen. Cynics, including the Kirkcaldy economist Adam Smith, later explained this as bounties being paid by Government to covertly 'augment the number of its sailors and shipping' in the run-up to the Napoleonic Wars in Europe.

Whaling grew in importance as a commercial enterprise in the relatively small-scale economies of the Scottish east coast ports. Yet just as quickly as a large British fleet became engaged in the northern fishery, it rapidly discovered that the industry's future was not going to be plain sailing. Growing unease over international relations in Europe had three important effects on the reinvigorated Arctic trade. Firstly, the Royal Navy resorted again to press gangs in order to man warships. Secondly, the government commandeered whale ships as troop and supply transports. Thirdly, heavily-armed privateers – private ships with permission to attack enemy shipping – viewed whale ships as easy prey. What mariners in every port feared was to become involved in the messy, underpaid, dangerous work of war. Men were pressed into service during the Seven Years War (1756–1763) and especially during the War of the American Revolution (1775–1783) and the Napoleonic Wars, which lasted to 1815. Whale men did their very best to avoid conscription. Petitions from whaling companies secured an exemption from the press gang for experienced personnel who were contracted for essential whaling duties in what was effectively a strategic industry. Customs records show the ships, such as Frogett's *Rodney*, petitioning the authorities for protection passes for boat crew officers and occasionally being quizzed by Customs officers over the numbers of exemptions requested for harpooners, line-managers and boat-steerers. Doubtless Royal Navy press gangs also scrutinised each pass for irregularities. Perhaps because of this, two boatloads of *Rodney*'s crew fled ashore at Aberdeen in 1798 to escape being pressed.

Protection passes were frequently ignored in practice. There were incidences of men being taken off whalers prior to departure, or being confronted by the wooden coshes of the naval gangs when they returned, unsuspecting, to port. The press gangs also visited the shipyards of the fledgling Alexander Stephen company: 'Ships carpenters were particularly suitable for the Royal Navy and the best place to find them was naturally the vicinity of the various shipyards'. A ruse used by east-coast whale men was to jump ship before they reached port. Gordon Jackson records 32 men of a Montrose whaler in 1790, 'upon being informed of the report of a Spanish war', leaving the ship at Duncansby Head and going into hiding. The master of the *Mary Ann* of Dundee reported 15 men and five Greenland apprentices leaving the ship at Aberdeen in 1813 to avoid being impressed; and, the following year, part of the crew of the Dundee-registered *Three Brothers* were landed 'at midnight at Stromness'. But in 1779 the whaler *North Star* of Dunbar lost two harpooners, four steersmen and four line-managers to press gangers. Another Montrose vessel, the faithful *Eliza Swan*, was even less fortunate, losing 19 men to the naval squads in 1805 and, 10 years later, being taken as a prize by the US frigate *President*, costing insurers £5000 for her release. It is unlikely, however, that press gangs or privateers had things entirely their own way against brawny Scottish whale men brandishing a range of ship's tools which, in 1765, included 40 harpoon irons. Owners were equally resistant to surrender to hostile shipping. A letter to the Collector and Comptroller of Customs at Dundee in February 1804 asked if the Dundee whaler *Estridge* could be armed for her defence. Permission was granted with the proviso that arms and ammunition be returned on completion of the voyage. And while any enemy warship could probably outgun a whaler, the four Bo'ness boats in 1755 were equipped with cannon and shot 'in readiness to salute any polite gentleman they meet'.

To the first *Dundee* of Dundee is owed the distinction of being one of the first whaling ships to become 'beset' in ice. She left the Tay for Greenland on May 4, 1782 under Captain Robson with a crew of 54 and reached 'ice' on June 1. Three days later she struck a heavy floe at the dangerously-high latitude of 78°N and was badly damaged. With six feet of water in her hold and sinking fast, the master ordered the *Dundee*'s six whaleboats to be lowered and the crew took to the ice. Provisions saved amounted to 'some fresh beef, a half dozen pork hams, a half dozen beef hams and 12 gallons of whisky' – which was contained in two chests, the captain holding the key. Two kettles were also saved and wood from the wreck allowed the men to keep a fire going on the ice until June 11. Herbs stored on the ship for the previous two years – lemon, thyme, sage and balm – were found to be fresh and Captain Robson astutely ordered his men to melt snow for herb tea two to three times daily as a precaution against the Arctic whale men's 'poison' – the dreadful disease scurvy. Watch was kept through the night and bears were dispersed by musket fire.

On June 11, the men of the *Dundee* set out in whaleboats to attempt to reach land at Cape Horn some 40 miles distant. Progress was slow. It was difficult to row through the floes, and the boats had to be dragged on to the comparative safety of the ice at the end of daylight hours. On June 19 a large polar bear was shot. Against the captain's advice some of the crew cooked and ate its flesh, which resulted in 'violent after effects, victims' roving eyes rolled, vomiting gave instant relief'. On meagre rations the men continued their perilous journey day by day until, on June 24, 1782, three weeks after being stranded, they reached Magdalen Point, where English whaling ships called. The entire crew of the *Dundee* was saved. Fifty biscuits and four hams remained.

The French Revolution and the Napoleonic Wars slowed the pace of the fledgling industry – as they did modest contemporary attempts at Arctic exploration. Further growth merely awaited peacetime, by which time the heart of the industry had moved north. By 1814 Hull had overtaken London as Britain's chief whaling port. And, that year, as if to demonstrate the movement of the industry's powerbase, Captain Souter in the *Resolution* of Peterhead brought home the greatest cargo ever landed at a British port in a single vessel – the bone and blubber of 44 whales. These were also profitable times for the Dundee whaling fleet. In seasons 1805, 1806 and 1807 the return of Dundee's six ships was 116 whales, representing a seasonal average of 6.5 fish per vessel. And in 1806 the *Horn* under Captain William Valentine was the first British ship home and made a name for herself with a full cargo from Davis Strait. In 1810, the *Advice, Mary Ann* and *Calypso* returned full with 16, 14 and 14 whales respectively. The total catch of 73 fish in 1812 represented a record return of £40,000 in oil and whalebone. And in the four seasons 1814, 1815, 1816 and 1817 Dundee sent out 32 ships, an average of eight per year, with no losses, and secured 248 whales, an average of 7.7 per ship. It is difficult to compare like with like, as the fleet and catches changed so much over the years, but the safe return of all 10 ships to Dundee in 1823, with the bounty of 268 whales lowering their hulls in the estuary, shines out in the firmament of star catches at this time.

One of the distinguishing features of the fleet which left Dundee every spring for Arctic waters in this period was its preference for the long voyage to Davis Strait, separating western Greenland and Baffin Island, where larger whales were thought to migrate in narrower channels. This vast stretch of ice-ridden water, 500 miles at its mouth, narrowing to 200 miles as it entered Baffin Bay and unknown lands to the north, was bounded at the southern point by the ominous-sounding but familiar landmark of Cape Farewell. As early as 1807, the Dundee fleet split four to one in favour of the more distant western hunting grounds, the *Advice, Jane, Horn* and *Mary*

Ann sailing to Davis Strait. Only the little *Rodney* sailed to the traditional Greenland fishery. Greenland whaling took place in waters around Spitzbergen and Jan Mayen Island and grew to be considered the preserve of the Peterhead fleet. Eventually the northern port focused and thrived upon sealing activities in that region.

DUNDEE'S WHALING FLEET AND CATCHES, 1823

SHIP	MASTER	WHALES	TONS OIL
Princess Charlotte	Adamson	26	230
Achilles	Valentine	37	260
Dorothy	Deuchars	27	225
Advice (1)	Webster	23	210
Estridge	Deuchars	28	193
Fairy	Thoms	18	150
Friendship	Ireland	12	90
Horn	Jeffers	32	240
Thomas	Thomas	37	240
Three Brothers	Foreman	28	220

It took brave and resourceful men to make the journey to Davis Strait in the knowledge that depleted whale stocks moved the hunt to the inhospitable and inaccessible areas to the north and west – and the notorious ice barrier at Melville Bay. At 66°N masters steered over the imaginary line of the Arctic Circle. At about 70°N they crossed the point after which there were no more trees, and where only bleak, permafrosted land lay northwards. At any latitude around 70°N, midway between Cape Farewell and Melville Bay, there was a chance a ship would be caught – or 'beset' – in ice. It would certainly encounter foul weather, heavy squalls of rain and snow, dense fogs and howling winds, while, all around, the pack ice creaked and threatened to squeeze it into the deep. Such was the danger that the Government had been informed by John Barrow's expedition ships of the early 1800s that no vessel could penetrate beyond about 80°N. This was given as a reason why interest in a commercial route across the top of the world was finally discounted, leaving the North Pole as an object of curiosity in its own right. As it happened, William Scoresby Snr reached 81°31N on the whaler *Resolution* in 1806.

In 1817 the *Larkins* of Leith, followed by the *Elizabeth* of Aberdeen, bravely ventured to open waters north of Davis Strait, beyond the dangerous ice barrier that guarded Melville Bay, and reached Lancaster Sound. It was the first time whalers had found a path through the ice pack of Baffin Bay. As the industry's boats followed, more ships fell victim to the ice than before. Some 12 whalers were lost in July 1819 alone, littering the sea bottom between Greenland and what are now Upper Canadian waters. They included the *Tay* and *Mary Ann* of Dundee, both crushed in ice in July of that year. Before that, losses in more accessible Greenland waters and the southern reaches of Davis Straits were negligible.

Melville Bay, which the whalers had to reach before crossing to Lancaster Sound, proved the whalers' graveyard. A later master, Captain Walker of the *Wildfire*, recorded an extraordinary episode in the bay when the Dundee fleet was gripped in some of the worst conditions experienced in the Arctic. The fleet was at a latitude of 70°N, some 35 miles off Cape Seton when:

> We were brought to a standstill – in fact to our wits' end. We could neither advance nor retreat . . . we were jammed and unable to move the ship in any way to a place where we could have the least protection. In short, we were six of the finest vessels that ever navigated these congealed seas, lying close together to be shoved up at the mercy of the immense floes . . . I have been on a lee shore more than once, and have seen death staring me in the face. We had to stand with our hands in pockets; could do nothing but look on, expecting every moment to see our good ships made mince-meat of.

Walker and the 300 men of the Dundee fleet were powerless to interfere with nature's work. His ship was twisted by a floe, her stern split from top to bottom. Two companion ships were thrust together in collision by the pressure of the ice, sending dangerous shards of timber across their decks. Another, with her bow in the air and her stern under water, slid out of sight as her men scrambled on to the ice and relative safety. The stern of the yet another was ripped away, and she quickly added to the number of stricken vessels below the dangerous waters of Melville Bay.

Writing his journal on board the Dundee whaler *Arctic*, Albert Markham reflected on the harrowing history of this menacing passage: 'The water below the ice in Melville Bay could indeed unfold a sad tale. Many is the stout ship, manned by a daring crew and commanded by a skilful and brave master, that has perished, crushed into innumerable fragments by the insatiable and ponderous floes rapidly closing upon the unlucky and doomed vessels, swallowing her so rapidly as barely to allow time for the escape of the crew'. The surgeon Thomas Macklin, who sailed through Melville Bay on the *Narwhal* of Dundee the following year, paid his own tribute to the whalers' graveyard: 'So much danger there is, of losing ships in the bay that all the ships before entering get up all their provisions on deck so as to be ready to leave at a moment's notice'. Often luck played a role in the narrow distinction between success and tragedy. The naval explorer Edward Parry took 54 days to pass through the bay in 1824. Sir John Ross, just five years later, took only five.

Losses reached a peak in 1830 when of the 91 ships in Melville Bay, 19 were lost in storms and 21 returned to port 'clean'. It was the worst year in British whaling history. Two Dundee vessels, the *Achilles* and the *Three Brothers*, were among those to sail into the bay and oblivion. The *Advice* and *Dorothy* were damaged and the *Princess Charlotte* returned 'clean'. The remaining six Dundee boats took only eight whales. The remarkable sight of 1000 men stranded on ice, free from masters' orders and taking liberal advantage of salved rum casks, entered whaling folklore as the Baffin Bay Fair. The 1830 losses marked a watershed in the industry. Every port was affected. Companies failed, men were laid off, and port revenues dwindled. Shareholders and partners faced ruin. Peterhead's fleet, then Scotland's largest, was forced to return to sealing in the calmer waters of the east Greenland Sea, reducing tension with the Dundee fleet which had arisen the previous year over the capture of a whale to which ships from both towns had made fast. Moreover, ship losses, poor catches and unprofitable seasons were not made easier to bear by the withdrawal of the Government bounty system in 1824.

In 1835 several ships, including the *Viewforth* of Kirkcaldy and *Middleton* of Aberdeen, were beset by ice near Disko Island after lingering in Davis Straits in hope of sighting whales. The Admiralty was persuaded by owners to mount a relief expedition and the famous explorer James Clark Ross was dispatched in the *Cove* to search for the missing vessels. The *Viewforth* scrambled clear towards the end of January 1836 and arrived in Orkney three weeks later with 14 dead. Only eight were saved from the *Middleton*, which was lost. A log detailing the sufferings of the *Viewforth*'s crew, 'from a journal taken on the spot by an officer' – its author was William Elder, probably the ship's mate – was published in 1836 and revealed how the men existed on starvation rations for four months, at one point devouring in their desperation the stinking, leather-like fins of the captured whales: 'I feel that I am really starving, two days in the week we get only a biscuit and a half'.

One consequence of this drama was new legislation providing for whaling ships to carry sufficient stores to see them through the possibility of overwintering – although, in practice, this seldom happened. The surgeon John Wanless, who travelled to Davis Strait on the *Thomas* of Dundee in 1834, commented forcibly upon the food provided to his shipmates: 'Poor sailors are imposed upon by every person in whatever line of business they deal almost. It should be looked after by a judge, the material before it is put on board a ship of this sort or any sort. What does not answer the sample sent to the committee of managers should be returned with a verdict proving the vendor to be a thief and a robber . . . the rascal should be imprisoned or he should be made walk the decks in heavy showers as some of our men are just now doing, squeezing the water from the end of their jackets in bowlfuls, their face and hair shining, their southwesters scarcely keeping it out of their necks'. Nor, in these years beyond the bounty-regulated victuals, was there any training in winter survival, nor extra supplies of fuel, nor adequate heating devices. In Dundee's case, the lessons were not learned. In the saddest episode in Dundee's whaling history, 70 men were lost, 'leaving 100 fatherless children in the port'.

The tragedy began in August 1836. With most of the British fleet on their way home, six ships lingered in Davis Strait to avoid returning 'clean' – the *Advice* and *Thomas* of Dundee, on which surgeon Wanless had served two seasons earlier, the *Dee* of Aberdeen, the *Grenville Bay* of Newcastle, the *Norfolk* of Berwick and the *Swan* of Hull. Within days the six were trapped by the rapidly widening ice field and had to rush through plans to move as far south as possible and to make fast in ice docks for winter. Contemporary journals record subsequent events – the alarm at being squeezed by ice, the emotions of watching a ship disappear, the exhaustion and exposure, frostbite and scurvy, starvation, failing health and, ultimately, the deaths of men by the dozen. Remarkably, some of the eventual mortality appears to have been due to listlessness and despondency among the crew: . . . 'They fell into a reducing slumber under the soporific influence of the cold'. *A Narrative of the Suffering of the Crew of the Dee*, an anonymous account of the Aberdeen ship involved in the incident, reveals how the *Dee* became fast in ice with the *Thomas* and *Advice* of Dundee at 73°10′N, with the *Norfolk* and *Grenville Bay* nearby. The ice was soon so thick that 'the men could travel from either vessel without danger'. The procedure to protect the ships by carving ice docks for them with large saws, five or six men heaving on blocks and tackle to achieve the sawing motion, was only partly achieved before the sun disappeared over the horizon on November 15 – 'a sorrowful day'. Conditions deteriorated and 'the melancholy spectacle' of the *Thomas* of Dundee succumbing to the grinding pressure of ice was recorded on December 12. Although the stricken Dundee ship was five miles away and could be reached only by a highly hazardous trek across ice boulders, the *Dee* immediately sent 22 men to provide assistance, while the *Grenville Bay*, some seven miles from the *Thomas*, quickly dispatched 21 'volunteers' to help. Forced to spend the night on the second Dundee vessel, the *Advice*, which lay between the *Grenville Bay* and the *Thomas*, the English crew found the *Advice* so short of supplies that only 'half a pound of meal' was available to each man for supper. Next morning 60 men from the *Dee*, *Grenville Bay* and *Advice* assisted the crew of the *Thomas* in salvaging stores and equipment – but the chief point of regret in regard to the loss of the *Thomas* was the distance, 'because that precluded the possibility of breaking her up for firewood'. Three days were then spent in the dangerous work of moving stores, and when as much as possible was recovered the captains made an equitable division of men and provisions among the surviving vessels.

Not all of the *Thomas*'s crew reached safety. One man drowned, falling through the ice in the night. Another lay dead in his tent in the morning, 'with part of his hands burnt off in the fire' – a polar phenomenon where frozen limbs were placed too close to heat sources as all feeling in them dissipated. On the *Viewforth* of Kirkcaldy the surgeon found a sailor's feet frozen into lumps:

> Having cut away the legs and uppers of his boots, I found it necessary to go through the same operation with the soles and stockings. The latter tore away the flesh from the insensate mass. So completely frozen were the poor man's feet that when he attempted walking on the deck, the sound was like the knocking of a pair of clamps on a wooden floor. When carried to the fire he was not satisfied with being near it, but he actually thrust his feet into the midst of it, and it was with the utmost difficulty I could prevail on him to withdraw them.

Horrible fates also awaited the Dundee men from the stricken *Thomas* and beleaguered *Advice* in 1837. Scurvy attacked them one by one as exposure to extremes of temperature and lack of exercise took their toll. Scurvy was a disease that appeared at first in the mouth and was recognisable by a swelling of the gums. It caused great pain and discomfort when anything touched these parts and one can only wonder at the anticipation of excruciating pain when the standard fare of salt beef was distributed amongst sufferers. Frostbite was also common, and even a short walk across ice proved likely to initiate this painful condition. Painful stomach complaints affected many and 'rheumatism caused some to move with agony'. With a third of the *Dee*'s crew ill of scurvy by the end of December 1836, the ship's log reveals disquiet among members of the joint crews as the deplorable conditions continued and rations were reduced. On one occasion, a deputation approached Captain Gamblin of the *Dee* to ask for extra food. Declining the request, the captain added with considerable diplomacy that he was aware that the crew had it within its power to compel him to comply with their wishes. The men, as he assumed they would, had no wish to go against their master's orders. The account of events on the *Grenville Bay* of Newcastle also revealed mutinous thoughts: 'Some of the crews were rather rebellious and threatened to take charge of the vessels from the masters and some of our crew seemed to lose all reason. Where ever there were ten men together there were ten different opinions thinking of his own the best'.

The year drew to close with the *Advice, Dee, Grenville Bay* and *Norfolk* beset in ice with the crew of the wrecked *Thomas* shared among them. The *Swan* of Hull had drifted south. The first death on the *Dee*, on January 11, 1837, served to concentrate the men's thoughts. There was a sensitive burial: 'As soon as possible the body was carefully wound in a blanket, sewed up, laid out on the carpenter's bench . . . and then the corpse was carried in mournful procession, to an opening in the ice, through which it was consigned to a watery grave'. However, such was the weakness through illness of the *Dee*'s crew that men from the *Grenville Bay* eventually had to cross the ice by foot to help in the burial of a Dundee crewman from the *Thomas*. It is impossible to express or imagine the hardships endured on ships in such awful circumstances. In stupefying cold throughout the long, dark Arctic winter, many men with frostbite to their faces, hands and feet, hardly capable of moving or speaking through scurvy, the crews also faced the prospect of many months of loneliness parted from their loved ones. In their own imagination they had nothing before them but darkness, cold, hunger and death. And when they retired to their bunks at night, their tired bodies fell upon 'blankets covered with solid ice . . . the pillows frozen in every part, but where the head lay'. As if to add to their nightmare, lice appeared:

> In some of the beds they were literally swarming, and these vermin were of a most rapacious kind. In many cases they found a lodgment underneath the skin, and fed on the flesh like cancerous lechers. Besides scurvy and vermin, the sufferers were almost all seized with the most violent diarrhoea; and so dreadfully did it affect them, that relief for a single half hour would have been hailed as an invaluable respite.

By March 1837, with still no hope of relief, the *Dee* had buried 22 members of its own crew and that of the *Thomas* of Dundee.

It was, ironically, another Dundee ship which came to the rescue of the *Dee*, five months and eight days after she had been beset in ice, during which time she had drifted without direction for 670 miles south, from 73°N to 63°N. On April 25, the barque *Washington*, bound for New York, sent over her captain and four men with provisions to the ship, a considerable act of trust and friendship when she must have been aware of the disease and conditions on board the stricken vessel. The *Washington* commendably interrupted her voyage to tow the *Dee* to the safety of the Butt of Lewis. This gave one passenger time to dash off a letter to the Editor of the *Dundee Advertiser*:

> Sir, I feel it is my duty as a passenger by this vessel to New York to call your attention to the following truly heart-rending and distressing fact. Yesterday, about 7 o'clock pm, we met the Dee of Aberdeen whaler on her way homeward from the Frozen Regions. I may also state the very painful intelligence that has been communicated to us regarding the Thomas of Dundee, amounting to this, that all the crew, with the exception of only three individuals, have perished.

The letter caused consternation in Dundee throughout the day, and until the arrival of the next postal delivery from Aberdeen, 'the space in front of Sinclair's Inn was thronged with people anxiously waiting for further intelligence'. Prior to this revelation, with still no knowledge of the magnitude of the disaster, politicians, owners, merchants and others had petitioned Parliament for a relief expedition to be mounted when their ships had become conspicuously overdue. Under pressure for its failure to act in previous years of tragedy, the Government instead offered inducements for their rescue. Some £300 bounty was offered to the first five ships sailing before February 5, far earlier than the customary start of the whaling season. A letter of January 1837 to HM Customs collector at Montrose, from F. Baring, secretary to the Lords of the Treasury, reveals that the search ships were to carry extra provisions and sail to the edge of the ice, south of 55° latitude, where the missing whalers were anticipated to be. Additionally, the sum of £500 was offered for providing assistance in the ice and £1000 for rescuing a ship beset in ice. Two Dundee whalers, *Princess Charlotte* and *Horn*, sailed for Davis Strait towards the end of February and the former was able to help in the later stages of the relief operation, coming across the *Swan* of Hull, which earned her owners £1200 for her efforts.

When the *Dee* finally arrived in Aberdeen on May 5 with only 15 men alive, 'weeping widows rushed on board with their helpless orphans in their arms'. A letter from the *Aberdeen Observer* to *The Courier* listed the names of the three survivors from the *Thomas*. And when Captain Davidson of the *Thomas* finally arrived in Dundee by rail on June 17, his wife was so completely overcome that she fainted into his arms.

The total number of deaths on board the *Dee* on arrival was 46, nine of them belonging to the *Thomas* of Dundee. The *Grenville Bay* arrived in Stromness on April 27, after being re-supplied by ships on the crossing to Scotland. She had 10 dead plus another 10 from the *Thomas*. The *Norfolk* returned to her own port of Berwick with only eight dead out of 50. The *Advice* of Dundee, meanwhile, staggered across the Atlantic on a more southerly bearing before being sighted west of Ireland wallowing under a few rags of sail on June 3. Ten days later, thanks largely to the crew of the *Grace* of Liverpool, the *Advice* crept into Sligo. A letter was immediately dispatched to the *Shipping Gazette* in London:

> Sir, aware of the anxiety there must be of obtaining the earliest information respecting the missing whalers, we hasten to inform you of the arrival in this port of the ship Advice of Dundee, Captain Deuchar. We at same time regret to inform you that out of forty-nine hands, including ten of the crew of the Thomas (lost in the ice) only seven poor fellows remained living, three of

whom were sent to hospital immediately on arrival of the ship apparently at death's door.

The losses and death associated with the pursuit of whales in more northerly regions, culminating in the disastrous seasons of the 1830s, served to stall the industry and make shareholders uncertain and prospective investors cautious. The ending of the Government bounty in 1824 only precipitated the industry's decline from a peak in 1815 when 164 British ships left for the Arctic; in 1838 only 33 sailed, seven of them from Dundee. Whaling faced other challenges. The expansion of the coal-gas industry in the early decades of the nineteenth century threatened a hitherto vital economic benefit of its catch. The Select Committee on Gas-Light Establishments recorded in 1823 that gas was 'a rapidly increasing means of adding to the convenience of society'. Moreover, as the whale was ruthlessly hunted or frightened away, reducing populations in accessible waters, so the hazards faced by whalers increased – as the 100 'fatherless' children in Dundee knew to their cost.

Whaling had always offered a highly variable yield and the risks were known but, as stocks fell and longer voyages into ice-ridden waters were required, so the industry fell into recession. London abandoned whaling in 1835 and Leith in 1840, with the loss of her last ship *Prince of Orange*. Aberdeen, which boasted 14 ships in 1815, had only three in 1839 and lost her last vessel in 1858 after attempting to deal with the decline by the dangerous practice of 'over-wintering'. Between 1830 and 1840, three Aberdeen firms, the Dee Company, the Union Company and the Greenland Company, sold or attempted to sell their boiling yards and stores. At the end of the 1833 season the Montrose Whale Fishing Company went into voluntary liquidation and its two whalers and boiling house were put up for sale. No one was interested. A year later the Union Whale Company of Montrose had an easier passage into liquidation when its only ship, the *London*, was lost in ice. Bo'ness sent out ships until 1858, when the *Jane* was lost. It was the *Jane*, in 1853, which lodged a harpoon in a whale eventually killed by the *Terra Nova* of Dundee 40 years later and returned as a trophy to Dundee in 1894. Hull, which had packed Stromness Harbour with 25 ships in 1816, discontinued whaling with the loss of the *Diana* in 1869. And Newcastle's last ship, the *Lady Jane*, the longest-serving and best-known of the Tyne whalers, was lost in 1849, ironically a century after the 40 shillings Bounty Act had first encouraged the town's merchants to enter the trade. Dundee was not immune to the fall-out from the succession of tragedies. After the poorest season on record in 1840, when three out of four Dundee boats returned 'clean', the *Fairy* was placed on the market at £1500 and the *Friendship* sold to Newcastle. The *Eber* was put up for sale after returning to port without catching sight of a whale. An advertisement in October 1849 proclaimed the sale 'by public roup' of the entire stock and fittings of the Greenland Whale Fishing Company of Seagate, Dundee. The same year the Dundee New Whale Fishing Company was dissolved while the Fairy Whale Fishing Company, operators of the 50-year-old *Fairy*, offered its ship, boats, lines, guns, harpoons, fishing stores, casks, blubber and oil all for the knockdown price of £800.

The 1830s were a watershed for the industry. Only 30 years earlier Scotland as a whole had fitted out nearly 50 ships. Now, as the few remaining whalers returned empty, if they returned at all, financial strain told on owners and investors. In Dundee the very survival of whaling was questioned for the first time. Returns had dropped from 2000 tons of oil from nine ships in 1833 to just 260 tons from four ships in 1840. Vessels left the industry as quickly as they had previously entered it. Managers in Dundee began using whalers for other purposes. The *Fairy* carried cargoes of emigrants to New York in 1837 and Quebec in 1842, while the *Dorothy* abandoned whaling in 1838 and sailed to Nova Scotia to load timber. Filled with apprehension and fears, faced by economic uncertainty and a community's loss of confidence, the industry went into rapid decline. Indiscriminate harvesting of immature whales in the pursuit of short-term profit had contributed to the ruinous seasons and investors suddenly understood that reduced stocks had serious implications for the trade's future. Nothing in the news from the Arctic encouraged the replacement of lost whalers, which had cost £2000 a time to send there. Sanger concluded: 'It had become painfully obvious that proceeds from the sale of vessels, facilities, and utensils probably offered the only opportunity for individual shareholders to recover even a portion of their investments'.

It was coincidence, but the empty whaling ships which entered Earl Grey Dock in the 1840s were piloted past the first vessels unloading raw jute in Dundee. And while the final triumph of gas lighting and mineral oil threatened the industry with extinction elsewhere, the recognition that whale oil was a uniquely suitable ingredient in the manufacture of jute guaranteed its continued importance to the Dundee economy. With the fortuitous development in Dundee of steam power for her fleet, coincidentally in the year that the threatening new invention of petroleum was made, the way was opened for the town to become the pre-eminent whaling port in Europe – and a centre of Arctic excellence able to offer the Heroic Age of polar explorers the men and ships to take them to the ends of the earth.

TWO

'Blubbertown'

In October 2002, BBC News reported the launch of an urgent police investigation after the discovery of 20 dead seals at Pool of Cletts on Orkney. The seals had been shot. Orkney police and island welfare organisations described the scene as 'unbelievable' and 'despicable'. A century earlier, in October 1902, the 2000 seal and 650 whale carcasses landed by Dundee whaling masters caused hardly a second glance, far less comment. Nor did the 168 dead polar bears swung over the vessels' sides and dumped on the oil-blackened quayside. For a century, the Dundee Arctic fleet culled whales and seals in vast numbers. In 1827 the *Dorothy* of Dundee returned sinking low in the water under the weight of 27 dead whales – a slaughter that would be condemned by conservationists today. In 1866, just four vessels landed an immense haul of 58,000 sealskins at Earl Grey Dock. It was a normal working day in Britain's foremost whaling town.

Whaling and sealing had vastly different practices and procedures, seasons and traditions. Commercial seal fishing from 1750 and for the next 100 years was regarded as a makeweight cargo when whales were scarce, yet later made the difference between profit and loss. Whaling involved more of a chase and much more danger for the hunters, but an equally unedifying end for the hunted. Yet the Dundee whale ships which retain emotional ties to the city today – among them the *Balaena*, the *Active*, the *Polynia*, *Polar Star* and *Terra Nova* – did not actually catch whales. They were expensive transport ships, taking the hunters to the hunting ground.

The first task for those entering the whaling industry was to fit out a ship for the trade. Early Scottish whalers were usually converted merchantmen purchased secondhand, rather than built new. When their role changed from Colonial trading to sailing to the margins of Arctic ice fields, they had to be fortified to withstand severe shocks and concussions. This made them expensive options for those willing to gamble funds on the northern fishery. Hulls had to be secured with double or treble planking, bows reinforced by iron plates and interiors strengthened with crossbars. Scoresby, writing in 1820, recommended 320-ton ships as the most desirable for whaling, possibly to maximise bounty returns. This size of vessel, some 35 metres long by 10 metres broad, was the most common from 1750 to 1850, when larger Dundee steam whalers overtook them. Whaling ships were never cheap. The 291-ton *Resolution* in 1803 cost £4570 to build and £3200 for fitting out. New-build prices rose sharply after the Napoleonic Wars, from £8000 in 1805 to the £14,000 recorded for a Montrose vessel in 1814. Dundee-built steam vessels of the 1860s cost from £8000 to £14,000, depending on size, with the *Glasgow Herald* in 1877 estimating the 'average cost' of a Dundee whaler and its equipment at £12,500.

Smaller ships of the eighteenth and early nineteenth centuries carried between five and six whaleboats of around eight metres in length, which were stowed upturned on deck on outbound and inbound voyages but otherwise kept hanging on davits on either side of the ship, ready to be launched on arrival at the fishery. The larger vessels of the steam fleet frequently accommodated eight boats. Technology was somewhat in retreat as far as whaleboats were concerned, however. Size and equipment at this sharp end of the industry – harpoons, lances, ropes, axe and indispensable bailing bucket – remained largely unchanged over the years.

Those signing on for the 1200-mile round-trip to the whaling grounds agreed to conduct themselves 'in an orderly, faithful, honest, careful and sober manner' when they signed ship's articles after they had been read out by a clerk in the whaling company's office. The articles offered by the Tay Whale Fishing Company to the *Princess Charlotte* crew in Dundee in 1845 were binding in every respect:

> It is Agreed by and on the Part of the said Persons, that they severally hereby engage to serve on board the said Ship, and the Boats belonging thereto, in the several Capacities against their respective names expressed, on a Voyage from the Port of Dundee to Davis' Straits or Greenland and back to the Port of Dundee, and the said Crew further engage to conduct themselves in an orderly, faithful, honest, careful and sober Manner, and to be at all times diligent in their respective Duties and Stations, and to be obedient to the lawful Commands of the Master, in every thing relating to the said Ship, and the Materials, Stores, and Cargo thereof, whether on board such Ship, in Boats, or on Shore.

Further articles debarred the men from leaving the ship without the captain's or commanding officer's permission at the risk of losing their oil and bone money, as well as 'two days pay' for short absences and 'six days pay' for every 24 hours of absence. Also, if any of the ship's company, 'either intentionally or through Cowardice, refuse or decline, or shall not use his or their utmost Endeavours to Strike, Take, or Secure Whales, or other Creatures living in the said Seas', the penalty was to be reduced to the station of able seaman with a severe cut in wages and bonus money. It was no summer holiday in the said seas, weatherwise or otherwise.

A ship's complement was determined by its size and by the number of whaleboats that it carried, but around 45 was normal on the bounty-limited 300–400-tonners before the introduction of larger auxiliary steam vessels in the 1860s. Dundee, like other east-coast ports, sailed with perhaps half a complement of locally-recruited men and added between 15 and 20 crew members in the Shetland or Orkney islands, the last port of call before the Atlantic. These men, hardy souls brought up with boats, would be dropped off on the return journey. This practice continued until the 1870s, when it was sometimes found more economical to bring the Shetlanders south by train to Dundee than to have a ship make a stop in Lerwick, Kirkwall or Stromness.

Ships were carefully prepared for the season's spring departures. An inventory of ship's whaling tools was recorded for the *Union* of Peterhead in 1830. It included 11 seal knives and 28 seal clubs, 30 'bluber' knives, 34 lances, 44 harpoons, 38 lines, 17 hand hooks and seven 'choping' knives. The equipment carried by the crews of each of the *Arctic*'s six whaleboats was listed some 50 years later. It included: '1 harpoon gun, 1 hand harpoon, 5 pulling oars and 1 steer oar, 4 lances, 5 whale lines of 120 fathoms each, or a little over half a mile, 1 tail knife, used for cutting holes in the tail and fins of a dead whale, 1 hatchet for cutting the line, if necessary, 1 flag staff and jack, which is only displayed when a whale is struck, 1 mik or rest for the hand harpoon, 3 spare thole-pins for each thwart [to muffle oars], 2 snow shovels, 2 piggins, or small buckets, used for bailing the boat out and for pouring the water over the lines to prevent their catching fire from excessive friction, 1 fog horn, 2 boathooks, 1 box of ammunition, 1 tow rope [for towing dead whales] and 1 fin tow [a rope used to lash the two fins together across a whale's belly, prior to towing]'.

Equipment was made ready on the lazy outbound voyage. John

Wanless, ship's surgeon on the *Thomas* of Dundee, noted in 1834: 'The coopers have been making piggins or bailing dishes for throwing the water out of the boats, which has got in by means of a leak . . . the carpenters have been making oars in order to have a few in store if any should happen to be broke or lost when every person is engaged during the hard work of catching the whales . . . the sailmaker has been making bags with canvass for boiling puddings into, a very excellent thought among the men'. Captain Murray of Wormit recorded various outbound duties in 1903: 'the watch busy cleaning harpoons below . . . coiled one line in each boat today . . . put guns and other whaling gear in boats'. Another entry reported contrasting roles for the men: crew busy cleaning decks, sailor men setting up main topmast rigging'.

Whale men were paid a monthly wage, plus oil and bone money determined by the tonnage of the catch returned to port. By the time a ship sailed, some wages were already spoken for – a month or half-month paid in advance to allow whale men to purchase appropriate clothing costing about £5 to £7. Oil and bone money, which could greatly exceed salaries, was made months later after blubber and bone had been sold at market value – and accounts detailing purchases made by crew members from the ship's stores had been prepared. One of the earliest accounts of wages, for 1765, lists the salaries for the voyage for the ship's senior officers as: captain 21 guineas (£22.5p), spectioneers nine guineas and the harpooners eight guineas each. The monthly pay of the crew was: mate, carpenter and surgeon £3.10s each, second mate and carpenter's mate, £2.10s each, boat-steerers £2, line-managers £1.15s, seamen and cooks £1.10s each. The captain and spectioneers also had six shillings for every ton of oil and the harpooners 5s 3d each. The reward to the harpooner who struck and killed a fish was half-a-guinea, besides which the captain received three guineas, the surgeon 21s, the mates, spectioneer and carpenter 10s 6d each, the carpenter's mate and boat-steerers 5s each, line-manager, seamen and cooks 2s 6d for every fish killed.

In 1834 the master of the *Superior* of Peterhead is recorded as having a monthly rate of £5, giving him an annual salary of £30, but total earnings for the year of £120 when oil money was added. This sum would have placed him in the 'gentry' class of the north-eastern fishing town. In the same year the *Superior's* mate, second in the ship's hierarchy in terms of basic wage, earned £43 and six other members of crew £30. Captain Middleton, out of Aberdeen, detailed crew's wages in 1838: 'From the Captain, who received five pounds per month, a guinea and half per ton of oil, and twelve pounds per ton of whalebone, with jaw bones, tail and fins, as prerequisites, there was a sliding scale through the intermediate ranks of First and Second Mate, Harpooners, Carpenters, Coopers, Boatswain, Boat-steerers, Line-Managers, etc, down to the able-bodied seaman who got one pound per month and one shilling per ton of oil, while the green hands and apprentices had to be satisfied with something still less'. In comparison, wages for male weavers in Dundee's linen industry in 1833 were around £2 per month.

TYPICAL MID-NINETEENTH CENTURY WHALING WAGES
(1856, MONTHLY)

Captain	£8.00
Mates	£4.10s
Spectioneer	£2.15s
Harpooners	£2.15s
Carpenter	£2.10s
Boat-steerers	£2.10s
Ordinary Seamen	£2.00

(excludes oil and bone money)

The spectioneer, who organised the cutting of the blubber, the skeeman, who was in charge below decks, in particular for stowing the barrels of blubber in the hold, and the harpooners, received three to four times as much bone and oil money as the others, in addition to 'striking money' during a successful whale hunt. Striking money, for example, for 'a sizeable fish' on the *Princess Charlotte*'s voyage to Davis Strait in 1845 was 10s 6d each for senior officers. Given that the ship took 30 whales, earning each man over £15, with a reduced rate for lower ranks, in addition to oil and bone money, the attraction of whaling at this time was not confined to the chance to escape naval impressment. Thus, for instance, the mate on the *Princess Charlotte*, 49-year-old William Latho from St Monan's, received £3 for each of the six months of his voyage, less £3 advance on signing articles, plus 10s 6d per whale strike money, plus 6s 6d per ton of oil, less an advance of 7s 7d. His take-home pay amounted to £15.3s wages, £15.15s strike pay plus £63 in oil bonus for the 30-whale catch, making nearly £100 in total. And there was nothing to stop him finding other work over the winter.

Basic wages reported by 'second mate' Commander Albert Markham RN on signing on for a whaling voyage aboard the larger steam whaler *Arctic* of Dundee some 30 years later, in May 1873, were considerably lower – for himself: 'My wages were to be one shilling per month, and I was to receive in addition the sum of one penny for every ton of oil brought home in the ship and one farthing for every ton of whalebone'. Markham's salary appears irrelevant given that whalebone sold on the quayside in Dundee the previous season for £500 a ton. But his purpose in joining the Dundee fleet was solely to gain experience for his future as a charismatic naval explorer. He knew no one was allowed to travel on a whaler as a paying passenger. It was as a crew member, or not at all. Markham detailed the crew, duties and scale of pay (see over).

Men might be in debt at the end of an unsuccessful voyage – on the other hand, they might make £50, a small fortune from this most irregular of regular employments. It was all part of the excitement of being a whaler, where life on board was based on communist principles – everybody from the captain to the ship's boy shared proportionally in the season's profits. Consequently there was every inducement to work with a will. Although remuneration depended on a successful season in terms of 'fast wages' in the fishery and a bonus conditional upon the amount of cargo returned to the town, these were not always happy eventualities. Analysis of Dundee whaling-fleet returns revealed many 'clean' ships and losses to local companies. Three of Dundee's small fleet of four ships returned clean in 1840, for example. Nine vessels in the 12-strong fleet were clean in 1867 with the financial loss to the Tay Whale Fishing Company, which operated the *Wildfire* and *Victor*, estimated at £6000. That year 800 men in Dundee depended directly on whaling for their incomes and some must have been left destitute. Come the 1890s, only half of the fleet were able to meet the expenses of their voyage from their catch. When whales were scarce as this, men fell into a depression they called whale sickness. Yet, such were the dictates of fashion that whalebone for use in corsets and female foundation garments pushed the price of bone up to an astonishing £3000 in 1904 – the year that the social pioneer Mary Lily Walker recorded one in five Dundee mill lassies earning less than 15 shillings (75p) a week.

Warm clothing was a prerequisite for a voyage to Arctic regions. A wardrobe generally comprised woollen mittens, flannel shirts, a thick tweed waistcoat and heavy coat, trousers, underwear, socks, boots and headgear. Such costly preparation was often provided to seamen in advance of monthly salary, but this debt against future wages was one of necessity before the days shortened and the cold became numbingly intense. Photographs show whale men wrapped from head to toe against the elements, yet the word 'warm' is not prevalent in log books. However, after four months of sub-zero temperatures, men found the return voyage across the Atlantic equivalent to walking into a sauna: 'anything more than a pair of canvas trousers and a cotton shirt was burdensome to us'.

NINETEENTH-CENTURY WAGES, WITH OIL AND BONE MONEY (1873)

RATING	NUMBER IN EACH RATING	MONTHLY PAY	OIL MONEY PER TON	BONE MONEY PER TON
Master	1	£8	£1.4s	£7
Mate	1	£5	7s 3d	10s 6d
Second Mate	1	£3.15s	7s	10s 6d
Doctor	1	£2	2s	2s
Spectioneer	1	£2.15s	7s 9d	10s 6d
Engineer	1	£7	7s 3d	10s 6d
2nd Engineer/smith	1	£3.5s	3s 6d	10s 6d
Carpenter	1	£3.10s	3s 6d	6s
Carpenter's mate	1	£2.15s	2s 6d	4s 6d
Harpooners	2	£2.15s	6s 9d	10s 6d
Loose Harpooners	2	£3.5s	3s 6d	10s 6d
Cooper	1	£3.10s	6s 9d	10s 6d
Ship-keeper	1	£2.10s	6s 9d	10s 6d
Boatswain	1	£3	2s 6d	5s
Skeeman	1	£3	2s 6d	5s
Boat-steerers	6	£2.10s	2s 6d	5s
Line-managers	6	£2.5s	2s	4s
Cook	1	£2.10s	2s	4s
Steward	1	£3.5s	2s 6d	6s
Cook's mate	1	£1.15s	1s 6d	2s
Firemen	3	£2.15s	2s 6d	6s
Able seamen	10	£2	1s 9d	2s
Ordinary seamen	5	£1.10s	1s 6d	2s
Boys	3	£1. 0s	1s 3d	2s
Myself (Markham)	1	£0. 1s	1d	one farthing

Provisions on early whalers were governed by minimum standards laid down by the Government's bounty system, as no supplies were obtainable in Greenland. On early voyages, food usually consisted of hard biscuits, beef, pork, barley or pea soup and potatoes. In February 1811 the Dundee Whale Fishing Company advertised for carcasses of '25 fine bullocks' to be delivered to the company's warehouse in time for the start of the season. In 1837 the Tay Whale Fishing Company sought tenders for eight tons of best ox beef, as well as 40 bolls of oatmeal, 14 hundredweights of potato barley, rum, brandy, wine, tea and coffee. Legs of beef were kept fresh by hanging them in the ship's rigging, where they quickly froze in northern latitudes. 'Our fresh beef was taken from the hold and hung up on deck after getting some brine sprinkled on it,' noted John Wanless on the *Thomas* in 1834. Forty years later the daily allowance provided on the *Arctic* consisted of butter, cheese, oatmeal, bread, beef, pork, flour, tea, sugar, lemon juice and water. A supply of fresh eggs and milk was sometimes added when ships called at Orkney or Shetland – and on Dundee ships especially, 'that godsend Keiller's marmalade' was served.

'Store Day' was the name given to the day early in the voyage when each member of the crew was served his share of the provisions – including the all-important tobacco ration – to last two or three months. This was kept in individual sea-chests next to the men's boxed bunks. In describing the 'internal economy' of a whaling voyage in 1838, Captain Lewis Middleton also remarked upon a weekly 'shop' on board the *Bon Accord*, where men could purchase supplies against wages:

> A Grocery and Slop Shop was kept open for a reasonable time every Monday, when we could buy Sugar, Tea, Coffee, Tobacco, Soap, Jackets, Trousers, Vests, Drawers, Stockings, Boots, etc, in fact everything required, which was charged to us and the amount deducted from our pay on our return home.

Whaler provisions after the withdrawal of the bounty system in 1824 left a lot to be desired. The problem that emerges from the contemporary journals is that while food supplies were adequate for routine sailings, they were seldom sufficient to support a crew stranded in the Arctic over the winter – something that seldom occurred in the bounties era when whales were plentiful in lower northern latitudes. A whaler imprisoned in ice had exhausted its fresh food by autumn and its crew had to turn increasingly to salt beef and hard ship's biscuits, a reliance that made them less healthy and more prone to scurvy. Such situations proved controversially fatal for some Dundee whale men. In 1837, following a succession of tragedies, the former Prime Minister Sir Robert Peel presented a petition from Dundee to the House of Commons in an effort to increase and improve provisions. Moreover, the commendable practice of absorbing members of a stranded crew often exacerbated difficulties. 'We have 21 extra hands, over and above our own men, to feed,' reported Thomas Macklin of the *Narwhal*, after the *Tay* and *Arctic* had been nipped by ice in 1874. In the disastrous season of 1830 the *Horn* of Dundee had nine crews aboard, and when seven vessels were beset in 1850 it was found that they were provisioned for only half the men. The masters had to resort to asking for volunteers to trek over dangerous ice floes to make contact with the nearest ship in open water.

Prior to arrival at the fishing grounds the captain would give the order for the crow's nest to be hoisted to the topmast, or top gallant mast. The historic initiative of William Scoresby Snr, the crow's nest was essentially a large wooden barrel through which a lookout entered by way of a trapdoor, pushed up with the head at the end of a long climb up the mast. When the trapdoor was fastened, the lookout sat on a small seat, his eye to a powerful telescope, scanning the icy horizon. There he endured many hours in temperatures far below zero, with only a screen to protect him from biting winds. Some captains kept a speaking trumpet in the crow's nest, or a large painted arrow, which they used to give directions to boat crews. In such an event, the boat-steerer could react to the captain's signals even though he could not see his quarry. Similarly, the master could shout orders to the mate at the ship's wheel, to enable him to follow a lead through pack ice seen from above. The shipowner William Crondace reported in 1884 that the captains and officers replaced each other in the crow's nest every four hours. Despite this uncomfortable shift, the seamen's sentry box was always manned in the whaling grounds and the crew alert for action day and night, at a moment's notice.

The sighting of a whale brought a shouted signal from the heights of the crow's nest for two designated whaleboats to be launched almost at a run, the crews grabbing whatever clothes they could find before scrambling down Jacob's ladders into the bobbing boats. Whaling ships normally carried six boats which, as Wanless explained, might not all be of the same quality: 'The harpooner draws out of one of the men's bonnets numbers upon pieces of paper and each got the boat the number corresponded to'. This was a crude but efficient means of ensuring that quarrels would not arise over boats which might not pull easily, or sail smoothly: an important consideration when 'strike' money was paid to harpooners and boat crew. A crew numbered six, with each crew pulling five oars, leaving the boat-steerer to use a long and broad-bladed oar for steering. There were no rudders. The hand that pulled the stroke oar also acted as the line-(rope) manager when the harpoons were released. The harpooner would pull the oar nearest the bow until called to his principal task when a fish was sighted. The harpooner was in charge of the boat, the line-manager responsible for ensuring that potentially dangerous lines coiled in every spare corner of the boat were clear to run when a fish was struck. Each whaleboat normally carried five lines, each 120 fathoms, or half-a-mile, long, and they were frequently spliced together to provide greater length. Whaling journals talk of several miles of ropes played out after a running whale.

Reliable deck-mounted harpoon guns replaced hand harpoons and earlier mounted harpoons – invented in 1731 but laid aside for many years – after Svend Foyn's technological advances in 1864–65. They were introduced to Dundee in 1872 and underwent a trial in Victoria Dock. The *Advertiser* commented, 'It is of a very ingenious construction, and by it the harpooner can take aim as with a gun'. The results of the Dundee trial were deemed 'highly satisfactory', with the harpoon head hitting a barrel in the dock and throwing it into 'one thousand pieces'. In subsequent seasons, the harpoon gun was fixed on a swivel in the bow of the boat, and could be traversed around, depressed or elevated by the harpooner. Each harpoon had the name of the ship to which it belonged stamped on the shank and was operated by pulling a lanyard attached to the trigger. Four to five feet in length, the harpoon fired by such a gun had an arrow-sharp point, with barbs to prevent 'drawing' out once it was fast. It was made of Swedish soft iron, and contemporary illustrations of harpoon heads which remained in whales, despite being pulled for many miles, show them in a great variety of contorted shapes, but never broken. When fired, the harpoon pulled the 'foregoer' – a rope lighter than the whale line itself. Only when the whaleboat was fast to a fish would the main heavily-tarred whale rope be played out. A harpoon seldom killed a whale, however. Its purpose was to remain fixed and prevent a whale's escape during its violent, convulsive movements. The *coup de grâce* was inflicted by razor-sharp lances which were thrust deep into its vital organs until 'the chimney caught fire' – the unfortunate analogy for blood spurting from the whale's blow hole, dyeing the sea and drenching the boats and crews, as the exhausted animal rolled on to its side and expired.

Hand-held harpoons remained the favoured option by experienced harpooners for many years. Boats would be rowed as quickly and stealthily as possible, often adventurously to a position five to 10 metres from the fish if surfaced, and always from behind the whale, to allow the harpooner to strike its back, or intuitively guided by the boat-steerer to anticipate where it was likely to surface to breathe. The back-breaking rowing could go on for hours, the oarsmen following the pointed finger of the boat-steerer, with the ship following under sail, making the least possible noise. The responsibility of the captain and the harpooner's important role should not be underestimated. Whaling masters had no manuals or training courses to lead them into the Arctic unknown. Early Admiralty charts were hopelessly inadequate and often based coastlines and depths on conjecture. 'I do not understand its position being so much out on the Admiralty chart,' wrote Albert Markham in 1873, on finding Cape Garry not where it was expected to be. These were the days before radio, radar, sonar or global positioning systems. Reading the weather and the instinct for careful navigation were part of inherited whaling knowledge. Experience was the great teacher – when to sail north or return south, whether to risk the ship or to cautiously withdraw. Masters learned practical skills and the uncanny know-how of visual navigation orally from veteran forebears. They were students of geography and scientific exploration, and often grew up in the trade, the greatest examples being the household-name father-and-son Scoresbys of Hull, Grays of Peterhead and Adams of Dundee. At times of peril, masters confided in each other, sharing their pooled knowledge in the wardrooms of rival whalers, making the most difficult decisions less hard to bear. To the harpooner, meanwhile, a good-sized whale could be worth £2000. If he missed his prey, and missed again with replacement harpoons, the unfortunate whale man would face frustrated, surly shipmates. The *Dundee Advertiser* in 1894 bemoaned: 'Nowadays masters and the older men engaged in the trade lament the decadence of the modern harpooner. There was a time, they say, when a man was only appointed to this responsible position after he had served eight to nine years as line-manager and boat-steerer. Now men who have two years' experience claim to be harpooners'.

When a harpooner struck, his boat hoisted a signal flag and the cry that rang out from the ship's watch was 'A fall! A fall!' – alerting other boat crews that a fish was 'fast'. This brought men leaping from their berths to tumble the remaining boats into the water. It was a critical moment for the 'fast' boat crew. A whale would instinctively react on being harpooned, throwing its mighty tail in the air in violent movements, before crashing it to the water with a crack that could smash a whaleboat to pieces. This was a permanent danger. Many lives were lost in freezing seas in this way. James Lamb, harpooner on the *Erik* in 1881, died 'a few hours' after being struck by a whale's tail. More commonly, a harpooned whale plunged into the depths, or retreated to the bottom beneath the ice. Lines on the fast boat would be played out and the boat rowed at all speed in the direction of the running whale, which could attain speeds of eight to 10 miles an hour for many miles. 'Not only were we being towed by the monster through the pack, but with such rapidity that we were frequently brought into violent contact with the heavy floes,' wrote Markham, safely back in his bunk after a 15-hour chase. This was when the line-manager earned his keep. A whale in flight, dragging the thick rope attached to a harpoon, would be slowed by means of a short wooden post, called a bollard, in the prow of the boat, which the towing rope would be wound once or twice around. Playing a massive whale in the way an angler toys with a fish was a tantalising but dangerous practice. If the line tightened, the boat dipped into the water and risked dragging the men under. Too loose, and the line whirling around the bollard caused so much friction that the harpooner was enveloped in smoke. The piggin, the wooden bucket used for bailing, was immediately brought forward and water thrown on the bollard to stop it catching fire. Similarly, an entangled line drew the bow of the boat under the waves in such a dangerous fashion that an axe was always kept ready for slicing the dragging rope.

With the harpooner's job done and the line-manager controlling his part of the process, the next display of acquired skills came from the boat-steerer who would use his Arctic cunning to predict where the wounded whale would surface. By this time 'loose' boats from the ship would be moving swiftly to the scene, 'loose' harpooners at the ready, to at least be within a distance called 'a start', perhaps within 200 metres of the rising. This would give other boat harpooners the chance to attach extra lines before the leviathan again descended. In time, perhaps one hour, perhaps five, perhaps a day, the exhaustion of pulling miles of two-inch rope and several boats astern would tell on the whale, bringing it to the surface and allowing killing lances to be thrust into it. Albert Markham, hungry and exhausted, recalled being fast to a fish for six hours, 'during which time we had been towed a distance of upwards of fifteen miles . . . until it gave up through sheer fatigue and was dispatched in a dying flurry by the harpooners using lances thrust up to the hilts of their long handles, drenching them in a shower bath of hot and oily blood'.

A typical description of a day's hunt was provided by Dr Kerr's narrative of the 1871 voyage to Lancaster Sound, aboard the Dundee steam whaler *Esquimaux*. His story provides an insight into the men's practices and philosophy, as well as offering a glimpse of the shivering savagery endured in Arctic regions. On reaching Lancaster Sound through Baffin Bay, Captain Charles Yule took the *Esquimaux* to where the water had a dark green tint, the assumed evidence of the whale's feeding ground, and cruised in the hope of falling in with a whale or two. In fog he issued a command for all-quiet to listen for the 'blast' from the Right whales to identify their position. Dr Kerr described how important it was not to scare away whales on approach – a matter which much exercised experienced whale men when steamships replaced the Dundee sailing fleet. Indeed, in January 1880 a meeting took place in Dundee at which whaling captains agreed that ships should be navigated under sail north of 74°50N, and that no ship should steam towards another ship among fish or in calm water. And yet there is no doubting the men's eagerness for the kill when a school of whales was sighted:

All the boats were lowered, or rather tumbled into the water, with all the indescribable excitement that always happens on such occasions. The fish appeared to be 'dodging' – that is playing about in various directions – and one of the boats soon got fast to a fine fish. Our boat was not long in following the example, the flags indicating 'struck fish' of both boats being hoisted almost simultaneously. Our fish 'sounded' with great momentum, going right down under the ice and jerking out the line with such surprising velocity as to threaten momentarily to drag the boat under the ice too. After half an hour's absence, the fish rose a quarter of a mile away in the open water and lay on the surface, rolling his huge bulk in great agony. We were in desperate circumstances. Our line was running fast out, and we had to allow the fish to drag the boat after it in the sudden jerks it occasionally made. Two boats had gone out of sight round the ice in pursuit of another whale and the rest of the boats were engaged in a desperate struggle with the whale first struck. Seeing our signals of distress [sometimes a flag, sometimes raised oars], a boat with the mate at last came to our assistance, and fired two harpoons into the animal's broadside, at which the fish 'made a back' under the boat, and nearly capsized it. The fish now appeared much exhausted and lay on the surface blowing with evident distress. The mate then pulled upon his line, and, getting close to the fish, bled it freely with the long whale lance, after which it spouted blood, and turning quietly on its side, died. We had no sooner got this whale towed alongside the ship – which we had some difficulty finding, in consequence of a dense fog – when the report of a harpoon gun, and a cheer from out of the fog, signalled another capture; and having got a fresh harpoon, we started off again to be 'in at the death'.

Such carnage could hardly be countenanced today. Whales riddled with lance wounds lashed to the sides of the ships, men returning exhausted and soaked in blood on bloodstained slippery decks. The process was gory and relentless, but for a share of the profits the work continued, on the sodden decks or among the blood-soaked floes. Robert Goodsir, aboard the Dundee whaler *Advice* in 1849, told how there was no escape for a Right whale which had sought refuge in an ice hole:

One of the harpooners immediately proceeded over the ice with a hand-harpoon, trailing the end of the line with him, assisted by part of his crew, and from the edge of the hole drove his weapon into the body of the poor whale: whilst some of the others following plied the bleeding wretch with their long lances, so that she was soon obliged to betake herself again to the open water outside the floe. Here more of her enemies were waiting, for our boat was immediately upon her, and a gun-harpoon was at once driven almost out of sight into her huge side.

The carcass of a killed whale would be laboriously towed back to the whaler by ropes passed by deft hands through two holes pierced in its tail. It was secured to the starboard side of the vessel by means of the ropes, blocks and pulleys of the 'cant purchase' mechanism, which allowed the carcass to be turned on all sides for cutting up. After a rest, a celebratory dram, and likely the meal missed during the hunt, the men expert in removing blubber and baleen – the harpooners – would begin the grisly task of flensing under the direction of the spectioneer, the head harpooner. The flensing process involved the men balancing precariously on the oily, floating carcass in boots bristling with spikes, or hacking at the blubber from two whaleboats tied alongside the heaving carcass under the charge of the ship's apprentices. With deep-cutting flensing tools their practised strokes expertly sectioned off the blubber in long parallel strips, before undercutting the strips with short-handled blubber spades in the manner of cutting turf. The large strips of whale blubber were then winched on board and cut into smaller pieces, which were thrown into the hold under the direction of the skeeman. As soon as the spectioneer's flensers had completed the whole surface of the whale lying above water, the cant machinery was cranked to expose another side of the carcass to the cutters. A century after they were last used in this ritualistic practice, examples of flensing tools at Broughty Castle Museum retain razor-sharp – and thankfully protected – blades. When flensing was finished, perhaps after two to three hours, the remaining mass of carcass was allowed to sink into the deep. This was a moment called the kreng, which would be accompanied by more cheers from the drenched and dirty crewmen, aware that it was also a moment a good captain would call for a measure of grog to be distributed. Calculations of the likely bonus occupied the conversation of the men as they retired exhausted and stiff with cold to their cramped wooden bunks.

Some time later, perhaps when the weather was rough, or whale sightings were not anticipated, ship operations were suspended for the tedious but famous whaling ritual known as 'making off' in which whale blubber was separated from skin and further reduced in size for storing in casks. This meant officers and crews forming an assembly line on deck around a metre-high making-off board, where the harpooners' flashing knives cut the blubber into blocks, before removing skin and other fibrous tissues that accelerated decay. The boat-steersmen then reduced it further by chopping it down into smaller pieces. These were dropped into the hold, where they were packed into barrels through bungholes under the direction of the skeeman and two below-decks men nominated as 'kings', who then stowed the casks, winning a double dram as a reward for their messy work.

The making-off process on the *Narwhal* in 1874 was described by surgeon Thomas Macklin in the small notebook journal he kept on the voyage:

> The blubber is hoisted on deck again, it is then seized by two men either side of the deck, who with their pickies, drag it to two men – generally harpooners stationed on each side – whose duty it is to cut it up into pieces about 12 or 16 pounds in weight, and who remove from it all kreng ot extraneous matter. The blubber is thrown forward to the remaining harpooners, who are stationed on each side of the deck, near a 'clash' which is an iron stanchion firmly fixed into a socket in the deck, standing about three feet high, and having five iron spikes on the top. Each skinner has an assistant who picks up the pieces of blubber having skin on it with a pair of clash hooks, and places it on top of the clash. The skin is then separated from the blubber by the skinner armed with a long knife.

In addition to wooden casks, later steam-powered vessels incorporated substantial iron tanks in their holds for storing blubber. These were described on the first converted screw steamer *Tay* in 1858: 'She has on the floor of her hold 51 square iron tanks, so that the blubber, as cut off the whales, can be immediately placed in them ready for boiling. These tanks will keep the blubber much handier and sweeter than in ordinary whale ships'.

On the return passage across the Atlantic, fish or no fish, whale-boats were hoisted aboard and stored upside down on deck, harpoons, knives and blubber spades were washed, cleaned and oiled, and the vessel was thoroughly scrubbed and repainted above the water line. Midway home, the fires in the officers' cabins were allowed to die out for the first time since leaving Dundee. Crew members, usually greenhands attempting to replenish tobacco stocks or sometimes because they had not made enough to pay off their advance wages, would hold auctions of warm winter clothing, books, carved scrimshaw and other personal belongings. 'I acted as clerk to the auctioneer,' wrote Alexander Trotter on his return from Greenland in 1856. The return voyage also gave the officers time to write up journals, weather permitting: 'I am stuck up to a post writing with my knees pressed against the table and seat to make me and my book tumble along with her,' wrote John Wanless on the storm-tossed *Thomas* in 1834. Until the establishment of shore stations in the late nineteenth century, the 'self-contained' Dundee fleet brought its blubber to port for processing to oil, floating or carting its cargo of 252-gallon wooden casks ashore on rafts amid a scene of bustle and excitement, as the wives and families of crew enjoyed the safe arrival of their loved ones – while anxiously anticipating the oil and bone bonus on the horizon. Oil was never extracted on board, and only rarely were slabs of blubber brought home in bulk as they caused an excess of gases in confined areas. Eleven of the crew of the *Eliza Swan* of Montrose nearly died in 1802 after being overcome by blubber fumes in her hold. In any case, by the time Dundee was reached, ships' holds would be rancid and swarming with maggots. Whisky or rum was distributed liberally to overcome the squeamishness of unloading. Jackson points out: 'Whalers were – save perhaps for slavers – the foulest ships in the mercantile marine'.

After the necessary forms were completed, the cargoes of raw material were taken to the large boiling yards in the harbour area. Their task was firstly to store the raw material prior to the extraction process. In due course it took over an hour of boiling in large copper vats for oil to be separated out from the blubber. It was then allowed to cool and stand before being casked for the market. An account for the British Association's meeting in Dundee in September 1867 explained: 'The blubber is not boiled immediately, for the purpose of extracting its oil, on being discharged from the ship. The oil is contained in a cell of fibrous tissue, forming the framework of the blubber, and these cells must be burst before the oil can be separated from the fibrous matters. Various schemes have been tried to crush and cut up the blubber with the view of effecting this, but nothing better has been yet arrived at so effective as to allow the blubber to reach an early stage of putrefaction, which has the desired effect of breaking up the fibrous cells and allows the oil to be extracted or separated'.

The undesirable consequence of the putrefaction, however, was the smell which hung over much of Dundee following the whalers' return. Because of this Dundee became an east-coast 'Blubbertown' – a place, in short, to avoid. The storage of the blubber for a month or so after its arrival left a putrid smell in the east port area, which the boiling process only served to exacerbate. The *Advertiser* reported in November 1825, 'For several days past a most disagreeable, suspi-

cious sort of smell has accosted the olfactory nerves of the inhabitants of this town'. By 1858 the smell of whale oil being boiled in the
yards was still, sniffed the *Advertiser*, 'a disgusting nuisance' and
'sickening'. As late as 1891 one of the paper's correspondents
relished the prospect of an experimental whaling voyage to Antarctica as the 'people living in the east end of the town would no longer
have to complain of the wholesome smell' because he believed,
wrongly as it turned out, that the oil would be boiled on the long
voyage home. Whaling merchants and masters faced loud complaints from the town and eventually had to call in science and apply
to 'three of the most eminent of the medical profession' to tackle the
problem. What the scientists came up with was an ingenious system
– similar to a modern-day catalytic converter – where a system of
conducting pipes and cylinders cooled the blubber vapour in porous
engine coke before passing it as a fluid into the town's sewage
system.

Much to the relief of the townsfolk, 'Blubbertown' was concen-
trated within smelling distance of Dundee's quaysides, where ancillary trades such as ships' chandlers, sailmakers and candle
merchants lined narrow, cobbled streets alongside marine instrument makers, clothing emporiums and insurance offices. Along
these hemmed-in harbour fringes horse-drawn carts brought barrels
laden with decaying blubber over oil-blackened cobbles and into the
high-walled boilyards around the restricted thoroughfares of Candle
Lane, Whale Lane and Trades Lane. Although the boiling yard of the
Mary Ann, a whaler lost in ice as long ago as 1819, is remembered
today by Mary Ann Lane, where it was once located, few descriptions remain of the cask-littered yards. A report for the British
Association meeting in Dundee of 1867 provided only a brief
description of the facilities: 'These yards are large and ample for
storing great cargoes of the bulky raw material after a successful
voyage, and are conveniently fitted up with all the prerequisite
tanks, boilers, coolers, presses, cooperage, etc, necessary for extracting the oil on the most efficient methods on a large scale'. William
Burn Murdoch, the freelance artist who sailed on the Dundee
Antarctic Expedition of 1892, described the office of Robert Kinnes
& Co, where he signed articles as 'surgeon' of the *Balaena*:

> Round the walls were a few maps, mostly of the Arctic regions,
> much soiled by many voyages of skippers' fingers. A pile of
> rusty, greasy rifles, mostly old Henrys, leant against the counter,

and in the far corner of the room was a collection of whaling-
gear and old ledgers.

By and large the yards were also subject to the vagaries and
vicissitudes of the Arctic. If a yard's ship or ships returned 'clean'
– or failed to return at all – then the business was at risk. It was not
uncommon for the Dundee press to advertise the 'public roup' of
boiling yards, warehouses and equipment belonging to a whaling
company – often along with stores salvaged from its stricken ship.

   When the catch was finally in a suitable condition to go to market,
whether as oil or valuable whalebone, the men of the crew knew that
the time had come for their wage packets to be calculated. Whaling
could be a high-earning industry, yet there was never a stable
relationship between the values of oil and bone.

SELECTED WHALE BONE AND WHALE OIL PRICES, 1786–1904

YEAR	BONE	OIL
	£	£
1786	230	19
1790	170	22
1800	65	39
1824	125	23
1833	150	20
1861	350	35
1866	525	52
1874	500	40
1880	720	33
1890	2,550	20
1904	3,000	20

Source: *Dundee Advertiser*, Dundee Year Books

The average price paid for oil in the nineteenth century was around
£35 and for whalebone about £750. Sealskins sold for between four
and six shillings (20–30p) over the same period. Of course, these
averages hide wide variations. In 1830, for example, the loss of so
many ships in Davis Strait, 19 in total, plus the return 'clean' of 21
British whalers, served to push up prices, and the *Fairy* of Dundee
secured a hefty £60 per ton for its precious oil. By 1833 the price had
dropped to £20 per ton and remained around this lower level for

many years as mineral substitutes were developed to supersede oil. The rise in the price of bone towards the end of the nineteenth century is explained by the diminishing quantities harvested and the tight-waisted demands of fashion.

When whales were plentiful, such prices resulted in large revenues in Dundee. In 1874, for example, Captain Fairweather of the *Active* took 25 whales which yielded 160 tons of oil and nine tons of bone. He also returned to Dundee with 3200 seals, yielding 60 tons of seal oil. Thus his catch represented £6400 in whale oil, £4500 in whale-bone, £864 for skins at the equivalent of 27p each, and £2100 in seal oil. Fairweather's total of £13,864 represented a net profit of some £10,000. The dramatic increase in the value of bone towards the end of the nineteenth century did not guarantee huge dividends, however. It only reflected the balance of natural supply against industrial demand, as whale stocks dwindled. In 1906, for example, the Dundee fleet numbered nine vessels. One of them, the *Scotia*, recently returned from the Scottish National Antarctic Expedition under William Speirs Bruce, had been converted into whaling trim. That year whalebone was selling for a princely £2500 and the *Scotia* returned with four whales, a number greater than that of the other Dundee vessels combined. It also brought back two walrus, 16 bears and eight seals. The *Scotia*'s revenues totalled £5051, but the cost of its voyage to the North-West Passage was put at £3956, leaving an annual profit of just £1095. This meant the former exploration ship still had not paid for itself since joining the fleet after its Antarctic adventures. No dividend was paid to investors. Matters could have been worse. The profit from the *Diana*'s trip to the whaling grounds in 1907 exceeded expenditure by £194, while the *Morning*, which had famously helped to relieve Captain Scott's *Discovery* in the Antarctic in 1904, made a loss. It had income of £1750 in whalebone and £284 in oil from the three small whales it had caught, plus £228 from various skins, but the expenses of crew and provisions over six months amounted to £4176, resulting in a net loss of £1914. Whaling, as the whiskered retired captains on the wharves at Dundee knew to their cost, was a gamble in more senses than one.

At such times, the makeweight cargo of seals returned to port often made the difference between profit and loss. Dundee is not generally regarded as a sealing port, yet it actually imported more seal oil than whale oil and eventually boasted an impressive two-storey factory for grading sealskins for the fashion industry. Early commercial sealing took place in the vicinity of Jan Mayen, an island to the east of Greenland at 70°N latitude, or at locations off Greenland's east coast. Later the hunt moved to the huge body of seals among ice floes off Newfoundland, where the Dundee steam whalers were the first outsiders to take part in the cull. Seal oil was used for machinery lubricants and for lighthouse oil; the skin for harnesses, boots and the fashion trade; and, later, the refuse for fertiliser.

Ships fitted out for sealing left Dundee in early March and timed their voyage to reach their destination as the seals were pupping. The killing season would commence towards the end of March. In the light of the massive and indiscriminate culling of seals by the 400-strong Newfoundland fleet – 686,000 in 1831 alone – ships were eventually not allowed to leave St John's, Newfoundland before March 1, and steamers not before March 10. This law was strictly enforced. Once the killing floes were reached, whaler boat crews would take to the ice and walk among vast herds, seeking out pups too young to take to the water but which had already developed a fine white fur – rapidly fattening seals that they called 'white coats'. The ruthless kill was mostly carried out by a crew member striking a seal on its forehead with a heavy club, and then skinning it, sometimes before death had occurred, with a long knife by 'making a cut along breast and belly from snout to tail and dexterously stripping off the fat and skin together'. On a 'good' day the men would club up to 3000 seals, though increasing numbers were dispatched by a single rifle bullet. It was brutal, relentless, impassive, labour-intensive work, which turned the ice red with blood. It was also dangerous. There was an ever-present danger of falling into freezing water as the men courageously leapt from floe to floe to carry out the slaughter, particularly when the movement of heavy seals affected the stability of the floes. Frequently men were crushed or simply disappeared.

Skins, each weighing six to eight pounds, were piled in heaps, called 'pans', on safe ice and marked with a boat's flag to indicate the ship to which they belonged. After further slaughter and the creation of other pans the exhausted men dragged the harvest of heaps across the ice before transferring them by sagging boat to their waiting ship. Later, the blubber would be slashed from the skin by whetted steel in the making-off whaling procedure. Some eight to 10 days were spent on the kill and the slaughter would begin again and again until the season ended when the seals took to the water. A meeting of British Association scientists in Dundee in 1867 was told that it was enjoyable 'sport' – and much more 'exciting and grander' than a grouse shoot.

The extent as well as the nature of the seal kill makes harrowing reading today. In 1868, by which time Newfoundland waters were the preferred sealing grounds, the Dundee fleet reported a 'pack' of seals 10 miles long and from half-a-mile to three miles broad. It was estimated to cover eight square miles of ice, on each of which it was computed that there were from 7000 to 8000 seals. Of these 'scarcely one escaped'. Bad seasons provided some balance. The additional cost of fitting out a whaling vessel to make the week-long voyage to the spring sealing grounds was estimated at £2000. In the event of failure, this was a total loss, and not just for shipowners. Crews missed out on 'oil money' payments. More often, however, the short sealing season was lucrative. When Captain William Adams Snr of the *Arctic* returned to Dundee in 1872 with 8000 seals, representing 80 tons of oil, it earned him £3120 before he even set his compass for the whaling grounds. The *Dundee Advertiser* spared its readers the details of his slaughter, merely remarking that, 'It is hardly necessary to say that the seals found no quarter. The crew commenced to kill them with a will and in the course of two or three days what proved to be the cargo of the *Arctic* was taken on board'.

Dundee, however, was never the top sealing port, as it was eventually the premier whaling port. This is illustrated in returns for the 10 years before auxiliary steam engines allowed a spring sealing voyage and a summer's whaling expedition.

TOTAL CATCH OF SCOTTISH SEALING FLEETS, 1848–1858

PORT	SEALS
Peterhead	725,312
Fraserburgh	79,707
Aberdeen	10,734
Kirkcaldy	9,005
Banff	7,045
Dundee	1,690

Source: Dundee Year Books

Over these years, Dundee masters confined themselves almost exclusively to whaling in Davis Strait, taking only those seals they came upon, leaving Peterhead to claim the sealing crown through its massive catches around Jan Mayen Island, east of Greenland. This position changed after steam power was introduced in 1857. The spring

sailing to either Greenland or, when stocks were exhausted there, to
Newfoundland provided whaler owners with an extra route to profit-
ability by allowing two voyages each year. They were not alone in the
hunt. In the boom years of Newfoundland seal fishing, half-a-million
kills a year were not unusual for the 15,000 men and 400, mainly
American, vessels on station in these waters. Said the *Advertiser* with
considerable compassion in 1894: 'With this extraordinary and, it is to
be feared, sometimes indiscriminate slaughter going on for the greater
part of a century, the wonder is not that the fishery has declined, but
that the seals have not become altogether extinct'.

Even with the coming of steam power in the 1860s, the Dundee
masters were not completely at ease with sealing. The newcomers SS
Camperdown and SS *Polynia* were first to make passage to Newfoundland in 1862, but the trip was unsuccessful. Few seals were
discovered and, to add to their troubles, the *Polynia*'s propeller was
damaged in a collision with ice and she had to put into St John's for
repairs. Morale was sufficiently lowered to preclude another attempt
until 1867 when Captain Charles Yule took the *Esquimaux* to Newfoundland waters. The *Advertiser* reported ruefully: 'A sailing master
who went with the ship to the ice had the misfortune to miss the
seals, and the trip was a failure'. Yule must have viewed with
frustration the *Camperdown*'s catch of 22,000 seals at Greenland
the previous season. With confidence dented, it was a further decade
before Captain William Adams of the *Arctic* and Captain Charles
Dawes of the *Aurora* used auxiliary steam power to engage in the
Newfoundland sealing. This time the former secured 21,493 seals
and the latter 14,634 seals on their inaugural visit, then returned to
the sealing grounds after the whaling season to secure a further 6092
and 1592 seals respectively. After that, the large Dundee steam ships
sailed regularly to the March-April seal cull, filling almost 300 spare
bunks on board with hardy and fearless Newfoundlanders to carry
out the slaughter. The subsequent catch noted in records at St John's
provides useful data in establishing that sealing eventually became
an important industry in Dundee (see opposite).

With such harrowing totals in mind, the last word on the brutal
undertaking of seal-killing is a journal entry which suggests how
indifferent to their savage task the human hunters must have been
. . . and how oblivious to proceedings their victims were:

Unused to enemies on land, the seals merely slept or dozed, or
looked up with indifferent, dog-like eyes as steel slashed the

coat off a neighbour. The blood spurted in hissing fountains, drenching the men, spraying the neighbouring seals. These, with unbelievable apathy, dreamily watched a nearby skinning or casually fell asleep among reeking remains.

TOTAL SEAL CATCH OF DUNDEE AUXILIARY STEAM FLEET, FROM 1867

SHIP	SEALS	NO OF YEARS	AVERAGE
Aurora	245,655	18	13,647
Arctic	151,254	11	13,750
Esquimaux	206,692	17	12,152
Narwhal	75,123	7	10,732
Resolute	107,763	6	17,960
Terra Nova	176,134	10	17,613
Thetis	42,734	3	14,245

Source: Dundee Year Books

THREE

There She Blows!

A maritime enterprise as dangerous and exciting as whaling was bound to be awash with as many superstitions as it was customs and traditions. The ships left to great enthusiasm and excitement before every Arctic voyage. Crowds of well-wishers flocked to the harbour to say emotional farewells. Wives reeled and wheeled on the decks until it was time to leave – 'spirited dancing to the music of a tin whistle'. To a chorus of cheers, children, sweethearts and friends on the quayside threw 'good luck' red herrings, ribbons, apples, or-anges and pennies from shore to ship. But the crews would never catch any of them through the 'shrouds' – the rigging holding up the masts – for fear of an unsuccessful voyage coming of it. Nor would any seasoned harpooner accept the weapons of his trade passed through the rigging instead of round it, rigging which cheering small boys would cling to on the flag-flying flotilla in the estuary six months later – unless, of course, a ship was returning 'clean'. Nor would any master risk setting sail on a Friday – 'never on a Friday' – which was considered unlucky, or, indeed, do anything important on the day Christ was crucified, such as engaging crew members or coiling the harpoon lines into readiness for the whaleboats. And only after casting a pleading eye to the sky for fair winds and fine weather, and a look in the same direction as a sailor's psalm was said, would Dundee whaling captains send their ships on their way to the lingering cheers of their loved ones.

Whale men, like other seafarers, created superstitions to accom-modate occasions, outlooks and decisions. Superstitions offered a sense of control to their dangerous and often chaotic occupation. Horseshoes on a mast would turn away a storm, gold hoop earrings protect the wearer from drowning, and 'open' eyes tattooed on the eyelids warn a sailor of danger whilst asleep. They were constantly on the lookout for omens or lucky charms that could guarantee a safe voyage or, better, economic success. Left largely to themselves with little contact with the outside world, they were subsumed by fears and prejudices – why were fish abundant there and not there, why was his ship successful and not mine, when and from where will the wind blow? Superstition was the natural answer to such questions. And, as they stuck their knives into the aft side of the mast to ensure a fair wind, and the compass needle swung north, Dundee whale men fingered prophylactic talismans in waistcoat pockets and re-called the rituals that might make the difference between felicity and failure.

Useful references to whaling traditions were recorded by the British naval explorer Albert Markham who sailed on the Dundee whaler *Arctic* in 1873 to gain experience of handling steam vessels in polar ice. Markham's narrative, the first full story of the northern fishery in Baffin Bay and Davis Strait, provides a fascinating insight into day-to-day activity aboard Captain William Adams Snr's famous whaling ship. Other journals and contemporary accounts, notably William Scoresby's *Arctic Regions* of 1820, add to his evidence to complete a picture of the idiosyncratic lives of the superstitious men forming the crews of the Dundee whalers among the crushing ice packs, furious winds and freezing fogs of Arctic latitudes.

Perhaps superstition as much as tradition was at the root of the heavy drinking, singing and dancing, raucous start of every whaling voyage. Intoxicated men upset boats and were thrown into the Tay on the way to joining the whaler *Advice* in 1808 and the *Horn* in 1830. The causalities on the first occasion were a few hats and shoes. The five men involved in 1830 were rescued with difficulty and required 'urgent' medical treatment. Captain Lewis Middleton noted in 1838 men so drunk that they had to be craned aboard: 'We never could get our whole crew together before leaving, so, after being towed out of the harbour, we had to lie in the bay until the delinquents could be hunted out of saloons and other drunkard factories, brought along-side in boats and hoisted on deck like bales of goods'. Middleton, who recorded the whaler *Oscar* being wrecked outside Aberdeen harbour because her crew were too drunk to handle her, believed that a temperate sailor then 'was the exception'. Clearly the tem-perance movement that flourished in Dundee, making it home to the national Prohibition Party and Britain's only-ever Prohibitionist MP, never extended to its whale men. As the SS *Arctic* set off on her seventh voyage to Baffin Bay in 1873, Albert Markham noted scornfully: 'The departure of a whaler is marked by a total incapacity of the crew to perform any duties whatever connected with the ship, in consequence of the numerous parting glasses of which they have partaken with their friends and acquaintances'. The log of the *Active*, compiled by one of Dundee's last whaling masters, Captain John Murray, describes her uncertain departure from port on June 10, 1903: 'At 2.30 pm took in mooring. Pilot onboard. Steamed down into Camperdown Dock and out into the Tay. Nearly all the crew drunk'. Murray regarded the sorry crew with wry humour as they eventually surfaced from their bunks, 'with swelled heads on the hunt for the hair from the dog that bit them'.

Vast crowds would give the bunting-adorned ships a hearty and emotional send-off – blasts from sirens announcing that vessels were ready to leave – but the Dundee fleet would often get only as far as mid-estuary before dropping anchor to allow men aboard who were the worse for wear to recover, or those who missed the departure, with perhaps one too many a shanty sung or yarn told, to swim or take a small boat to catch up with her. These men were called the pierhead jumpers. They would burst through the crowd on Broughty Ferry esplanade, three miles downriver from Dundee, and take a high dive into the water to try to overtake their ship by swimming. The human tide flowed in both directions. Willie Anderson, a crewman on the *Morning* for four seasons, reminiscing in *The People's Journal* in 1970, recalled that 'there'd aye be one or two who'd strip doon tae just the essentials, jump overboard and swim tae the Ferry. There they'd sit and have anither drink or two – till they were taken back aboard that night'. This tradition did not always end happily. A 21-year-old boat-steerer from the anchored *Eclipse* died while attempting the swim to Broughty Ferry in the spring of 1907. He had boasted of his swimming abilities during merrymaking on board.

Whaler crews were not permitted to stow alcoholic drinks in their personal sea chests. On board a whaler drink was at the behest of the master, usually in the form of grogs of rum, and most typically after a successful whale kill. Indeed, the late-Victorian Dundee master Tom Robertson won the nomenclature 'Coffee Tam' in the whaling fleet as he would allow no strong drink aboard the SS *Active*, while other captains permitted regular rations of rum, often on Saturday evenings. Perhaps Robertson, and the Dundee owner-managers who eventually imposed the teetotaller's habit on their ships, had learned the lessons of history. One of the saddest traditions of the whaling industry was the inevitability of discipline disintegrating if ships were abandoned or wrecked. The first 'port of call' for the displaced crews was usually the drinks casks. 'Nipped' men would rush aft, providing there was time, and possess themselves of 'anything that may please their fancy, and, sailor-like, immediately broach the ale and spirit casks'. There was a goodly supply to be had for the men who suddenly became their own masters. When the three Tay Whaling Company vessels *Estridge*, *Advice* and *Princess Charlotte* left Dundee in 1824, they were provisioned with 228 gallons of rum, 12 hogsheads (large casks) of beer, five gallons of strong ale, one hogshead of port, a gallon and a half of gin and 18 bottles of wine.

So much rum was rescued from stricken vessels during the disastrous season of 1830 that the thousand men who found themselves 'homeless' on ice with the merged liquor of 19 British ships faced an 'ordeal' that entered whaling folklore as the Baffin Fair Day! When the *Advice* of Dundee was later lost in Cumberland Sound, Captain Simpson of the Hull whaler *Emma* unselfishly sent 20 of his own crew across 12 miles of dangerous ice to locate any survivors. They found around 70 men staggering around next to the stricken ship after excessive imbibing from her rum casks, some of them barely able to walk. Three men died, and several were badly frostbitten.

After the 'drink' delay, the ships would set off northwards, often into the teeth of April gales. By now, discipline aboard was sober and severe, as befitting an occupation which took its employees to the most inhospitable region of the known world, and one that frequently developed into a matter of life or death. Still, it was customary to give three cheers when a ship left harbour; in the case of the *Balaena* in 1906, for example:

> The blue peter was brought down with a run, indicating that the voyage had commenced, and then the captain [W. Guy Jnr] sang out, 'All hands aft.' The nimble sailors ran aft, and lining the taffrail gave, on the call of the skipper, three rousing cheers, waving their caps the while. The scene was repeated as each of the succeeding ships left the dock.

The crews of whale ships were always ready to cheer on the slightest provocation. Three cheers would be called when a 'fish' was killed and when the last of it was taken on board. There were more 'huzzas' when the stripped carcass was finally allowed to sink beneath icy waters. Another custom was ringing cheers when a ship broke through the Baffin ice to reach the north water, at which time a master usually allowed a tot of rum to be served. But the loudest cheers were saved for the great day the captain announced a 'full ship' – presumably in anticipation of the unlocking of the grog cabinet.

Whaling vessels were equally well fortified – and generally surrounded by superstition and tradition. Double- or even triple-planked, reinforced internally, five or six clinker-built whaleboats stashed to their decks, two coats of tar to their underbellies, painted black topside, a white line along their covering board, they languished over winter in east-coast ports awaiting the spring fishing season. But a ship which had been brought down from the yard stern first was usually given a wide berth by seasoned and superstitious mariners until it had been sent back and brought back down bow foremost. Whaling was enough of a risk without gambling with time-honoured traditions.

With a voyage under way, meal times were regulated: breakfast at eight, dinner at twelve and 'tea' at five. It is clear from Arctic narratives that these habits were jettisoned when the fishery was reached. On one occasion Markham mourned that he had had three hours' sleep in sixty-four, and he often noted that the men suffered confusion over the time of day. 'The state of irregularity in which we live is positively delicious. I never know when I am to have anything to eat, nor even when I am to get any sleep. On some days we breakfast at 5am, on others at 5pm, and the remaining meals are served in the same charming irregularity.' Clearly enjoying the phenomenon, he added in a later diary entry, 'The men were turned out at four, having an hour given to them to collect their scattered senses and to get some breakfast, dinner or tea – it is impossible to say by which name this meal ought to be called'. Dr Rae, the surgeon on the SS *Arctic* two seasons before Markham, complained of not being able to distinguish between night and morning: 'There have been fifteen meals on the cabin table between midnight on Sunday and half-past nine this morning. A fellow begins to doubt his correctness as to whether it is morning or night when tea-time arrives at 11 o'clock am'. A fascinating comment on the seasonal nature of the industry was made by the captain of the ill-starred Dundee whaler *Thomas*, who complained in 1834 that he had never been able to taste fresh strawberries during 21 years of Arctic attendance.

With sizeable Dundee fleets operating in the waters of Davis Strait over much of the nineteenth century, a system of recognition evolved to avoid any possibility of confusion, not least because of the impenetrable Arctic fog which attended many journeys. When the ships were fishing in company, for example, it was customary for the vessel whose boat succeeded in getting 'fast' to a fish to display a special 'fishing' flag from the mizzen mast head, which was kept flying until the fish was killed. Each ship had a different device or pattern for her flag, and the whaleboats that each carried were painted in different colours to distinguish them from other boats when fishing in company. The boats of the SS *Arctic*, for example, were painted blue, white, blue, horizontally. Its fishing flag was white with a blue five-pointed star. After one successful hunt Albert Markham recorded, 'One of the boats was literally drenched with blood; so much so, that when I saw it coming alongside, I imagined it was painted red, and inquired what ship it belonged to'.

The process of catching and processing whales was also steeped in tradition. In whaler parlance a whale was always a fish, nothing else in whaling vocabulary coming under that designation. When a harpooner struck successfully, the cry that rang out from the watch was 'A fall! A fall!' – the stamping boots on the deck alerting boat crews below that a fish was 'fast'. Such was the custom to respond to such calls with precipitous haste that young hands are recorded as believing their ship was going down. In an instant the deck would fill with semi-naked men with snatched bundles of clothes under their arms, running to get into the first boat in temperatures seldom above freezing. Robert Goodsir, who sailed on the *Advice* in 1849 to try to find out more about the fate of his brother Harry, assistant surgeon of the lost Franklin exploration vessel HMS *Erebus*, described being alerted by men shouting 'A fall! A fall!' at the pitch of their voices, 'whilst the rest of the crew are tumbling pell-mell into the remaining boats, which are lowered almost by the run, and without the loss of a second are off towards the 'fast one,' which is now seen, with its 'jack' flying, a happy sight to the master, who directs it to be replied to, by hoisting the ship's 'jack' at the mizzen'. Flags, or jacks, formed an important whaling tradition. Each wooden whaleboat, besides its harpoons, lines and oars, was equipped with a slim flagpole and 'jack' in the ship's colours. Flags instantly denoted success or otherwise. In the 1884 log of the *Nova Zembla* Matthew Campbell recorded the crew's joy as 'our cautious spectioneer an old Greenlander Jack Knight fired his gun and got fast, hoisting his flag'. Just five days later, Campbell was able to watch the Dundee sister ship *Arctic* getting 'fast to a fish with one harpoon, but it must have got loose again as the jack was pulled down'.

The speed of response to a 'fast' harpoon was a feature of whaling and a matter of great pride and rivalry among crews. The master in the crow's nest, bawling directions to the fast boat out of a speaking trumpet, would, like the men, realise that upwards of £1000 was at the end of the line . . . but it would likely stay there only if other harpoons were got fast. Thus the last man reacting to 'a fall' was greeted by oaths and the last boat lowered was disgraced. Basil Lubbock commented in his history of whaling, 'It did not matter how cold it was, the men never waited to dress; this was done as the boats were pulling their hardest towards the fast boat, each man of the boat's crew being allowed to put on one article of dress in turn until all were completely clothed. Sometimes a boat had been rowed several miles before her crew were fully dressed, and sometimes when the fast boat was near the ship, the men of the other boats had no opportunity of dressing and frost bites often resulted'.

Once the kill was achieved, it was traditionally the duty of the crew of the first 'fast' boat to prepare the whale for coming alongside – always on the starboard side of the vessel. After a period of rest, which followed exhausting occasions when whaleboat crews might row in fields of ice for anything up to 20 miles in deepest silence in pursuit of a fast whale, and then have to tow a dead animal back to the ship at a mile an hour, the order for flensing, removing the blubber from the whale, was given, and the crew was primed 'with a glass of grog'. This was often a compound of Morton's Dundee rum and water and it was viewed by the men as necessary food. In the early days of whaling, men lowered on to dangerously-thin bay ice were roped together to enable them to approach whales surfaced in isolated pools of water. Several men could fall through the ice, but those who endured this freezing fate were hauled to safety and given a tot of rum on their return to ship. Although it was the hardest grog ever earned, William Scoresby concluded that some took the plunge on purpose in order to qualify for the liquid compensation! A further honour secured by a successful whaleboat concerned the messy operation of flensing. Before it began, the massive, rubber-like tail of the whale was cut into square sections to form the whaler's equivalent of a butcher's block, on which blubber was subsequently chopped into pieces without damaging the blades of the men's cutting tools. It was customary for the boat-steerer of the first 'fast' boat to have the choice of blocks, after which each man marked his own block by cutting his initials upon it.

For the superstitious on board, a successful season's fishing could be guaranteed by exorcising any spirits remaining from 'clean' ships. This involved a ceremony described by Markham in mid-Arctic waters in 1873: 'The men attribute their good fortune today to the fact of their having last night burnt in effigy two of the crew, who are supposed to bring ill-luck, having had the bad fortune to serve of late years in ships which have returned "clean," or after very poor voyages'. This incident may have owed its origins to a custom practised in the early days of whaling in which burning 'the witches' who brought bad luck involved placing salt on the end of a flat stick, which was then pushed through the ring of the anchor. The salt was set on fire, with the master of ceremonies reciting an incantation to ensure good fortune for the ship during the voyage.

Salt was also a component of a rough-and-ready cold cure tried on the SS *Arctic* that year when an 'old salt' among the crew, despairing of ever getting better through the ship's medicines, applied a raw, salted herring to his neck, tied a handkerchief over it, and kept it on overnight. Next day he assured everyone of the benefits from its effects. This, too, may have had origins in ancient custom as seafarers of former days wore nutmeg round their necks to cure scrofulous or other glandular swellings. Of course, if a ship caught no fish there was inevitably a Jonah on board. A Jonah was the bringer of bad luck on a voyage – bad weather, bad catches or bad accidents. The two crew members on Markham's voyage who were thought to be carriers of ill fortune would not necessarily have had an easy time of it on the *Arctic*. Belief in luck in whaling crews was very deep-seated, and it was known for the 'ill luck' of such men to be readily believed in by the crew. Men were occasionally discharged from vessels because of their reputations as Jonahs and tensions heightened as their reputations followed them from ship to ship. Sometimes whale men resorted to strange customs to rid themselves of being seen as carriers of ill luck. One journal tells of superstitious hands gathering filthy clothes, shaping them into a human figure, packing it with gunpowder, attaching it to the mast, then taking pot shots at it until 'Jonah' was blown to smithereens.

Some ships, too, had the unenviable reputations of being Jonahs. These vessels had difficulty getting crews until their luck changed. Thomas Macklin in 1874 watched the *Tay* being nipped and crushed by ice just as she was getting out of Melville Bay, and there was no hint of regret as he recorded that 'she was a leaky old ship anyhow, and nobody will be sorry but the underwriters'. Conversely, certain vessels, and in particular their masters, acquired the enviable reputation of being the luckiest in the fleet. It was always thought a piece of good fortune to be able to ship on board such vessels or in the company of such men. Macklin, for example, held the little *Victor* in high regard: 'she is a brave, stout little ship and will take them all safe home'.

Another day of celebration in the whaling fleet was Old Horse Day – the end of the first month at sea, which the sailors, given wages in advance, all spent, considered they had worked for no money. They constructed a dummy horse and had a procession around the ship, singing whaling shanties or chanting bawdy rhymes. Shanties were sung whenever the crew were working in unison, but particularly when considerable effort was involved, such as the backbreaking job of towing a ship over ice to a lead of free water, constructing an ice dock or the aching task of boring a hole for an ice anchor. Some whaling songs passed into the city's folklore, the best known being the tribute to the *Balaena*:

> Oh, the noble fleet of whalers out sailing from Dundee,
> Well manned by Scottish sailors to work them on the sea;
> On the western ocean passage none with them can compare
> For there's not a ship could make the trip as the Balaena, I declare.

> Chorus:
> And the wind is on her quarter and her engine working free,
> And there's not another whaler a-sailing from Dundee
> Can beat the aul' Balaena and you needna try her on,
> For we challenge all both large and small from Dundee to St. John's.

> And it happened on a Thursday, four days after we left Dundee,
> Was carried off the quarter boats all in a raging sea,
> That took away our bulwark, our stanchions and our rails,
> And left the whole concern, boys, a-floating in the gales.

> There's the new built Terra Nova, she's a model of no doubt,
> There's the Arctic and the Aurora, you've heard so much about,
> There's Jacklin's model mail-boat, the terror of the sea
> Couldn't beat the aul' Balaena, boys, on the passage from Dundee.

> Bold Jacklin carries canvas and fairly raises steam
> And Captain Guy's a daring boy, goes ploughing through the
>   stream,
> But Mallan says the Eskimo could beat the bloomin' lot,
> But to beat the aul' Balaena, boys, they'd find it rather hot.

And now that we have landed, boys, where the rum is mighty
  cheap,
We'll drink success to Captain Burnett, lads, for gettin' us ower the
  deep,
And a health to all our sweethearts, an' to our wives so fair,
Not another ship could make that trip but the Balaena I declare.

Note: The song, c. 1890, refers to Captain William Guy of the *Polynia*,
Burnett's previous ship. 'Mallan' is Captain William Milne of the *Esquimaux*.

A further tradition involved a painfully cruel ceremony which befell
newcomers to whaling on May Day, or as a ship crossed the Arctic
Circle, as a parody of the equator-crossing ceremony common in
shipping generally. The Arctic ceremony was so awful that it
dominated the conversation of anxious young hands on the *Thomas*
of Dundee in April 1834 even as she left the Tay estuary – and it
made them 'sailors at once' on its completion. Its initial stage was
described in Alex Trotter's *Journal of the Voyage of the Enterprise* in
1856:

> Tues 1 May: This morning, immediately after 12 o'clock, a
> curious ceremony was gone through on board . . . About 10
> minutes past the midnight hour, although it was clear as mid-
> day, I was startled by the sound of a horn blazing three loud
> blasts and on looking up I beheld two strangely-attired figures
> leaping over the bows of the vessel, not however, before a voice
> had thundered, 'Ship ahoy,' which words had been set to music
> by the ringing of bells. The one figure was the great Neptune;
> the other was his wife. Their appearance was very remarkable.
> Let me describe the nobler animal first: his headpiece bore a
> striking resemblance to a red nightcap such as human beings
> wear; his face was covered with a beautiful veil which, however,
> allowed his beard, white as the coat of polar bear, to fall
> gracefully down on his breast; his habitments were first, cover-
> ing the crown of his head to the waist and including his arms, an
> Esquimaux coat made out of seal skins and sewn together with
> sinews of the whale; second, his inexpressibles or trousers were
> also made of sealskins, which is very natural as what else could
> the so-called God of the sea get to clothe himself with? In one
> hand he carried a trident, an emblem of his authority, and in the
> other the trumpet through which he had summoned our vessel.

His beloved loving spouse was attired in a pair of moleskin trousers and was otherwise wrapped up in a large green shawl.

Thereafter Trotter described how Mr and Mrs Neptune, two of the *Enterprise* crew dressed up, of course, accompanied by burly servants bearing long whaling lances, subjected blindfolded Arctic novices, or 'green hands' as they were known, to a cruel initiation rite as their rite of passage. Firstly, the unwitting hands were invited to 'kiss' Mrs Neptune. At this point a little box filled with gunpowder mixed with flour, and with a lighted candle next to it, was placed in front of them. Mrs Neptune's blown kiss served to ignite the mixture and set fire to the unfortunate crewman's whiskers. Inevitably there would be a yell of pain. At this point, a frothy broth of filth made from oil, soot and grease was shoved inside his mouth and lathered over his face. Then his painful chin would be 'shaved' with a razor made from an iron hoop saw. Skin torn off, face bloodied and burned, he was saluted as a freeman of Greenland!

The May Day initiation ceremony was also practised on the Aberdeen whaler *Bon Accord* and recalled by Captain Middleton in 1838:

> A gruff voice is heard from over the bow demanding the vessel's and Captain's name, nationality and destination, Neptune then (for it is the veritable Sea God) orders that the ship be hove to till he comes on board. He then, armed with his trident and accompanied by Aphrodite, his wife, steps over the bow and the royal pair take their seats on the gun carriage, and are drawn round the deck, serenaded by music from the ship's bell, the beating of frying pans, and other discordant sounds. All the preparations had been made to initiate those who are making their first whaling voyage; of these there are usually from ten to fifteen, who are stowed away in some convenient place and watched over by old hands detailed for the purpose, who bring them forward one by one, blindfolded, as they are wanted to undergo the process of being shaved.

One report of this rough ceremony tells of Mrs Neptune kissing the blindfolded crewmen while wearing a moustache made of the points of nails. Another suggests the hoop saw was garlanded with ribbons from each of the crew undergoing the rite – ribbons given to them, by tradition, by their loved ones on departure. Afterwards the ribbons were knotted into a garland and hung from the foremast head where, out of superstition, it remained until the whaler docked safely in its home port, a token of good luck bleached white by the elements. In his *Account of the Arctic Regions*, published in 1820, William Scoresby describes one of the garlands as being an effigy of Neptune himself, but often a model of the ship was placed at the centre of the ribbons. A 'Dundee' garland was noted by the surgeon R. H. Hilliard on the *Narwhal*'s maiden voyage in 1859:

> Hanging from the top mast stay in a state of the most deplorable wretchedness this specimen of a garland was the production of our most disreputable-looking hand, who had been married for several years, his wife being about as bright a specimen of humanity herself. Between this pair of turtle doves I understand a squabble arose, the male bird coming off with his red flannel shirt in tatters and she with a broken nose and a black eye. The tattered shirt was, along with an iron hoop, hoisted to the mizzen top mast and there it was allowed to remain.

No one was exempt from the May Day ceremony, noted Captain Middleton, but it appears that sea gods were not beyond bribery. Some officers, such as ship's surgeon and 'visiting' explorers or scientists, like the writer Arthur Conan Doyle who voyaged to the Arctic as surgeon on the *Hope* of Peterhead in 1880, were excused the painful process if they presented a sufficiently valuable gift to the royal couple. A bottle of rum was usually acceptable. As for the more troublesome novitiates, they were given the added taste of a bucket of cold, salty seawater – to help, they were told, to extinguish the flames.

A gentle irony which mirrors the cruel humour of the initiation of the youngsters is that Neptune's entourage effectively had the run of the ship as the day progressed, to the extent that 'Neptune' could boldly demand a cup of grog in the captain's cabin. Such was normal ship's discipline that the hands would not dare walk on the same side of the quarter deck as the captain, and would not normally speak to him without touching their hats. The ceremony always ended with good-humoured singing and dancing, however. Parties on board Dundee whaling vessels were called 'mollies' and usually involved a shipboard melodeon, or bagpipes as in the case of the screw whalers *Narwhal* and *Nova Zembla* in 1877, much to the envy of the remainder of the dozen-strong fleet. 'Mollie' participants were usually the officers and experienced hands, and often extended to other ships in the fleet. The traditional signal that indicated a captain was offering hospitality was the presence of a bucket hoisted high at the mizzen-top-gallant masthead. Very soon his guests would arrive by whaleboat. Markham on the *Arctic* in 1873 reported ruefully, 'I am now writing amidst a perfect chaos of empty bottles, broken pipes and glasses, and cigar ashes, inhaling a strong perfume of stale tobacco. And the cause of all this is, we have had a "mollie" '. The bucket-on-mast signal served a dual purpose. It was also used by captains to order the return of whaleboats, perhaps after a hopeless chase, or when weather conditions were worsening. It could also be used to signal the return of a shore party. The most urgent signal of all was one that remains with us today. When a whaling ship flew its flag at half-mast on its main masthead, it was a cry for help that usually signalled disaster had struck.

Interaction within a whaling fleet served other purposes. Captains often conferred over incoming weather, oncoming ice or the coming or non-coming of whales. The survival of the crews as well as the success of the voyage often depended on individual or collective experience of the characteristics of ice and weather conditions. There were no training manuals. Admiralty charts were notoriously way-ward. Hard-won practical skills usually outstripped current scien-tific thinking, and seldom did captains return to port without surveying a new coastline or sounding a new channel. It was also an unwritten custom that masters of endangered vessels sought the advice of colleagues in times of peril. Three experienced Dundee masters decided in October 1878 that the SS *Camperdown* should be abandoned in Davis Strait when she developed a leak, for example. Another congregation of masters gathered in 1880 to examine the long serving *Victor*, before deciding to abandon her at Coutts Inlet. Six years later, Captain Souter of the *Triune* consulted on board with Captain Adams of the *Maud* as ice squeezed the life out of his vessel in Lancaster Sound. She was abandoned not a moment too soon, disappearing beneath the ice 90 minutes after the veteran master disembarked. Thomas Macklin records the captain of the *Narwhal* desperately searching for safe anchorage in terrible gales and driving snow, and about to give up all hope of reaching safety when a crewman caught a glimpse of a blue light 'which Captain Yuille of the *Esquimaux* burned, just for fear some ship might be close at hand, and very fortunate it was for us'.

Otherwise, life was a solitary experience above the 70th north parallel. There was no communication with Scotland for up to eight months and no post office in Davis Strait. Homebound whalers would take the 'home letters' for delivery in Dundee. Incoming whalers would bring letters, and copies of the *Dundee Advertiser* and *Courier*, to be distributed among ships stationed in the fishing grounds. One can sense the men's joy at contact from home while becalmed and inactive in polar seas. Dr Wanless on the *Thomas* in 1834 recorded, 'I went on board the *Charlotte* of Dundee to see my friend Mr Milne and to deliver two letters'. Dr Macklin on the SS *Narwhal* 45 years later noted, 'We left [after a visit to the nearly-full whaler *Victor*] on the understanding that if they got full they would speak us [make contact] and take letters home for us'. And surgeon R. H. Hilliard on the *Narwhal*'s first voyage in 1859 commented: 'No sooner up with the Dundee fleet than we are boarded by boats to get and give news and (as we carry mail) to receive letters from home'. This was an important function and men on a six-month voyage must have been sorely disappointed to receive no communication from home. The Danish station of Upernavik, on Greenland's west coast, and in the lower regions of Baffin Bay, was generally the last settlement where post could be left on dry ground. Even here travellers were infrequent. Alexander Trotter's journal of the voyage of the whaler *Enterprise* in 1856 reveals that 'a boat came on board and told us a lot of news, such as that the war was finished' – a reference to the end of the Crimean War. And when Captain Adams called in June 1873, no European intelligence had been received at Upernivik for nearly 12 months, 'so that the finding of Livingstone, the death of Napoleon, and the abdication of the King of Spain were all news to Dr Rudolf [the Danish governor and chief trader]'. The only contact between the men and the outside world was the arrival of another whaler.

Some traditions appear irreconcilable. On the one part, there was intense rivalry between ships and their crews. There would be rejoicing if a whale was missed by one and gathered by another. Rival Dundee harpooners, for example, were recorded by Dr G. A. Rae on the *Arctic* in 1871: 'The *Intrepid*'s boat had already got fast to two ships. One of our harpooners had a race for a fish with one belonging to the *Intrepid*, who played the same trick with our man last year, and got the fish. Both boats fired – ours getting fast, and the other missing the aim. The *Intrepid*'s man was hauling in the loose line, and said, "We are all right!" "And so are we," said our man, in a derisive tone. "One good turn deserves another; perhaps you re-member an occurrence last year?" ' A Captain, on sighting a fish, would use stealth and quietness on his approach, not solely to avoid scaring off the whale but to prevent neighbouring ships from witnessing the action or seeing 'his' whale. 'The whaling is a very selfish trade: if one ship is unsuccessful, nothing delights her master and crew more than to observe others equally unfortunate,' revealed one journal. When the *Camperdown* got fast in Davis Strait, the *Narwhal*'s boats were recalled and hoisted up by a clearly dejected crew, 'our consolation, a very poor one, being that it was only a small fish, "no larger" as one of the harpooners informed me, "than a sardine" '. On the other hand, a whaler crew seldom ignored a plea for assistance from another, and the history of the Dundee fleet is criss-crossed with tales of bravery involving crews risking lives to assist others.

Superstitions also existed for the waters north of Upernavik, and for the inevitable deterioration of climate which awaited those who ventured towards Melville Bay. When a south wind blew, causing loose ice to be packed hard against the thin water leads in Davis Strait, it was called the 'strong ale' wind by old-time whalers. In this situation, ships were more liable to get 'nipped' and therefore destroyed. Another wind was called 'the barber'. This was not so much a wind as a situation where frozen snow particles were blown by the wind. Its name was given when it pierced the men's scarves and mufflers, causing their faces to sting and bleed. It has been said that whaling high above the Arctic Circle was always a gamble. Dundee's most famous whaling master, Captain William Adams, was as superstitious as he was knowledgeable enough to counter the risks. Adams always carried with him what he called a 'lucky penny'. With this, from first thing in the morning until last thing at night, whether on deck or below, 'he is always anxious to toss with the doctor for the best of five successive guesses. It is most amusing to watch the cunning manner in which our worthy skipper puts his coin down, and the delight beaming on his jolly countenance when he succeeds in winning,' wrote Markham in 1873. The Canadian writer Dorothy Harley Eber noted that, 'In treasure boxes carefully stored by families in Cape Dorset and Lake Harbour [in the Canadian Arctic archipelago] are much-cherished collections of big British pennies. Often these are inheritances passed down from whaler ancestors who travelled on the *Active* [presumably with Adams]. The pennies once decorated women's amaautiit [sealskin costume] along with beads and spoons'. The taking of coins on a whaling voyage was usually regarded as an unnecessary practice, but they were not entirely unknown on superstitious ships – a silver coin placed under the masthead ensured a successful and profitable voyage. In *Moby Dick* Captain Ahab nails a gold coin to the mast as a reward, making the crew of the Nantucket whale ship *Pequod* swear they will assist him in killing the famous white whale for revenge.

Whether it involved nearly a full day of daylight, or the dreary months when the sun remained below the horizon – when the tradition of carving scrimshaw from whale's teeth or bone took hold in long periods of inactivity – long-in-the-tooth Arctic whaler hands could find something in nature's phenomena to praise for good fishing or blame for bad. It is hardly surprising that the combination of climatic and physical extremes and the inhospitable and lonely Arctic environment heightened the men's spiritual awareness. Voyages seldom began without prayers the preceding Sunday in Dundee and Broughty Ferry churches, and a missionary's blessing was often delivered in Baffin Bay as whalers anchored to take on water at Danish settlements. As early as 1818 a society to provide Bibles and prayer books for the spiritual welfare of whale crews was launched at Hull and besides his classic *Arctic Regions* of 1820, Scoresby compiled a *Seaman's Prayer Book* that was used extensively in the whaling fleet. Thereafter Bibles and books were frequently donated to Dundee's whale ships. The *Advertiser* noted novels, books on history, travel and biography and added: The sailors are condemned to six months of almost complete isolation amidst unavoidable discomfort, and they very much enjoy the books provided.

In his entry for 'Sabbath, 25 May, 1834' John Wanless records activity at the slop shop on the *Thomas*: 'eight testaments were sold and four Bibles, at 2/6d Bible and 1/6d Testament, cheap enough. They were got from some of the ministers of the Sabbath School Union of Scotland'. Curiously, a famous seaman's tradition holds that reading the Bible at sea carried considerable risk unless a burial was being performed. This is thought to have originated in 1707 when a condemned sailor being marched to the yardarm gallows aboard HMS *Association* shouted out the 109th Psalm – 'May his days be few; may another seize his goods! May his children be fatherless, and his wife a widow!' – to curse his commanding officer. The following day the *Association* was lost with all hands and another seafaring superstition took hold.

The weather in Davis Strait was no friend of the written word. One ship's library in 1856 was frozen into blocks of ice and had to be thrown overboard, and the compilation of officers' logs was often interrupted by heaving seas or crashing floes. But it is clear from various journals that the value of religion was felt more readily where dangers was present. On the occasion of Captain Gamblin's death during the *Dee/Advice/Thomas* tragedy in 1837, 'all seemed more than ever sensible of early preparation for eternity. . . . The mind was in a peculiar manner disposed to listen to the instructions of the sacred volume'. The journal of the *Viewforth* of Kirkcaldy's troubled voyage to Davis Strait in 1836 refers many times to the power of religious belief, in this instance recording the drowning of a crewmate on a Sunday: 'He fell into a hole, the brush ice met over him, and he disappeared for ever, to give an account at the judgment seat of Christ. What an awful warning to us, when we think of a man ushered into the presence of his Maker in such a [blanks here] and on the Lord's most holy day'. Later, the writer recorded the willingness of the men to pray: 'Oct 22d. It was unanimously agreed to by the men that we should assemble in the half-deck to give thanks to that God who has so mercifully preserved us through the past week. Sung the 29th Paraphrase and part of the 107th Psalm. It was truly sublime to hear our voices ascending to the throne of the Most High in such an awful situation, and I am sure many of them sung from the heart'.

And on the occasions when death struck in these northern latitudes, in circumstances other than when ships became the tombs of their frozen crews, the whale men of Dundee had a traditional manner of disposing of shipmates. If the death occurred at sea, the body was sewn up in a blanket, with a heavy iron bolt fixed to its feet, and placed on a flat board. After a short service led by the captain, it was slipped off the deck into the sea. If a death occurred while a ship was nipped, marooned or docked in ice, the body was carefully wound in a blanket, then 'carried in mournful procession' to a hole drilled in the ice, through which it was consigned to a watery grave. Dead officers, though, were sometimes preserved in barrels of brine and returned to port!

While the fear of death was usually eclipsed by the lure of whaling, the risks remained great – and occasionally they presented themselves closer to home. Just as it was one custom for whale men to doodle sketches of whales in the ship's log as and when a 'kill' occurred, another tradition was for whale ships to fire a large-calibre gun on entering harbour to indicate the number of fish taken. In 1810, however, a powder horn in the hand of crewman David

Lorimer ignited and caused an explosion on board the Dundee-registered *Calypso*, which was returning with a full hold of 14 whales. He was severely injured.

One final tradition was the custom of boys trying to 'escape' from Dundee by stealing aboard her fleet of whalers. It seems incredible that youngsters would voluntarily stow away on a ship sailing to the most inhospitable region in the world, where life and death often depended on an otherwise insignificant change in temperature, and where work was bone-crushingly difficult for no guaranteed remuneration. Edgar Allan Poe's only novel after all had described the life of a stowaway as one enmeshed in the dark side of life at sea: mutiny, cannibalism, savagery—even death. Perhaps Dundee boys simply craved adventure or, more likely, the hopelessness of life in Dundee persuaded them to stow out of sight until sailing day. They were boys who would be men in a man's world, lads as young as 10 or 12 who perhaps saw no future in their lot as half-time bobbin shifters in a mill.

The prospect of the 1892 Dundee whaling expedition to Antarctica, for example, captured the imagination of more than whale men and explorers. As the *Balaena* sailed out of port and down the estuary on a sunny September afternoon, a dozen sobbing boys were removed from hideouts on board, placed in small boats and returned to the shore. The ship's surgeon William Burn Murdoch noted with astonishment that 'some of them were crying with disappointment'. Two boys managed to escape the customary search for stowaways – which also turned up 15 on the *Polar Star*, another of the quartet of vessels on the Dundee Antarctic Expedition. William Brannan, aged 16, and his friend Terrance McMahon had originally tried to hide on the *Diana*, but opted instead for the larger *Balaena*, a polar vessel of considerable pedigree and one believed to have been the first merchant ship to reach Franz Josef Land. Brannan and McMahon concealed themselves among cans of paint and oil. But a smaller boy, looking for a hiding place, set the cans clattering over them. Together they used whaling tools to open a small harpoon chest, in which they hid while the commotion of departure took place above them. With the *Balaena* in open sea by the following afternoon, Brannan and McMahon gave themselves up to the mate and were set to work by a sympathetic Captain Alexander Fairweather, who, a native of Dundee himself, had gone to sea as a cabin boy on a coaster, aged 10. When the *Balaena* reached the Falklands, two of her able seamen quit the ship. Brannan and McMahan signed articles and took their places on the crew.

Stowaways became commonplace in the era of steam whaling, which coincided with the heyday of the city's jute industry, rapid industrialisation and soaring population. Like Brannan and McMahon, boys hoped to be taken on as crew, perhaps having heard from grandfathers that whalers were once obliged to carry apprentices in order to secure a pool of naval recruits. Whalers, too, preferred local recruitment where possible and sturdy young lads were the choice of many a captain for their greenhands. In a way, stowaways simply accelerated that process – and there appears to have been no limit to their ambition. In 1882 the *Resolute*, bound for Newfoundland, landed eight stowaways near Wick. All were Dundonians, with ages from eight to 21. All claimed that they wanted to disembark at St John's and then to walk to New York to find work! The *Resolute* appears to have been the conveyance of choice for the wayward youth of Dundee. In February 1885 she was obliged to land eight boys in the vicinity of John o' Groats, two aged 17, five aged 16 and one aged 14.

Boys were also drawn like moths to ships in port. They watched until the hurrahs from departing whalers grew faint and the last of the fleet had left the Tay for another season. They considered it their duty to welcome the whalers home, and to attend on them daily during their stay in port. When, in 1894, Dundee police court dealt with a complaint that boys climbing on whalers had become an 'intolerable nuisance', there was a show of indignation. The *Dundee People's Journal* remarked that a dearth of boys was entering the Royal Navy and here was Dundee Council trying to terrify them back to the shore. *The Courier* called the issue a judicial fuss and remarked that if a 'bevy' of affluent West End residents could visit a whaler to gawp at a visiting Eskimo, 'why not 40 boys from the east?' But stowaways were a different matter and most were put ashore. Mathew Campbell's log of the *Nova Zembla*'s voyage to Davis Strait in 1884 records: 'While anchored off the Buddon light, the mate came aft and informed the captain that there were some stowaways on board. The captain went to the tween decks and ordered the men to make a search, whence they were found concealed amongst the coals, so we drummed them on deck and gave them a couple of biscuits each and put them ashore in our boat to find their way back the best they could'. The greatest number of stowaways landed by a Dundee whaler was probably the 20 returned to shore by the *Esquimaux* in 1900, two days after leaving port. Perhaps the most fortunate, however, was the single lad who fancied his chances on the maiden voyage of the whaler *Columbia* in 1869. Luckily for him he was discovered and sent ashore at Kirkwall. A few weeks later the officers of the *Columbia* were at supper as she steamed through ice. There was a bump. She sank like a stone in the next four minutes. The surviving crew did not see Dundee again for 13 months.

FOUR

On Top of The World

Dundee dominated British whaling in the second half of the nine-teenth century, prompting the *London Standard* in November 1879 to offer its readers this tongue-in-cheek celebration of the city's whale-laden fleet:

> When the Greenland men come home is a great event in the annals of Juteopolis. For six months no news has been heard of ship or crew from husband, lover or son; and so, when the ice-scored vessels appear on the river to hundreds, they are freighted not only with whale bone and train oil, but with hopes and fears, and all the possibilities of the summer and autumn that have come and gone. The side of the Greenland Dock is black with women and children, and mingled with the 'heave-ooh' of the seamen and the sharp vocal duello of the captain and harbourmaster, rise a long-drawn blast of tenor cheers. In a few hours the ships are deserted, and happy is the wife who can escort her bag-laden 'man' to the home where for the next four months she will have him. Then the family who for half a year have been languishing on the seaman's scanty half-pay will revel in 'oil and bone money' galore; the riverside taverns will flourish and the mill girls of Dundee will wear gaudy sealskin slippers, while their fathers carry their tobacco in skin 'dossers' and their brothers play with Eskimo-modelled 'Kayaks' for the rest of the winter.

The 'nation is with her,' said the *Daily Telegraph* that year, praising the 'gallant Scottish mariners' in the Dundee fleet, and highlighting the importance of the premier whaling port to the British way of life. Yet the whaling world elsewhere was in decline. Ships lost in the tragedies of the 1830s and 1840s were not replaced. Whaling companies folded, yards closed, men were paid off. Accelerating the decline was competi-tion from coal gas for lighting. The joke was that whale oil lamps were good enough 'to let the darkness be seen'. In Dundee, though, whale oil and bone were so much in demand that they were almost a currency. The word decline was nowhere to be heard – and the industry flourished.

This timely restoration of fortunes can be attributed to two important factors: the decision to adopt new technology by the city's whaling companies, notably through the introduction of steam power to the fleet, and the coincidental discovery that preliminary processes in Dundee's vigorously-expanding jute industry could be smoothed by the application of whale oil. By 1858, when steam power for whalers was under test, it was calculated that Dundee's textiles industry, which by then was providing sacking, coarse cloths and carpet backing to the known world, required 2200 tons of whale oil annually in emulsified form for the preparatory process of softening raw jute – the equivalent of 15 full ships. This local factor stimulated quayside prices for oil and prompted owners to construct bigger and better vessels. It also encouraged Dundee's whaling masters to push towards new horizons in the Arctic, and what did not change was that the hunt for profit meant ships could be tempted to dally too long in unknown, unexplored seas. Thus whaling remained as risky an adventure as before. The deadliest enemies remained freezing fog and crushing ice, and the graveyard of their hopes remained Melville Bay.

As worldwide demand for coarse cloth, sacks and bags made from inexpensive jute reinvigorated the town's textiles industry, especially in the 1860s when supplies of cotton were cut at the height of the American Civil War, steam engines developed by local engineering companies to power the town's textile mills inspired her watchful whaling managers to introduce auxiliary steam power to her sailing fleet, a pioneering though rational advance in a century-old but largely unchanged industry. This, along with the increased value of whalebone as a commercial prize, made Dundee the centre of the whaling industry, a port, said the *Pall Mall Gazette* in 1873, 'where cargoes of oil from the Arctic regions may be seen discharging alongside jute from Calcutta'.

By 1860 Dundee, after Glasgow and Edinburgh, was the third largest town in Scotland. It had expanded exponentially from the ancient burgh that had sent out its first whale ship in 1753. Its population had multiplied eightfold to 90,000 and would, remarkably, increase by a further 50,000 in the subsequent 20 years as the most rapidly-urbanising city in Great Britain. There were commodious new schools to house its burgeoning working-class population, new parks for their leisure, and a rapid growth of charitable, literary and public institutions. Its outward-looking, cosmopolitan confidence was symbolised by its Robert Adam Town House (1734), an Ionic Trades Hall (1776), a Grecian-styled Watt Institution (1838), a Tudor-styled new infirmary (1854), a Royal Exchange building in Flemish style (1856), the Anglo-Italian Kinnaird Hall (1858), a classically-porticoed courthouse (1865), the Gothic Albert Institute (1866) and a colossal Royal Arch to commemorate the landing at her whaling harbour of Queen Victoria in 1844.

Dundee was also a unique industrial city in the grip of a staple industry. In 1807 the number of textile mills in the town was only four. By 1860 the number had risen to 60, containing 160 steam engines and employing 40,000 hands. It had 'transformed itself from the major linen town in Great Britain to the leading jute centre in the world'. Shipments of textiles from Dundee alone were as much as from the whole of Ireland. Another major transformation had taken place where the Tay estuary washed the town. Between 1815 and 1830 the King William IV dock and graving dock were constructed and the harbour widened, deepened and extended. Sea walls were built and additional quays provided. After 1830 a large part of the original harbour was converted into Earl Grey Dock. A magnificent Custom House was erected in 1843 and, later, the 14-acre Victoria Dock and the seven-acre Camperdown Dock were opened, greatly enhancing accommodation for shipping. If not exactly picturesque, Dundee made up for it 'by the romance of its crowded quays, as also in a degree by the magnitude and the whir of its numerous factories'. And, by 1865, over £1.2 million had transformed Dundee's docks into one of the 'finest, safest and most convenient in Britain' – a port suitable for the most powerful whaling fleet in Europe to ply full steam ahead for the Arctic fishing grounds.

Although auxiliary steam power has been claimed as a Dundee whaling initiative, the Peterhead master William Penny suggested the development in 1853. At that point many captains evidently feared that the noise made by screw propellers would alarm the whales, a rationale which also dispelled talk of introducing paddle steamers to the fishing grounds. Four years later, in February 1857, the Hull whaling ship *Diana* successfully tested an auxiliary steam engine. A year after that, in February 1858, a *Dundee Advertiser* reporter was invited to join a test voyage from Dundee to Broughty Ferry on the Dundee Arctic Fishing Company's *Tay*, which had been fitted with engines by Gourlay's of Dundee. The *Advertiser* felt the invitation justified, as it had been 'amongst the first to advocate the employment of the auxiliary screw on board whaling ships'.

There were significant advantages to the application of steam power

to whaling. Sail ships were frequently becalmed in high latitudes. It
became a physical trial of strength to reach seals and whales seen at a
distance if there was no wind to propel a sailing vessel. It could be
achieved only by rowing boat. Steam also allowed a faster passage to
the whaling grounds. 'The passage from the ice to Dundee in three days
and a half is one of unprecedented quickness and called forth the
wonder of many' – was the praise for the *Narwhal*'s maiden return
voyage in 1859. A sailing vessel with a fair wind could make five knots
and a steam ship more than twice that. Moreover, 'leads' of clear water
through ice were missed when a sailing ship was becalmed. With
steam, leads could be reached with stealth and speed whereas, in the
past, becalmed vessels had to be towed through the openings by
crewmen in the ship's rowing boats or physically hauled through
the slender passages of water by men on the ice. Steam power also
offered an additional dimension to a ship's armoury. Journals, such as
R. H. Hilliard's account of the maiden voyage of the *Narwhal* in 1859,
describe engines being thrust into reverse, and the powerful Dundee
steam whalers flying into ice at full steam ahead. The becalmed Captain
David Gray of the Peterhead whaler *Active* reportedly had the 'morti-
fication' of seeing the rival SS *Camperdown* of Dundee forcing her way
through hitherto impenetrable ice to a body of seals in 1866. And in
1884 Mathew Campbell describes the *Nova Zembla* battering an ice floe
by 'backing astern so as to get a better power of striking at full speed'.
Moving in for the kill or out of trouble were obvious benefits of steam,
and it was always kept in reserve for purposes of manoeuvrability or
improving safety, but the most important advantage was economic.
Auxiliary power made it possible for ships to fit in two fishing voyages
a year – a sealing trip to Greenland or Newfoundland in early spring,
and a summer whaling trip to Davis Strait. Thus steam presented
economy of working, and there was no better advance to bring a smile
to the speculate-to-accumulate shareholders of Dundee's whaling
companies.

The 1858 engine trial in Dundee lasted a little over half-an-hour
and involved the *Tay*, a 600-ton Dundee-built vessel owned by
Alexander Stephen's brother-in-law William Clark which had been
requisitioned from the jute trade. Size was important. While vessels
of 200 tons had been suitable in William Scoresby's day, the practi-
calities of fitting engines and boilers and providing storage space for
coal inevitably meant larger ships. A further consequence was the
inability of the longer, heavier vessels to berth in smaller northern
harbours, which not only prevented parallel large-scale develop-

ment in Peterhead, but contributed to that port's decline and eventual withdrawal from whaling. The *Tay*, meanwhile, was carefully prepared for her new role. A pair of inverted 70hp engines worked a screw propeller under the ship, and therefore beneath the general level of ice. The propeller was also designed to be manoeuvrable, so that when the vessel was under sail or in ice, it could be hoisted up clear of any impediment. The *Tay's* hull was doubled in thickness with some parts of it reinforced to seven feet. In other words she offered her captain what no other sail whaler could – the confidence to enter and manage Melville Bay.

The *Tay* featured another novel device designed to change the industry. A steam blubber boiler was installed below her decks to enable Arctic crews to boil whale and seal blubber long before it began to decompose and before it reached port in rancid condition. Said the *Advertiser*, 'Everybody knows the disgusting nuisance of the whale boiling yard in Dundee and the general sickening smell of whale oil. Well, if all our Greenland and Davis Strait fishing vessels were fitted out like the *Tay*, we should have no more occasion to complain of the Seagate nuisance'. At best estimates, it was said the boiler could accommodate the blubber of a large whale in 24 hours, producing from 12 to 15 tons of oil in that period. As it transpired, on-board boilers never replaced the return of raw blubber to Dundee, and this innovation was sidelined. A more useful arrangement on the *Tay* was the provision of 51 square iron tanks in which to store cut blubber ready for boiling. Each tank was designed to hold six tons, making a capacity of 306 tons in metal tanks, plus another 100 by way of traditional wooden casks, giving a total capacity of over 400 tons. The tanks, reported the *Advertiser* proudly, 'will keep the blubber much handier and sweeter than in ordinary whale ships'.

The financial risk did not extend only to the prospect of a steam ship foundering in Melville Bay. The cost of fitting out the *Tay* was put at £17,000. An auxiliary steam, sail-rigged whaling ship required a staff of engineers and firemen, some 300 tons of coal aboard and sometimes a smaller tender vessel to steam astern as a coal carrier. Not surprisingly, the introduction of these propeller-driven ships was viewed with mixed feelings by whaling men. Some thought they would be beneficial in terms of speed, power and economies of scale, and they were proved correct. Some thought the engine noise would scare away whales. They were also correct, and masters agreed guidelines in 1880 limiting the use of engines when whales were sighted. Above all, however, steam offered speed, manoeuvrability and safety and, crucially, two visits to the hunting grounds. There is no doubt that it marked a significant watershed in the industry. The thousands lining Dundee's docks to watch the *Narwhal* leaving on her maiden voyage – 'she floats majestically on the waters of the Tay, a thing of life and beauty' – must have been thrilled by her power as she effortlessly towed a dozen large fishing boats behind her, to 'save them the long pull to Broughty Ferry'.

Although the *Tay* was adapted to auxiliary power in 1857, and did well enough in her first season in 1858, the classic age of Dundee as a whaling port began with the construction of Alexander Stephen & Sons' wooden-hulled *Narwhal* in 1859 – ironically under the supervision of Peterhead's William Penny, the master who pioneered the initiative. The 533-ton SS *Narwhal* – built in only four months and described by her surgeon as 'the largest and finest whaler afloat' – set the new pattern. Messrs Stephen followed with the *Dundee* the same year, which was constructed in just three months and five days, the *Camperdown* in 1860 and the *Polynia* in 1861. After that any new vessels were built as wooden-hulled, sail-rigged, auxiliary steamers – while the process of conversion of sail ships went on apace. Such was the confidence, optimism and excitement in the town as ship after ship was launched and Dundee overtook Peterhead as Britain's leading whaling port that when the *Arctic* was ready, her luxurious cabin (for Captain Adams) was finished in 'pitch pine handsomely polished' and she was seen off by a boisterous crowd which 'not only filled the yard but occupied much of the available space on Marine Parade'.

By 1867 the Dundee fleet had grown to 12 fully-rigged steam auxiliaries at a time when the industry was declining elsewhere. In 1861, for example, 11 whalers were fitted out from Scottish ports other than Dundee and Peterhead. By 1870, there were none. The Dundee fleet was, according to the *Sheffield Telegraph*, the finest whaling fleet in the world – 'a fleet so good that the shipowners of North America, who are desirous of having the most approved of whaling ships, sent their orders across the Atlantic to builders on the banks of the Tay'. Of all the builders of whaling vessels, none achieved so great a distinction as Stephen's, an Aberdeen-born company that had moved to Dundee in 1844. The whalers built in Stephen's yard were regarded as institutions and 'every citizen watched their voyages and waited for news of whale or seal catches with all the zest of co-operating adventurers'. The succession of powerful ships were furnished with 70hp engines mostly supplied by the local engineers Gourlay Brothers, who had traded as builders of agricultural engines from a foundry in Whale Lane from the early nineteenth century. Gourlay's began producing powerful marine steam engines in 1853 by harnessing mechanisms pioneered by James Carmichael, whose inventions in relation to engines and reversing gears had been adopted on vessels operated by the Dundee, Perth and London Shipping Company, including their first paddle steamer in 1834. The marriage of these local industries – tied to a pool of experienced Arctic crews – contributed to Dundee's prominence as a whaling port long after most others had given up. While owners across the country withdrew their capital and ships, Stephen's workforce constructed 27 high-quality whaling ships rigged for sail and engine, and built them bigger than ever, the largest being the 828-ton *Arctic* in 1875 and the 744-ton *Terra Nova* in 1884, later, of course, Captain Scott's expedition ship.

Watchful of the Dundee developments, the rival ports of Hull and Peterhead opted to experiment with iron steamers, making the wrong choice in doing so. Hull sent three reinforced iron ships to the northern whaling grounds, all of which were damaged when ice buckled their plates. Peterhead built the *Empress of India*, a huge iron steamer with 12-feet thick bows and a crew of 110 men. R. H. Hilliard, the surgeon on the *Narwhal* in 1859, recorded his admiration for the beauty of the *Empress* when she was seen off Peterhead and yet, 'all our experienced hands shake their heads at the thought of an iron whaler'. Their misgivings were not misplaced. In mid-March 1859, in the Atlantic, Hilliard discovered 'the poor *Empress* in a state of great confusion, seven pumps working'. The luxurious ship duly sank beneath the waves on her maiden voyage after hitting the first rough seas she encountered. Reported Hilliard: 'Captain Martin was armed to the teeth, the whole of the men were pressing down demanding rum'. To aggravate Peterhead's wounded pride, 50 of her crew faced the ignominy of being rescued by the wooden-hulled *Narwhal*, whose own crew included a young Dundonian bo'sun destined to become 'the most famous whaling captain in the world' – William Adams.

Dundee was not entirely immune to calamity. The SS *River Tay*, built of iron in Kinghorn for Dundee owners by John Key of Kirkcaldy, and constructed supposedly with double the strength of normal iron vessels, complete with 'unsinkable' watertight compartments, sank in millpond calm on her maiden voyage in 1868 after being bumped by ice at Pond's Bay. As she was sinking, crewman David Walker drank a bottle of carbolic acid thinking it

1. Captain Alexander Murray, c.1885. The Arctic brought many dangers and crews also had to endure extreme cold. When the Peterhead whaler *Hope* returned from Greenland in 1880, her young ship's surgeon from Edinburgh, later Sir Arthur Conan Doyle, wrote, 'I came of age in 80 degrees north latitude'.

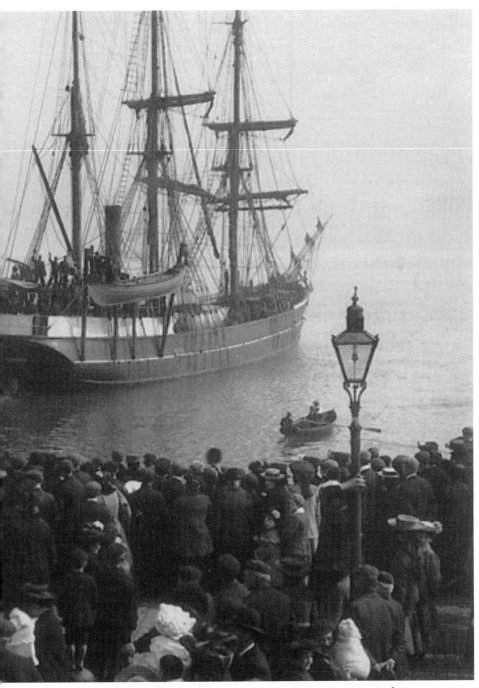

2. Whalers sailed to the Arctic each spring, returning in late summer or autumn. Traditionally crews stood waving on the stern rail until lingering cheers from the quayside crowds faded.

3.   Captain Thomas Robertson – 'Coffee Tam' – on the snow-covered quarter deck of the *Active*, 1894.

4.   Large strips of blubber on the SS *Active*, 1894 after being winched aboard from the whale lashed alongside.

5. Captain William Adams in the crow's nest of the *Maud* in 1889.
    The barrel crow's nest was invented by William Scoresby in 1807.

Captain Thomas Robertson, of the "Active."

Captain Alex. Fairweather, of the "Balæna."

Captain James Davidson, of the "Polar Star."

Captain Robert Davidson, of the "Diana."

6. The quartet of Dundee whaling captains who made the historic voyage to the Antarctic in 1892 – Captains Thomas Robertson, Alex. Fairweather, James Davidson and Robert Davidson – as illustrated in the *Piper o' Dundee* magazine.

7. The *Terra Nova*, Stephen's last whaler in 1884, and the last whaler built in Dundee. At 740 tons she was also the second-largest constructed in the port.

8. The *Windward* under sail off Greenland, 1888. Constructed in Peterhead in 1860, she found fame as an exploration vessel before being nipped with the Dundee fleet in 1907.

9.   The *Maud* reflected in the cold waters of the Davis Strait, 1889, where she took three whales, traditionally marked in the margins of the ships' logs with a silhouette of a whale's tail.

10.   The *Eclipse* under full sail, nosing through ice, Davis Strait, 1894. A figure is just discernible in the lofty crow's nest.

was whisky. The *River Tay* sank in 16 hours. Walker died in 20 minutes. 'Like other ships of her class,' said the *Dundee Year Book*, 'she was the last experiment of her kind.' Dundee's choice of wooden hulls for ice ships was the correct one, and it was borne out in the years ahead as the world's great explorers beat a path to the city to purchase Stephen-built whalers for polar purposes.

STEAM WHALERS BUILT AT STEPHEN'S YARD, 1859–1884

YEAR	NAME	TONS	OWNERS
1859	*Narwhal*	533	Dundee Seal and Whale Fishing Co.
1859	*Dundee* (3)	630	Alexander Stephen & Sons
1860	*Camperdown*	541	Dundee S & W Fishing Co.
1861	*Polynia*	472	Dundee S & W Fishing Co.
1863	*Wolf* (1)	400	*Walter Grieve
1864	*Alexander*	590	Gilroy Brothers
1865	*Erik*	533	G. Gibbs
1865	*Esquimaux*	593	Dundee S & W Fishing Co.
1865	*Retriever*	462	*Ridley, Son & Co.
1866	*Nimrod*	334	*Job Brothers
1867	*Mastiff*	360	*John Munn
1867	*Arctic* (1)	567	Alex Stephen & Sons
1870	*Commodore*	427	*John Munn
1870	*Hector*	473	*Job Brothers
1871	*Eagle*	506	*N.F. Sealing & Whaling Co.
1871	*Ranger*	520	*Robert Alexander
1871	*Wolf* (2)	500	*Walter Grieve
1872	*Iceland*	423	*D. Murray & Son
1872	*Bloodhound*	396	*Royal Navy's *Discovery*
1872	*Neptune*	684	*Job Brothers
1873	*Proteus*	687	*J. W. Stewart
1874	*Bear*	689	*W. Grieve
1875	*Arctic* (2)	828	Alexander Stephen & Sons
1876	*Aurora*	580	Alexander Stephen & Sons
1880	*Resolute*	624	Dundee S & W Fishing Co.
1881	*Thetis*	723	Alexander Stephen & Sons
1884	*Terra Nova*	744	Alexander Stephen & Sons

Sources: Lubbock 1937, Dundee Year Books, and others.

* Not registered as Dundee whaler, most for West of Scotland or Newfoundland owners.

The rapid expansion of jute manufacturing guaranteed a market for oil and encouraged interest in whaling among speculators. Direct imports of raw jute from Bengal rose from 30,000 tons in the mid-1850s to 100,000 tons in the early 1870s and to over 200,000 tons by the late 1880s. The jute industry's growth coincided with the peak of the town's whaling activity, and it was with considerable satisfaction that the *Advertiser* on January 12, 1863 announced that another whaler had been bought for the Dundee fleet, the pride of the Hull fleet no less, and that this was 'the first instance of Dundee manufacturers proposing to fish for the oil required for their mills'. In other words, a whale ship was specifically earmarked to supply the local market.

None of all this effort and expense would have been of much use if it had not translated into success in the Arctic fishing grounds. This it did. For upwards of two decades the technically superior Dundee fleet enjoyed catches that matched the heyday of the early 1800s – in terms of financial return if not in headcounts of whales. For the years 1865 to 1873 the port fitted out a seasonal average of 10 ships, most of which made two profitable trips to the fisheries.

By 1867 the capital invested in the Dundee fleet was reported to have risen to £180,000, with 800 men employed in the trade. The average value of produce of a successful season's fishing in whale and seal oil, whalebone and sealskins, was estimated at £120,000, equivalent to a dozen new ships. By 1873 Dundee was 'unquestionably Britain's leading whaling port'. Its ships averaged nearly eight whales per voyage, with highs of 17 whales per vessel in 1871 and impressive individual returns such as the *Camperdown*'s 17 whales in three days, all lashed alongside for flensing at the same time, and her 23,000 seals, secured in just nine days, in 1866. The slaughter of seals – some 460,000 – says Henderson, should be seen in the context of the 'estimated, three million' taken by all ships in the sealing grounds between 1865 and 1873. Yet clearly the steam fleet profited enormously from its disturbingly-high seal catches during the period. Four ships – the *Camperdown, Polynia, Tay* and *Narwhal* – amassed massive receipts of £91,000 in 1865, for example, with the *Tay* killing 5,000 seals on each of three consecutive days the following year.

For all the success, the vagaries of the Arctic elements and shortage of whales ensured that unsuccessful seasons remained a feature of the industry. Nine of the 11-strong whaling fleet returned 'clean' in 1867, for instance. The 13 vessels which sailed a year later, taking an astonishing 108 whales, must have raised eyebrows in ports to the

north and south with their brash confidence as, in 1868, the last
whalers sailed from Peterhead and Fraserburgh. The writing was on
the wall for these ports, and when the *Intrepid* was bought by Dundee
from Peterhead for £5000 in 1865, it was the first of a succession of
vessels to be added to the fleet from declining ports. A more exciting
arrival at Camperdown Dock that year was the 350-ton American
whaler *Reindeer*. Such was the fame of Dundee that her captain
revealed that her owners were interested in using Dundee as a winter
port. Nothing came of this potentially lucrative market, however.
Instead, the *Reindeer* was sold to Dundee owners for the Baltic trade.

CATCHES OF THE DUNDEE FLEET, 1865–1873: WHALES

	SHIPS	WHALES	OIL (TONS)	BONE
1865	7	68	630	30.0
1866	11	30	340	18.0
1867	11	2	20	–
1868	13	108	970	50.0
1869	10	6	140	7.5
1870	6	63	760	40.5
1871	8	134	1165	61.5
1872	10	105	1010	54.0
1873	10	163	1352	69.1

CATCHES OF THE DUNDEE FLEET, 1865–1873: SEALS

	SHIPS	SEALS	OIL (TONS)
1865	4	63,000	730
1866	7	58,000	690
1867	11	56,000	640
1868	12	16,670	190
1869	11	45,600	480
1870	9	90,450	870
1871	9	65,485	648
1872	11	40,621	429
1873	11	25,594	265

With powerful steam-propelled ships, a management motivated
by short-termist shareholders, experienced captains and crews and a
local monopoly of oil, Dundee tightened its dominance of the trade,
and in 1867 the cream of the nation's scientists at the British

Association meeting heard that 'Dundee is now foremost in respect of steam whalers of any port either in Europe or America'. The *Advertiser* did its sums in November 1874 and concluded: 'The gross financial result of the trade may be estimated at about £104,000 per annum, and the number of vessels engaged by it be taken at 10. When the whaling industry was in its prime some sixty years ago, the gross yield was £420,000. It would thus appear that the annual catch of the Dundee whalers is about one fourth the volume of the catch by 120 sailing vessels employed in the trade when bounties formed part of the inducement to engage in it'. Another way of putting it is that, thanks to steam power, a tenth of the number of vessels was able to make a quarter of the one-time record revenues – without the benefit of bounties.

CATCHES OF THE DUNDEE FLEET, 1874–1883: WHALES

YEAR	SHIPS	WHALES	OIL (TONS)	BONE (TONS)
1874	11	174	1290	66.5
1875	12	77	817	41.5
1876	13	72	891	44.5
1877	14	76	891	41.0
1878	15	6	108	6.0
1879	13	72	725	35.5
1880	12	112	1077	46.5
1881	12	48	514	24.5
1882	12	79	675	28.0
1883	8	17	524	9.5

CATCHES OF THE DUNDEE FLEET, 1874–1883: SEALS

YEAR	SHIPS	SEALS	OIL (TONS)
1874	11	46,252	567
1875	12	56,095	560
1876	13	65,984	808
1877	14	77,711	850
1878	15	85,820	999
1879	15	97,878	1228
1880	14	88,040	1215
1881	15	152,106	1998
1882	14	81,123	967
1883	13	113,353	1460

These, again, were profitable years for the Dundee fleet with an average of six whales taken each season. The whaling catch in 1874 represented about £87,000 at £40 per ton for oil and £540 for bone. The cull of seals that year brought in £19,845 in oil and £11,560 for skins. Captain William Adams in the replacement SS *Arctic* led the way as usual. In the period 1875–1881 he took 52 whales, which produced 725 tons of oil and 33 tons of baleen. The average price for whale oil was £35 at this time, while bone was rising rapidly in price, from around £540 in 1874 to £1750 in 1883, with an average around £750. His cargoes from whaling, therefore, amounted to £25,375 in oil, while bone brought in £24,750. His yearly average from whaling over these seven years was £3625 in oil and £3536 from baleen. (Adams went sealing in 1882 and 1883, and in the latter year loaded the *Arctic* with potatoes to offload at Newfoundland to help combat the shortage in North America caused by the Colorado beetle plague.)

The decade's cull of over 800,000 seals is startling and one can hardly imagine the heaps of flayed carcasses and the bloody trails leading back to the ships along which the men had dragged valuable pelts for storage in brine. The practice of engaging in Greenland sealing – begun in 1863 – continued, but from 1867 the fleet also steamed to Newfoundland waters. After that, it became the regular practice for ships to choose between Greenland and Newfoundland. In 1880, for example, five Dundee ships attended the Newfoundland sealing and nine went to Greenland waters. Some Dundee ships eventually employed Newfoundland masters at the sealing, including the famous firebrand skipper, Captain Arthur Jackman. Among the floes the huge colonies of seals proved easy targets:

> The seals are very foolish beasts. Sometimes they are so lazy with sleep that a man may dig them in the ribs with his gun, and, wondering what is disturbing their slumbers, they raise their head, which quickly falls pierced with a bullet.

It is clear from returns that the slaughter of seals for skins and oil often paid the whale men's wages. The *Arctic*, with Adams at the helm, returned to port with 169,373 seals over the decade. Adams' seal oil amounted to 1844 tons. In quayside cash, this represented a yearly average of £4234 for skins at an average of five shillings (25p) each, and £5532 for oil at an average of £30 per ton. In 1881 Dundee's fleet of six vessels in Newfoundland alone returned with 139,985 skins worth five shillings each, and 1797 tons of oil, worth £29 per ton, making a total of £86,109 or £14,518 per vessel. This was far in excess of the amounts earned by whaling at this time, giving a lie to the notion that Dundee was solely a whaling port as its rivals fell away from the trade. As Dundee came to be regarded as the principal whaling port in the United Kingdom, boasting the largest, most powerful and best-equipped fleet of steamers in the country, there was a physical effect on the town. Several whaling companies extended their premises. The Tay Whale Fishing Company was located in the aptly named East Whale Lane, just off the harbour area, and boasted extensive yards. The Dundee Seal and Whale Fishing Company, the successor to the Union Whale Fishing Company of the early 1800s, was situated in East Dock Street. There was also the Dundee Polar Fishing Company in Commercial Street in addition to Messrs Stephen of Marine Parade, and eventually several private 'oil' companies operated by the likes of James Mitchell, Gilroy Brothers, William Crondace and Robert Kinnes. By 1878 the *Advertiser* reported that, 'the establishments in Dundee for boiling the oil and storing of sealskins, whalebone etc, have been greatly enlarged', while a distinguishing feature of the trade was that the Dundee fleet was entirely locally owned.

Such was the success of Newfoundland sealing in particular that in 1878 shipbuilders Stephen's invested a considerable amount of capital to erect a new factory in Dundee for boiling and storing oil. This was appropriately named the Arctic Yard, and was situated in the south-west corner of Victoria Dock with 'no special architectural design adhered to'. Indeed, it was a functional brick, wood and corrugated iron-roofed building, some 60 metres in length. The lower storey was installed with boiling equipment and eight storage tanks, six of them six metres square. Two smaller rectangular tanks were used for cooling, while the blubber boiler itself comprised a large tank in the centre of the building. Beneath it were two tanks for the scum and 'a heavy lever press for squeezing every drop of oil out of the refuse'.

In 1881, the extent of the Newfoundland cull – 150,000 seals – persuaded Stephen's to open their own sealskin grading factory to furnish the fashion industry with best-quality young fur 'muffs, boas and capes', as well as quality leather goods ranging from women's purses to pocket books to bicycle gear cases. The Arctic Tannery, as it was called, comprised tanning pits, skin stores, drying lofts and various finishing departments, and was located in Marine Parade, roughly in the landfall area of the Tay Road Bridge today. From skins piled high in its warehouse a corps of male workers firstly completed the initial process of washing, cleaning and tanning before beginning operations of splitting, graining, and decorating until tanned and finished leather products were produced for 'London, Continental and American' markets. In 1890 the *Piper o' Dundee* magazine boasted, 'Even in the matter of bootlaces London appeals to Dundee, and a special department [at the Arctic Tannery] is required for the cutting and tagging of the famous porpoise leather laces'. The following year Messrs Stephen supplemented the Arctic Tannery by opening a new range of buildings for the manufacture of whalebone, of which the firm retained a large stock because of price fluctuations. 'There are only two of the manufactories in the United Kingdom, both situated in London, and the business is carried out with the utmost secrecy,' said *The Courier*, a reference to the processes involved in turning baleen into a commercial range of products.

Although the whaling industry formed an increasing part of the town's life, the businessmen behind the ventures to the Arctic accepted that some processes might be better carried out nearer the fishing grounds. As the steam fleet thrived, the companies diverted profits to establish impressive shore stations and boiling yards in the regions of Davis Strait and Baffin Bay to facilitate the catching of whales and seals, but partly, also, to offset the financial uncertainty of whaling. Although catches in the 1860s and 1870s had been anything but poor, and more ships were being added to Dundee's register, the omens were not good. In particular, the whales taken were noticeably smaller in size. Whaling also remained a hazardous enterprise, a business of risk for its financial backers and for the masters and crews who faced the uncertainties of Arctic conditions. Almost every year ships failed to return – and, as the whalers penetrated further into the pack ice of Baffin Bay in pursuit of diminishing stocks, the potential for damage and loss increased. It was thus sound business sense to consider shore stations as a means of reducing costs and exposure to danger. Besides, native labour was cheaper.

Dundee whaling crews were left at settlements in Arctic regions from the mid-1860s when the *Narwhal* deposited men at Exeter Sound to prospect for minerals. The shipbuilders Stephen & Sons had also, by the late 1870s, erected storage and boiling facilities at St John's, Newfoundland for the seals caught by the vessels under the firm's flag. Then, in 1899, in accordance with the instructions of her owner, Robert Kinnes, the *Active* left her mate John Murray and two Peterhead men on Southampton Island in Hudson Bay, having erected a large wooden dwelling and a sectional boat shed for them prior to departure. It was arranged that the three men should stay for three years' whale hunting with the assistance of the Inuit communities nearby. Their first winter proved to be as rigorous as it was adventurous. One small whale was taken and only half a ton of whalebone was uplifted by the *Active* on her next call. Wolves and bears were shot in considerable numbers, however, anticipating the revival of the region's fur trade in future years. The station represented a considerable investment for Kinnes. There was neither food nor fuel in Baffin Bay, and the creation of shore-based facilities involved expensive materials and supplies to cater for the men.

Following a calamitous illness in 1903, when dysentery was reportedly introduced to the community by a sick seaman on the SS *Active*, the station was abandoned in favour of a new location at Repulse Bay, on an isthmus north of Southampton Island, which had been first visited by the *Active* in 1886. Here, the company sent its ketch *Ernest William* to act as a floating station. The *Ernest William* spent the next eight years anchored in the bay, bartering with the natives while its catches were brought home each year, usually by the *Active* on her circuitous route around Davis Strait and Baffin Bay. The station was manned by successive crews recruited from visiting whalers. On the west side of Davis Strait, Robert Kinnes & Sons established shore stations at Kekerten, at 65°N on the north shore of Cumberland Sound, and at Blacklead Island on its southern coast. In 1910 David Cardno, who sailed on the *Polar Star* and the *Jan Mayen*, became manager of the two stations. Later he spent two years living in the Eskimo settlement at Kekerten, which is now part of an Inuit national park. From 1900 until 1913, Kinnes also operated a mica mine near Lake Harbour, in Hudson Strait, near the lower reaches of Davis Strait. A shore whaling station was also established by the whaler owner-manager James Mitchell at Albert Harbour near Pond Inlet, on the northern tip of Baffin Island, at the lofty latitude of 73°N, in 1903. There was considerable excitement at the station in 1912 when Canadian expeditions arrived to search for gold.

Such diversification was more a show of concern than confidence. The Dundee owners' quest to adopt practices of shore-catching – an Inuit tradition for a millennium – moved the industry from its traditional ship-based counter-clockwise voyage up Davis Strait, across the ship-destructive Melville Bay and down the bitterly-cold

Baffin Bay coastline in the pursuit of migrating Right whales. The new winter habitats were moderately successful in that the whale blubber, skins and furs passed to visiting whalers eked out modest catches made at sea. They also helped ships to avoid lingering and becoming prisoners of the ice. But they could not reverse the fact that the unrestrained harrying of the Right whale into northern waters had led to a reduction in stock estimated by W. Gillies-Ross to be 'a few hundred animals' by the turn of the century. In truth, the industry's short-term goal of maximum catches had destroyed the stock of whales on which it depended. Besides, leaving men and supplies to overwinter north of the 70th parallel did nothing to promote optimism or raise morale in Jolly's Bar in Broughty Ferry or the aptly-named Arctic Bar in Dundee's New Inn Entry, where the intrepid crews of the whaling ships that ventured out to the perilous northern seas spent some of their hard-earned wages.

Shore stations established by Dundee owners also contributed to changing forever the life and culture of the native Inuit population. Canada, which had taken control of much of the region from Britain in 1867, but which had paid scant attention to its population, or to the sporadic contact from British whaling activity, began to take notice of the physical expansion on its territory and the unrestrained activities of the men involved. As Canada became increasingly concerned that its sovereignty was being threatened by foreign crews, it established remote stations for detachments of Royal Canadian Mounted Police to enforce Canadian laws and, in due course, imposed taxes on whale operators and seasonal time zones in which their activities were not allowed.

The free-for-all which had acted to undermine the industry's own resource base was at an end – and the watershed year was 1884. In fact, 1884 was not an unsuccessful year. It was a good season – too good. Some 100 whales were taken, 'an indiscriminate killing of mother and young' that gave the Davis Strait fishing grounds no time to recover. The following year only 26 whales were secured as storms raged at Newfoundland. The industry's confidence was further dented by the losses of the *Intrepid*, 80 miles north of Iceland, and the *Cornwallis* in ice in Davis Strait. The irony was that this was Dundee's record year in terms of the number of vessels dispatched.

This time lost ships were not replaced. And when another disastrous year followed in 1886, when 15 ships caught only 18 whales, and four vessels were lost, questions began to be asked about the long-term future of the industry. 'Why has prosperity deserted the prosecution of the Davis Strait fishing industry?' the *Advertiser* asked in a headline. There was only one answer: 'Namely, that all appearances point to the fishing having been overdone'. Looking back in 1896, one captain confirmed the newspaper's view. 'No distinction,' he said, 'was, or could be made, in the sex or age of whales taken. Male and female, mother and sucker, were alike harpooned and cut up.' The high price of whalebone and the market for whale oil in Dundee were effectively propping up an expiring industry. In spite of the efforts and expense involved in opening up new 'fields of adventure and new methods of pursuit' the trade's long-term future was overshadowed by declining stocks.

Science had stepped in to serve Dundee well in terms of powering her ships and creating a market for the fleet's products – and it should not be overlooked that Britain's jute industry was almost entirely located within Dundee thanks largely to the presence of the whalers – but nature could not be circumvented in the manner that pack ice was. The writing was on the wall for the world's premier Arctic whaling port.

FIVE

Human Cargoes – Native and Natural

The Dundee whaling industry had comings and goings which did not involve whalebone and oil, skinned seals, toothless walrus or the daunting presence of very-much-alive polar bears. One inevitable result of the expansion of the industry northwards was the whale men's contact with the indigenous peoples of Greenland and the High Arctic – the Inuit, or as they were in the whaling era, the Eskimos. Eskimo is a non-preferred term nowadays. Its continued use here reflects contemporary usage during the era of northern whaling. Moreover, Inuit is not a name given to all of the native populations of the region, and Eskimo is perhaps a recognisable if not wholly acceptable single term for these peoples here.

There are two aspects of the lives of Eskimos that are relevant to the story of the Dundee whalers. There is the important presence of native populations encountered on voyages – of wide interest for reasons of geography, history and culture. Eskimos provided help, sanctuary and, ultimately, companionship to whale men. They were guides and traders, workmates and friends, and called their visitors *qallunaat* – the white men, or *Siikatsi* – the Scots. Yet they were viewed in British whaling communities as having no morality or religion and accorded the stereotype of savages, partly because of stories about their never washing, eating food raw and, even, enjoying cannibalism. Secondly, whale men were responsible for conveying the first sealskin-clad natives to Scotland, resulting in scenes as remarkable then as might be considered questionable in the early twenty-first century. They were placed on public display, encouraged to entertain by, for example, clumsily handling knives and forks, and forced to attend religious services. It often amounted to ritual humiliation, but notions of racial tolerance were still some way off – as were moratoriums on hunting whales.

The peoples of Eskimo tribes were called Eskimos, Esquimaux or just as often 'Yaks' by whale men – a slang term substituted by another, 'Huskies', by crewmen in northern ports. At the outset of the pelagic whaling industry, Eskimos were among the most isolated people on the planet. Captain William Adams Snr told a crowded lecture in Newport, Fife of a small group of Esquimaux in north Greenland, who, when discovered by the explorers Ross and Parry in 1818, thought they were the only people in the world. They had no boats, no sails, no guns and no fire. Much later, as whalers chased declining stocks to the very edge of permanent ice, new tribes were discovered and recorded in the men's journals. Mathew Campbell on the *Nova Zembla* of Dundee in 1884 reported on Duck Island that 'The natives here have no vestige of civilisation . . . I showed them my revolver and they roared out with surprise and squatted away together'. Captain Austin Murray of Newport recalled his father, Captain John Murray of the SS *Active*, telling him how natives from the far reaches of Baffin Bay would point rifles the wrong way round, and how one of them touched his father's face to see if the 'white' would come off.

It is worthy of note that the Inuit had 'fished' for bowhead whales for centuries before foreign vessels touched their shores. Whale meat was prized as food, and the communal nature of the hunt and the traditional sharing of the catch were part of an age-old native culture. The traditional method of Eskimo whaling contrasted with the commercial operations to come. It was shore-based, carried out from skin boats (umiaks) by hunters with hand-held harpoons. Whales struck were dragged back to shore and butchered at the ice edge. Meat from a single whale might last for a winter and was stored and preserved in underground ice cellars as a primary food source. Baleen was put to myriad uses – as weapons, tools, utensils and clothes, for example. Whales also had a spiritual dimension for Eskimo coastal communities. They provided life through food and fuel and were a powerful symbol of continuity.

Generally friendly, the native populations of the Arctic approached visiting ships in long, slender canoes constructed of bones or wood with a tan sealskin covering. Photographs show these low-slung craft to contain around 12 to 15 Eskimos, with the first boat to approach the ships often crewed by women, generating the generic term 'women's boats', as the craft were sighted by Scottish crews. Trade was their priority and the word 'trock' was used by the Greenlanders and their whaling visitors for barter. Trading in 1838 included sealskin boots, jackets, trousers, slippers, models of canoes and tobacco pouches in one direction, and, in the main, guns and ammunition, cotton clothing, tobacco, tea and foodstuffs in the other. In the summer of 1871 Dr Kerr logged a visit of around 20 native Greenlanders to the appropriately-named whaler *Esquimaux*: 'The men bartered, the women cut out sealskin gloves for the sailors, while the children ran about or danced to the music of a cracked fiddle and old concertina'. The naval officer Albert Markham, aboard the *Arctic* in 1873 to gain experience of polar conditions, described several boats of Eskimos coming alongside the Arctic 'all anxious to trock'. He recorded that the exchange principally involved slippers and tobacco pouches made of sealskin, for which powder, shot, coffee, shirts and trousers were exchanged. And in 1887 the crew of the *Maud* under Captain William Adams found that 'several of the gaudy petticoats were seized, and the women put them on above their sealskin dresses, being so fond of display that the most showy articles are always worn outermost'. Yet one medicine man, or shaman, who traded for a clock, thought its tick-tock sound was a devil's spirit with magic more powerful than his, and threw it into the sea.

Ship's surgeon John Wanless provided one of the earliest descriptions of Davis Strait natives from the Dundee whaler *Thomas* in 1834:

> They were tattooed upon the brow, cheeks, chin and things, by what I could not learn. . . . I fired a gun and all of them ran and put their hands on their ears very much surprised. Their cheek bones are high and are far separated, hair long and dark hanging over their shoulders; black eyes and skin of tawny colour; hands and feet are exceedingly small in proportion to their body; the cunas [women] had their heads adorned with ribbands like children.

Dr Kerr, the physician on board the *Esquimaux* in 1871, provided a description of the Inuit which should be viewed in the context of its time; an era in which the colonising British had a high opinion of themselves: 'The adults were of small stature – not over five feet – broad-chested, pot-bellied, and walked with a waddling gait. This was particularly noticeable in the women, who were inclined to "bow-leg" and decidedly "in-toe-ed." The "coonah," or wife, is hardly esteemed the "better-half," and polygamy prevails among them'.

'All the children are very fat, very interesting, full of fun and frolic, but generally very dirty,' added Thomas Macklin on an excursion from the *Narwhal* in 1874. 'The Yaks seem very fond of their offspring. The captain tells me one of them, a father, died of grief at the loss of his child.' Dr Kerr noted that the women were 'wonderfully expert at the needle', and made all the sealskin clothes of the tribe. 'The stitching is so neat as almost to defy detection,' he wrote in admiration. In terms of his profession, he treated one woman for facial wounds received in an attack by a bear, which her husband shot. A number suffered from inflamed eyes caused by the intense glare of the snow. Another physician, Dr G. A. Rae, medical officer on the *Arctic* in 1871, found numerous colds and influenza among the natives, and diseases and illness related to privation in the extreme temperatures. There were also cases of malnourishment and dehydration.

Among other observations made by Dr Kerr of the *Esquimaux* was the natives' manner of singing. This involved placing their hands by their sides and swaying their body from side to side and making striking noises, less like a song and more a repetition of sounds produced by the larynx during rapid respiration – 'They are said to charm the reindeer within gun-shot by means of it,' noted the Dundee doctor. The Eskimos' love of singing and dancing was recorded many times in whaling journals. John Wanless welcomed a boat crew of women aboard the *Thomas* in June 1834 and noted that 'they danced to a fiddler's notes most admirably'. At Disko Island in 1919 ship's steward William Walker took part in many enjoyable evenings of dancing and games with the scattered local population, and it seems every whale ship had a fiddler as part of its complement. 'Most of the native dances are done on the heel and they can dance as long as one likes to keep the music going,' he noted. Domestically, however, Dr Kerr confirmed the widely held view that Eskimos did not cook but ate everything raw and stripped meat with their teeth. 'I saw one woman throw herself on the ice, fill her mouth with water at a pool, get up and run towards a child sitting on a sledge, and squirt the refreshing draught into its mouth. The piccaninny was thirsty. Another woman pacified her crying baby with a piece of blubber nearly a pound weight, which it held with both hands and sucked with the greatest apparent relish.' Dr Kerr also reported seeing one male Eskimo bailing water out of his canoe by mouth. Eskimos in their natural habitat seldom found favour with their Scottish visitors. Matthew Campbell of the *Nova Zembla* recorded crawling into an Eskimo house on all fours at the Danish settlement of Godhaven, 'but we crawled out very quick as they had a terrible smell'. Albert Markham was also invited to inspect a settlement. Unimpressed, he suggested the native houses were 'most pleasing' when viewed from the outside – 'the greater the distance off the better'. He continued:

> If sufficiently brave to encounter the offensive stench which pervades everything, as to risk a visit to the interior, one passes through a long narrow entrance, having almost to crawl upon hands and feet, emerging into a small room, in which is the stove, the everlasting lamp, and the long bench or shelf on which they sit during the day, and on which, wrapped up in their skins, they sleep during the night. The number of people residing in one of these houses may probably amount to twenty or thirty of both sexes and all ages.

Markham paid not one compliment to the Inuit peoples of Greenland and Upper Canada – despite the sophisticated organisation of families, their inter-community distribution of food, their skills in hunting on land and navigation of offshore waters, their ability to read weather, and more. The state of igloos was 'better imagined than described', and the Eskimos 'particularly dirty and filthy in their habits'. The long and unkempt hair falling over their shoulders and their general appearance made them 'more like some amphibious animals than human beings,' he concluded. Many who sailed on Dundee ships, even the so-called educated men, shared his opinion. Dr Kerr labelled Eskimo lifestyle 'very filthy' and 'degraded' and claimed they were 'positively hideous in appearance'. He compared old women he came across to 'the witches in Macbeth'.

This polarisation of cultures was exaggerated by the insurmountable language barrier facing pioneering whaling crews and the natives they encountered. Jennifer Niven suggested that Eskimo words, once translated into English and then back into Eskimo, 'become nonsense'. The 23rd Psalm, for example, translated delightfully and alarmingly into: 'The Lord is my gate keeper; he does not want me. He shoots me down on the beach and pushes me into the water'. Unsettlingly, Dr Kerr found the same word being used for sleep and death. Such difficulties may explain why one or two Dundee whaling journals contain rudimentary Eskimo vocabulary sections and why, in time, Eskimos and Dundee whale men were able to converse quite freely in a mix of pidgin English and basic Inuit words.

Gradually – and particularly when overwintering of whaler crews began and whaling stations were constructed – the two peoples became increasingly interdependent. 'It altered the way the Inuit

lived and the way the whalers whaled,' the Inuit historian Dorothy
Harley Eber concluded. The usefulness of the native population was
never in doubt. From the start whaling masters sought their views on
the location of whales and seals, the possibility of precious leads to
open waters, the topography of unknown areas into which they were
venturing, the presence of mineral deposits, and their practical help
as guides and hunters, as oarsmen on whaleboats, or as manpower
to move beset ships. Explorers in the region also used them as guides
and porters. Peary's crusade to the North Pole in 1909, for example,
employed 22 Eskimo men, 17 women and 10 children. From an
earlier journey Peary had brought back five barrels of Eskimo
remains and six living Eskimos and, 'an eager public queued at
the quayside to inspect them'. Controversially, he also removed
three sacred Inuit meteorites and deposited them in the American
Museum of Natural History.

As the horizon smoke of the Dundee steam fleet became an annual
event, so Eskimos began to rely on their summer visitors from
Scotland. Their appetite for the material riches brought by the ships
grew and their participation in the whaling process became increasingly formal. They congregated near wintering whale ships and
signed on as crew, or guides, as hunters or shore labourers, all in
return for the coveted 'trock'. As time passed, Eskimos moved a long
way from being objects of curiosity. They had come a long way from
the days when it was often the practice on whaleboats to have them
shoot with bows and arrows at a biscuit suspended by a string. By
the late nineteenth century the bow was scarcely seen in their
possession, its place taken by the rifle, a more reliable weapon
against one of their chief predators, the polar bear. Eventually they
'could drink rum and swear round oaths in English', and strong
bonds were forged between the Scots and their Arctic friends as
customs and habits grew closer.

A change for the worse, however, was the introduction of 'western' disease to peoples largely lacking immunity from dreadful
complaints such as measles and tuberculosis. One elderly Inuit
woman in Dorothy Harley Eber's study of Arctic communities said,
'Every time a ship came in, the Inuit used to get colds'. There was no
natural immunity to many diseases. Eber believed 'hundreds, even
thousands died'. She estimated that the population of the Inuit of
western Canada, which was not the fishing ground of Scottish
whalers, fell dramatically from some 2500 people in 1850 to just
150 people in 1910. Inuit communities around Davis Strait, Baffin

Bay and Lancaster Sound also suffered, however. The Dundee whaler *Active* is said to have been responsible for the disappearance of a local tribe on Southampton Island in 1902–03. They were believed to have caught dysentery from the *Active*'s crew as they visited a shore station for water. Just a year later, John Murray, overwintering on the ketch *Ernest William* at Dundee's station at Repulse Bay – established after the closure of the ill-fated station on Southampton Island – recorded the death of the last adult survivor of the tribe:

> Saturday 25th March, 04. Fresh gale NNE thick blowing snow. Gave the natives a little blubber for their lamps. Afternoon a Southampton woman died after a long sickness, consumption, (In-you-co-sha) her name. She was the only surviving grown up person left of the Southampton tribe of natives. They rolled her into a piece of sailcloth and carried her away, and buried her in the snow.

Whale men frequently found Eskimo women worthy of closer examination. Journals kept by ships' doctors leave the impression that they were a reason why medical students from colleges in Glasgow and Edinburgh volunteered for such arduous voyages. As the *Narwhal* called at Lerwick for stores and additional crew before her maiden Arctic voyage in 1859, the Glasgow medical student R. H. Hilliard could hardly contain his anticipation: 'I have spent a not unpleasant time jaunting to and from the shore, making purchases of veils and shawls, and all sorts of Shetland wares for the fair "Neuglis Coonalis" as huskies would say'. Thomas Macklin, surgeon aboard the same ship in 1874, mentioned the belief that Eskimo women had a hankering for the 'officer class' among visiting whalers: 'In one thing they do, however, resemble the girls at home, that is in giving their preference to, or at least, receiving the attentions of the upper tier, rather more graciously than the lower class. In short, preferring officers to men.' When one explorer's Eskimo wife was safely delivered of a son at 82°N, Albert Markham mused, 'the little fellow has, in all probability, the most northern birthplace of any human being living'. It probably did not occur to the soon-to-be-famous naval officer that the natives he had 'discovered' were also human.

Personal relationships were placed on a more formal footing with regular and often long-lasting native partners taken by whaling crews, particularly those based at shore stations, where ships were deliberately frozen in and maintained for the winter. John Murray, overwintering at Repulse Bay, frequently referred to the presence of Eskimo men and women during his working day, and referred to them always as valued members of the station, reporting their comings and goings, births and deaths. A strong business relationship also developed between Scot and Eskimo as contact became frequent. By the 1890s the Dundee shipowner Robert Kinnes had established a mica mine near Lake Harbour employing up to 300 Eskimo, and John Murray's journal records cargoes of mica being loaded on to the *Ernest William* in the spring of 1904 to be used in Dundee for stove doors and batteries.

As late as 1935 the influence of long-departed Dundee whalers was still being felt. One article revealed: 'The natives of these remote regions still vary their own monotonous two-step dances with Scottish reels taught them by the crews of the Dundee ships'. They also retained a taste for tea – 'which they derived from the same source,' it added. In recent times families in the village of Pond Inlet on Baffin Island, one of the most northerly islands in the world, were said to have porridge for breakfast and considered mince and tatties a delicacy. Dorothy Eber met one woman from the dozens of families who left their scattered camps to work for the Dundee whaling fleet at the winter harbours in the 1890s who remembered how excited the tribe would be at the sight of the ships: 'Because now they would get tobacco, they would get tea, they would get bannocks, all the good things they'd be missing all winter'.

While the two groups co-existed in harmony, whaling had a detrimental impact on health and Inuit culture as interaction at winter harbouring developed. Disease decimated Eskimo populations. Guns, tobacco and fancy goods changed their way of life. The high murder rate common today among traditionally non-aggressive Inuit societies is blamed on the introduction of firearms by whale men and explorers, replacing the hand-held harpoon. High suicide rates have been attributed to the rapid culture change. On the other hand, one elderly woman confirmed to Eber that trade with the Dundee whalers was the priority of her people, and that the acquisition of firearms, surplus whaleboats, clothing and many other manufactured goods often made the difference between life and death for remoter communities. And she spoke of her delight in the food left behind for the Eskimo people by the ships – especially 'that orange marmalade' from the famous Keiller's factory in Dundee.

As to arrivals of Eskimos in Scotland, a sighting of native boatmen from northern latitudes was reported in the Orkney Islands as early as 1682. Doubt remains about whether these visitors were Greenland Eskimos, however. Elsewhere, it was a disturbing custom of explorer captains in polar regions to capture 'specimens' of tribesmen for 'examination'. Frobisher's expedition of 1576–1577 returned to England with three Eskimo captives who proved a 'great attraction' when they landed at Bristol. The male hostage demonstrated the use of his kayak and bird-spear to hunt ducks on the River Avon – an occasion recorded in an account of Frobisher's voyage in an early history of Bristol:

> Captaine Frobisher in a ship of our queenes of the burden of 200 tonnes came into Kingrode from Cattai, who brought certaine oare from thence, which was esteemed to be very ritch and full of gowld. . . . They brought likewise a man called Callicho and a woman named Ignorth. They were savage people and fed only uppon raw flesh. The 9th. of October he rode in a little bote made of skinne in the water at the backe, where he killed 2 duckes with a dart, and when he had done carried his bote through the marsh upon his back. The like he did at the weare and other places, where many beheld him. He would hit a ducke a good distance off and not misse. They died here within a month.

Not all died so quickly, and the gold ore from the bay which now bears Frobisher's name turned out to be worthless. But so many 'hostages' were taken by early whaling ships that the Dutch government issued a decree in 1720 prohibiting their murder or kidnap.

The first Eskimo to arrive willingly on a Scottish whaling ship was probably John Sakeouse, who was put ashore in Edinburgh in 1816. One later account claimed that he had stowed away on the Scotland-bound ship. He is reported to have enjoyed his visit to Scotland, and the *Edinburgh Courant* of that year describes a kayak demonstration he gave in Leith harbour. Sakeouse's presence in Scotland, or rather his familiarity with his native Greenland, did not pass unnoticed. He was named official interpreter for Captain John Ross's expedition to the Arctic in 1818, when he is said to have acquitted himself well.

Aberdeen provides the best-documented arrival of an Eskimo who had requested a trip to Scotland. Eenooloopik was aged about 18 when he arrived with Captain William Penny of the *Neptune* in 1839, apparently to help win support from the *Neptune*'s owner, William Hogarth, and from the Government, for a commercial expedition to the northern regions. He was, in effect, proof of the existence of the strange new land – and, ominously, of a new source of labour. Penny had used the native mapmaker to provide expert advice on the seasonal movement of whales. The two men apparently forged a close bond of friendship and trust, as Eenooloopik subsequently led Penny to bowhead whales in Cumberland Sound after the *Bon Accord* had returned him to his community in 1840. It was the first time the Sound, in the dangerous waters of west Davis Strait, had been re-visited by outsiders since explorers had stumbled upon it two centuries earlier. Eeno's arrival caused a sensation in Aberdeen and hundreds lined the dockside to catch a glimpse of him. Rather than the stereotypical savage, he was found to be 'mild and gentle in his nature, and modest, and even delicate'. Eeno certainly won admirers. Prior to his departure the British Treasury placed £20 at the disposal of his minders in Aberdeen for procuring whatever was necessary to establish him in his native community in more comfortable circumstances than he had formerly enjoyed. Similar scenes were experienced south of the border when Eskimos brought to Hull in 1847 were put on show to the public. 'During their stay in England more than 12,000 people in Hull, Manchester, York and other cities flocked to see them – "Admission Sixpence, Schools and Children, Half Price".'

Their cultural susceptibility and lack of immunity to disease exerted pressures on whaling masters to dissuade from such visits. Journeys to Scotland were also discouraged by Eskimo shamans, who forecast that travellers would succumb to the mysterious illnesses of the far-off home the whalers sang about in their shanties. Indeed, John Sakeouse – a 'good looking, healthy young man' when he arrived in Edinburgh in 1816 – caught typhoid and died in Leith in 1819. Eenooloopik, who had 'looked forward to his departure from Aberdeen with pleasure', died in 1847 of tuberculosis, and at least six of the Labrador Inuit taken to England in the nineteenth century died of smallpox. Equally, however, the number of Eskimos who expressed a willingness to visit Scotland increased, and bit by bit their curiosity and persuasiveness won the day. In 1846, for example, a 14-year-old boy called Aukotook Zininnuck pleaded to be taken to Fife by the Kirkcaldy vessel *Caledonia*. He was given lessons in English, drawing and Bible studies before being returned the following season bearing gifts from many of the 8000 people who flocked to the town's harbour to see him off.

The first visit of an Eskimo to Dundee appears to have occurred in

October 1873 when Captain Allan of the *Ravenscraig* discovered an Eskimo 'about 18 years of age' adrift on the ice at Cape Kater in the Davis Strait. The youth, called Ococock, was picked up 'half dead' by the Dundee-registered whaler's crew, with the intention of landing him safely on their southern journey. Owing to weather conditions, Captain Allan discovered that this was not possible and that there was 'no alternative but to go with him to Dundee'. The *Advertiser* reported that Ococock was 'very kindly treated on board, and though unable to understand a word of English, nevertheless appeared to be quite well pleased with the attention and kindness he received'. He appears on a surviving *carte de visite* photograph by James Gibb of Princes Street, Dundee as a small, shy, dour, almost insolent youth, squat and muscular, and dressed in western clothes.

Ococock's arrival was largely ignored by the Dundee newspapers because of the sensational reporting of the plucking to safety by the *Ravenscraig* of 11 members of the American *Polaris* polar expedition. The survivors were landed in Dundee, with much rejoicing on both sides of the Atlantic. Ococock was said to speak very limited English, though he could count slowly up to 20. One can only wonder how he felt at being exhibited in Macfarlane's Music Hall in Castle Street and elsewhere, though it was reported that the Dundee MP James Yeaman had 'manifested a particular interest in his welfare'. In the spring of 1874 Ococock was seen standing on the quayside in Dundee waiting for the *Ravenscraig* to leave because, ironically, he couldn't stand the Dundee cold. The following September word reached Dundee via Captain Fairweather of the *Active* that Ococock 'had died on the passage out'. The *Advertiser* reported, 'Notwithstanding every attention, [Ococock] died while the vessel was rounding Cape Farewell. He was on deck a few hours previous to his death supported by some of the crew. The poor fellow was carried off by consumption, and his body was consigned to the deep'. What was not reported was that the *Ravenscraig* had sailed without a doctor.

Dundee was honoured in November 1876 to receive an Eskimo chief called Olnick. Captain William Adams of the *Arctic* brought him to Dundee from Hudson Bay after he had made repeated requests to visit Scotland. Aged 38, about five feet tall, Olnick was reputed to have been a dead shot who had killed 11 polar bears in the year of his departure to Scotland. He was fêted wherever he went in the city. He gave spear demonstrations to crowds of devoted youngsters and had an interview with the Prince of Wales, later King Edward VII, during a visit to London. He took back many presents, including a small armoury of guns and ammunition which he apparently used to 'boss' the settlement.

Olnick later led the large Eskimo tribe that attempted to salvage the beleaguered *Ravenscraig* in 1879, a dangerous task that resulted in injuries to his people. A year later he visited the *Active*, introducing his two wives to Captain Fairweather – 'one to manage household, one to carry provisions'. While at Pond's Bay in 1888, Captain Adams, by then master of his own whaler *Maud*, received a visit from Olnick's tribe, comprising nearly 100 Eskimos. The tribe boarded the *Maud* and asked to be conveyed to the other side of the bay, some 40–50 miles distant, to reach a new fishing ground. Captain Adams acceded to their request and the whole encampment – men, women, children, dogs, sledges and tents – was squeezed on board for what must have been a memorable voyage. Olnick is said to have prized his friendship with the whale men of Dundee and visited the city's ships when they called at his settlement on the west side of Davis Strait. After a warm sleep near the boilers of the *Eclipse* in 1900 he took ill and Captain Milne was called to attend to him. Nothing could be done. The Eskimo chief, uncomfortable with western ways, was rowed ashore in a whaleboat to die in his native land.

Urio Etawango was a 'fine young fellow' brought by Captain Adams to Dundee in 1886 from Davis Strait. Etawango spent five months in the city, appropriately over winter, and on his return on the *Maud* the following year he received an ovation at Lerwick, 'where he appeared in his native dress in his kayak'. But the nearer he sailed to his homeland, the more moody and disconsolate Urio became. The conjecture aboard the *Maud* was that he was sorry to be going home. He had proved 'a good sailor, was beloved by all of the crew, and he was a dead shot while seal hunting'. In a surviving portrait photograph from 1886 the bearded Urio Etawango is seen dressed in sealskin Eskimo clothing and aiming his bow at some invisible quarry. He gave a canoe and seal-hunting demonstration at Claypotts, which was attended by 2000 people. He also addressed a meeting in the Kinnaird Hall, Bank Street, in which he provided harrowing details of the harshness of Eskimo life. Many men had been lost hunting, he said, and in some parts of his homeland women outnumbered men by five to one. Indeed, the *Terra Nova* in 1895 discovered 30 Eskimo skeletons in Dexterity Bay, the women and children lying separate from the men, the children's toys beside their bodies. They had evidently died of starvation. On his return to Davis Strait in 1887, Urio Etawango's young wife exploded with joy at the sight of numerous presents which the people of Dundee had sent her, among them 200 yards of flannel from Mrs Adams. Another of the gifts was a mandolin. To the astonishment of the ship's company, she lifted the instrument and played *There's nae luck about the House!* The popular song could have been written for her poor husband. Returning from Pond's Bay the following year, Captain Adams called in at the settlement of Durban to discover Urio in a state of dejection. His wife had deserted him – and had taken the gifts from Dundee.

Urio was followed by the best-recalled of the Dundee Eskimos, Shoodlue, who arrived with Captain Milne on the *Eclipse* in 1894. Prior to his departure from his 200-strong settlement at Blacklead Island on Cumberland Gulf, Shoodlue's daily life was probably spent killing seals, eating blubber and playing on the melodeon left to him by previous whaling expeditions. He was certainly able to 'rattle off a list of Dundee vessels, the majority of which have long since gone the way of all whalers', and Milne had known him for several years. As soon as he stepped ashore at Earl Grey Dock wearing a new tweed suit in November 1894, Shoodlue's life changed. He expected the tenements of Juteopolis to tumble down on his head, the way icebergs fell into the sea. He eyed the bustling harbour for whales and looked in awe at horse-drawn trams and the iron monsters in the railway stations nearby. He must have passed through a range of intense emotions that few experience.

As befitted someone who had swapped Greenland for the Greenmarket, reporters from Dundee's newspapers besieged Shoodlue. Yet the first thing that struck the townsfolk about their visitor was his extreme docility. He posed happily in sealskins as crowds of sightseers peered at him. 'Any barbarous instincts were quickly subdued, and the native became content to obey the every word and look of his new master, even as a dog thoroughly tamed in spirit is pleased to do his owner's will,' was *The Courier*'s insensitive opinion. What might have been viewed even then as arrogance did not prevent the satirical *Piper o' Dundee* wondering how Shoodlue must have felt setting foot in a 'civilised world' surrounded by beings of a 'higher race'. The Dundee *People's Journal* more respectfully described him as a 'medicine man' and 'Esquimaux priest'.

Shoodlue was a typical Inuit: a squat figure, with a broad, kindly face and tumbling glossy hair. He was aged about 40. The *Advertiser* added unhelpfully, 'He has the features of a Mongolian cast'. To anyone who listened, he was a great medicine man from Blacklead Island, on the shores of Cumberland Sound, an inlet in west Davis Strait. When it became known in the city that he was happy to attend church, he rose in the estimation of many and a good deal of fuss was made over him. He certainly showed patience, humour and long-suffering good temper during his stay in Dundee. He attended council functions, was paraded before schools and asked to sing in his own language at concerts. He delighted large crowds by giving demonstrations of his Arctic skills in Dundee's docks, paddling canoes and throwing harpoons. He was said to be the hero of all the small boys in Dundee and made a host of new friends. He also had a sense of humour. His English came and went depending on his mood, and in reply to questions his eyes would orbit the heavens before he replied, 'I don't know' to some, or to others 'I dinnae ken' in a dialect peculiar to Peterhead. As the weeks passed he was given European clothes, cut his hair and became a regular churchgoer. Often he would stand at the harbour to discuss the prospects of the ensuing whale-fishing season. He took to tobacco with alacrity, spending more than the odd sixpence on two ounces of his favourite bogie roll. But he insisted that alcohol did not interest him: 'Fire-water very bad thing,' he would say. On one occasion he polished off a 2lb tin of marmalade at one sitting.

A day before leaving, Shoodlue gave an insight into why he had to go home: 'Not care for squaw, but want to see piccaninnies,' he confided to a reporter. To the question of how many wives he had, he threw up a single digit and said, 'One, one much plenty'. In fact, he was twice married, turning the first wife adrift in Greenland. He also had two sons. Shoodlue the Esquimaux, or Sugar Loo as he was known around Dundee, dressed in a new suit and wearing a presentation cap, bade farewell with a barrowload of gifts from his adopted city – including huge jars of the Keiller's marmalade that he had eaten non-stop since his arrival. The *Eclipse* moved slowly into the estuary, leaving behind quays lined with many thousands who had adopted an Eskimo and grown to admire him.

Eskimos continued to arrive at Earl Grey Dock, including in October 1899 a youngster whose name was phonetically spelt Kid-law, a boy of around 15 who arrived on the *Esquimaux* with Captain Harry McKay. Kidlaw quickly dispensed with his Inuit garb and adopted Western clothes – knickerbockers, jacket, collar and gloves. The *Piper o' Dundee* commented, 'He is learning the peculiar patois of

Dundee, and no doubt when he returns to his folks in the spring, he will be able to explain to them how the Queen's English is spoken in this queer northern quarter, where sledges are unknown, and where a menu of blubber is not yet fashionable'. Kidlaw's visit to Dundee, where he is said to have been a passable imitator of the *Evening Telegraph* paperboys and a quick learner of football in the youthful kickabouts on Tayport Common, was followed by that of another native called Schaa or 'Billy,' who was brought to Scotland in 1900 by Robert Kinnes who had established the shore station and mica mine at Lake Harbour. Kinnes then brought Kingwatsiak from his shore settlement. Another called Inea arrived in 1910, and an Eskimo called Nwyabek was a visitor in Dundee as late as 1925 and stayed in a house in the Hawkhill area. Another called Chikanuk became a celebrity known as the West End Eskimo. 'To see Chikanuk in the Empress Ballroom on a Saturday night, waltzing in full Arctic regalia, was unforgettable,' recalled a correspondent of *The Courier*.

The view could certainly be taken that Eskimos were brought to Dundee to be exploited – though Captain William Adams, for one, acted with best intentions. Adams argued for years that the most remote, nomadic Eskimo dwellers in the northern British possessions, who were familiarly known as the Arctic Highlanders, should be united with the better-off communities supported by the Danes in Greenland. 'Surely some help could be extended to these poor, God-forsaken people,' he wrote in 1887. In less reproachful terms, Adams also suggested establishing a supported Eskimo settlement as part of Queen Victoria's jubilee celebrations that year, and never failed to arouse interest in them. In Scotland, however, they faced disorientation, bewildering difficulties of language and the strange culture of an industrial society. Despite the 'riches' they took home, they were exploited, used for self-promotion, and viewed often as objects of curiosity and figures of fun. As Shoodlue was taken to meet the town council, the Lord Provost allegedly greeted him with the words, 'Cold today'.

The lasting legacy of the whale men's contact with natives from the circumpolar communities was the indispensable help and companionship they gave to the Scottish strangers in their homeland. They acted as guides and as labour, but contributed especially to the success and survival of whaling crews at wintering stations by hunting for and cooking fresh meat, which prevented scurvy, and leading hunting and whale boat excursions as 'ships' natives'. It was undoubtedly the Eskimo family system that saved the lives of countless Dundee whale men. Wrecked crews shared in what they had, and whaling journals reveal they were supported with genuine kindness and compassion. When, for example, the *Snowdrop* was wrecked in Frobisher Strait in September 1908, the given-up-for-lost crew lived peacefully with Eskimo families for nearly a year, acquiring Eskimo skills in hunting, navigating, driving dogs and building snow houses.

The cost, however, was the erosion of traditional Eskimo beliefs and practices. The whaling industry changed settlement patterns and a huge range of manufactured goods entered Inuit society. A sizeable number of Europeans settled in their midst, including many missionaries, yet few of them took the trouble to record details of the cultures of the communities they encountered. Socially, Eskimos for the most part were regarded as curiosities unworthy of further examination. Gradually they lost control of their own lives.

Other live cargoes were greeted with more trepidation at the quayside in Dundee. Over the years, a succession of live polar animals was brought ashore – to the consternation of the townsfolk, as they made a habit of escaping. In 1874 a bear broke loose and with its chain dangling at its heels set out for a Saturday evening stroll down the High Street, generating considerable public panic along the route. The bear made its way to Victoria Road, calling on a crockery shop. There it broke a few dishes, but on finding nothing to eat, left the premises plainly in a savage mood for, according to *The Courier*, meeting a boy 'who had incautiously ventured too near the door', the bear made a snap at his hand and bit some of his fingers. It then looked into a baker's where it received a direct hit from a loaf thrown by the proprietor. At this the bear reportedly lay down and began to gnaw at the missile. In this docile condition it was ultimately secured.

Another pantomime occurred in 1877 when a polar bear escaped in Commercial Street. This was one of a pair in a wooden crate being transported to a showground. The crate slipped from a barrow, making a space large enough for the escape of one of the bears from the damaged compartment. It was reported that a dog that attempted to tackle it was sent away to lick its wounds and that the bear soon effected a clearance of the streets. It followed some people into a clothing shop, knocked down and sniffed at a dummy before placing its giant forepaws on a large mirror, 'delighted' with its appearance. It was eventually lassooed when it showed too much of its snout from beneath a counter and was dragged from the shop, half strangled.

When Captain Adams moored the *Maud* alongside Earl Grey Dock in September 1887, crowds witnessed one of the most astonishing sights ever seen at the port – the unloading of a live adult walrus. Newspapers claimed it was the first time a fully-grown walrus had ever arrived in Britain. Dundee ships had landed several young walruses in previous years – one of which had been sold for £500 and another offered to Barnum's Circus – but these 'had invariably succumbed after a few months' residence'. Determined to capture an adult specimen, Adams wisely dispatched four boats and 24 men for the task when a walrus colony was reached in Exeter Sound, in the High Arctic. To lessen the risks to the men from attack, 'ten of the foremost animals had to be shot to prevent mischief'. After a prolonged tussle, the men lassooed a female walrus. The fact that such beasts can weigh well over a ton was not lost on the *Maud*'s crew, who firstly had to heave the animal by ropes into an empty whaleboat, before towing it to their ship, where it was hoisted on board for the two-week crossing to Scotland. Although the walrus was never hunted in the numbers that the whale or seal was, it was taken as and when it appeared. This changed in the last quarter of the nineteenth century when walrus skins were sold at 1/6d a pound to make bicycle seats. The slaughter duly increased. In 1897, for example, Captain 'Coffee Tam' Robertson sailed to Franz Josef Land and returned with only one whale, but 600 walrus hides. The *Advertiser* reported: 'His special object this season was the capture of walrus, which have greatly increased in value in the past year or two'.

Perhaps the first live polar bear returned to Scotland was the cub captured by Captain Sturrock of the Dundee whaler *Alexander* in 1846. Her crew had seen two adult bears and the cub on an ice floe, and the larger male was eventually dispatched after 17 shots. (The crossfire also accounted for Captain Sturrock's son, who was fatally wounded.) The cub was roped, taken on board and 'cooped up in a cask'. It was subsequently transported by the Gourlay-built passenger vessel *Britannia* to Edinburgh where it 'became a tenant in the zoological gardens'. Polar bears became major attractions in subsequent years and it was rare sport catching them, according to the experienced whale man James 'Toshie' McIntosh: 'A lasso was thrown round their necks, and then they were dragged to the ship, and the rope reeved in a tackle on the yard-arm, we hoisted them on board. A big strong barrel was got ready on deck, and 'bruin' was lowered into the cask stern foremost. The cooper was standing by with a cover made of strong iron hoops, and as soon as the bear was fairly caged, he covered him up and secured him tight'. An advertising flyer from February 1886 provides an impression of the excitement the polar visitors offered on arrival in port:

> Last week of the bears!
> Positively Closing on Saturday 6th February
> TO BE SEEN ALIVE
> AT COMMERICAL STREET (Top of Seagate)
> The
> 3 Largest Polar Bears
> EVER IMPORTED from the ARCTIC REGIONS
> These Beautiful Animals, which are as White as the driven
> Snow, were brought to Dundee by the Brothers Captains
> Fairweather, in the whale ships 'Arctic' and 'Terra Nova', and
> will be Exhibited here for a few days only, previously to being
> sent to the Zoological Gardens, Dublin. Mr Woods, wishing
> the inhabitants of Dundee to have an opportunity of seeing
> them, has decided to make the Price of Admission merely
> nominal. ONLY 2d. On view from 9am to 10 pm.

Polar bears were hunted for their skins, often as gifts for ship shareholders rather than for their monetary value. Skins gradually increased in price, and in 1864 the *Polynia* brought home 22 dead bears, worth £50 each, and two live brown bears, which were exhibited to raise money for Dundee Royal Infirmary. At the time, a live bear could fetch only about £35 from zoological gardens and, in any case, 'the quantity of blubber they consumed on the voyage home was more than the profit'. One to go on public display was landed by the *Victor* in 1868. Some seven feet in height, it had been confined on the homeward voyage in a blubber cask. On the quayside at Dundee it was sold for £35 to Mandel's Menagerie, which was touring Scotland at the time. The account of the voyage tells how it was offered raw bear meat to eat, but preferred bread soaked in seal oil. Unfortunately, bears were worth more dead. Eleven of the 12 polar bears seen by the *Arctic* in 1873 were shot, and the sole survivor, described by Albert Markham as a 'savage little brute', was sold to a zoo in Bristol. And, in 1889, the explorer Walter Livingstone-Learmonth, born in Australia of Scottish parents and educated in Edinburgh, steamed to the Arctic with the veteran master of the *Maud*, William Adams, ostensibly to map the coastline, but spent most of his time 'bagging' 26 walruses, nine seals and four polar bears. James McIntosh, who lost both legs from frostbite in the *Chieftain* disaster of 1884, recalled a ruse used by whalers to attract bears to their waiting guns: 'When the man in the crow's nest sighted any bears on the ice, a bone was put in the fire, and if the wind was blowing in their direction, the smell was sure to bring them near us'.

Bears proved reluctant victims, however. They would suddenly be found sharing an isolated ice floe with crewmen. They would attempt to scale the Jacob's ladders to the ships' rails, or disconcertingly join in football games on the ice. Whaling journals contain many exciting tales. One account tells of a bear attacking a rowing boat and its sailors jumping overboard and resting on their oars as the bear, in the meantime, took possession of the boat. Another tells of three seamen from the *Intrepid* of Dundee who set out on foot across the ice to visit the *Perseverance* of Peterhead in April 1877. Some two miles from the Peterhead vessel a large female bear and cub confronted the men. Having no rifle – a major misjudgment later outlawed by skippers sending men ashore – the men chose to make a dash towards the *Perseverance*, which was by then closer than the Dundee ship. The bears gave chase. A quick-thinking crewman realised that the bears' pursuit would be stalled if they had something to distract them. All three began ripping off their clothing as they ran. The bears stopped, inspected the clothing for food content and tore the items to shreds before taking up the chase again. In the nick of time seamen on the *Perseverance* saw the men's plight and overcame their surprise in time to shoot the bears dead at the feet of their exhausted and semi-naked visitors.

The men's delight at the slaughter of such creatures is difficult to accept in today's world where the 'shooting' is done by the cameras and videos of polar tourists. Surgeon R. H. Hilliard aboard the *Narwhal* in 1859 logged an incident indicating the cold indifference:

> We lowered away a boat after an old she bear and two large cubs. We first shot the mother and then harnessed the cubs alive to the bow of the boat, and made them tow us to the ship, for which service we were kind enough to blow their brains out.

It was a brutal calling, and these tough men of the sea displayed emotional detachment from the cruelties they imposed on themselves – and on the life around them. But, as the satirical *Piper o'*

Dundee pointed out, one magnificent specimen of the animal kingdom was not as defenceless as others on the slaughtering voyages to Arctic waters:

> The poler bare is a citisen of greenland's icey mountains, where he romes abowt looking for Dundee sailors who are whailors. When he can't get a joly tar too eat he goes for the seals, the walrushes and the whails. The poler bare is the only man what nos were the north pol is fixt up and he wont tell no one. He is very devoted to his yung when he has any and will dye in their defens. He is all pure blak, except his skin wich is white as the sno. Yu can sea them in the Dundee musem on the days wich it is open, but they are so stufft full there that they lye dormouse.

SIX

Cauld Winter Was Howlin'

In February 1992 a Swedish naval salvage expert arrived in Dundee to make an audacious attempt to buy a Dundee whaler which had been abandoned in over 600 feet of Greenland's ice-ridden water 100 years earlier.* The *Vega* had known better days, said the expert. She was the first vessel ever to make the North-East Passage from Sweden to Japan, around the top of the world – and she was a maritime shrine for the Swedes. The *Vega* had known harrowing days, too. As part of the Dundee whaling fleet in Davis Strait in 1903 she had been caught in ice in the dreaded ship breakers' yard – Melville Bay – and holed below the water line. It was her maiden whaling voyage, and as her master John Cooney watched the crew of 44 men clamber scantily dressed into her flimsy whaleboats some 300 miles from the nearest settlement, he remained with arms folded in the stern of his doomed ship, refusing pleas to leave with them.

The *Vega*'s story was soon to enthrall readers of newspapers throughout Britain – 'Of what sterling stuff these gallant Scottish mariners are made,' said the *Daily Telegraph* in admiration, but the determination and heroism of her men was a reminder to the Dundee whaling community that the safety promised by the adoption of auxiliary steam in the 1860s did not mean an industry without risk. Far from it. When a whale man signed on for a small salary and a share of oil and bone money, he may have envisaged a speedier passage, more manoeuvrability and comparative comfort aboard the second generation of larger Dundee-built whaling ships, but the only guarantee that came with the job was a wretched existence in the most desolate place known on earth. Of Dundee's 60 nineteenth-century whale ships, 40 never returned.

Sometimes the greatest danger was not to be caught in ice but the threat of unforeseen accidents brought about by the combination of difficult work in perilous environments. Some calamities occurred

---

* Alas, nothing came of the salvage attempt as far as I am aware. She was certainly still in deep water off the coast of Greenland in 1998.

close to home in the less-hostile vicinity of Dock Street. In 1821 the *Dorothy* struck a sunken rock outside Dundee harbour and had to be towed off by the Tay Ferries' steamer *Unicorn*. On her return from Greenland that October, the *Achilles* struck the military's gunpowder store while entering harbour, wrecking half of its east turret and bringing down her masts – though fortunately leaving the town intact! In 1858 the SS *River Tay*, constructed with 42 watertight compartments, did not get beyond her launching slip without tearing away her side, and steamed not to Greenland, but to Granton for repairs. She was eventually launched on February 10 – and promptly sank on her maiden voyage. In 1872 Captain Grevill moved from the tiny *Victor* to take over the mighty *Camperdown* – and grounded her opposite Dundee baths on his outward journey. He restored his reputation within weeks by taking 17 whales in three days. In 1878 the Dundee-registered *Ravenscraig* left port in such a leaky state that her crew refused to proceed to Davis Strait with her. She was making over a foot of water an hour. Her master, Captain West, jumped overboard and committed suicide. In March 1900, the townsfolk abandoned desk and spinning frame to wish good fortune to the *Eclipse*, which proceeded to steam into the sea wall. In 1902 'great excitement prevailed' when the *Balaena, Diana* and *Eclipse* left Dundee for Davis Strait. Moments later the huge Bank Holiday crowd was 'greatly astonished to see the *Balaena* sailing back to Dundee again' with her tail between her legs. Faulty machinery was blamed. And the following year, the pride of the fleet, the majestic *Terra Nova*, simply rolled over in the graving dock.

Danger was an ever-present element in the working day of whaler crews. Men fell or were washed overboard, were scalded by fire, accidentally shot, or, in the case of the wave-lashed *Nova Zembla* in 1884: 'The fireman got his head badly cut in two places by the furnace doors swinging backwards and forwards . . . the weather we are having just now is frightening everybody, even the Captain, who has written down in his log for today, "Ship like to do damage" '. Wooden whaling ships were permanently liable to damage from fires – so much so that as soon as they were beset or anchored in ice, one of the first duties of the lower ranks was to cut a 'fire hole' close to the ship's bow to ensure a ready supply of water. Ironically, the most damaging fires occurred while the fleet was in port. The *Nova Zembla* herself went on fire while tied up in Dundee in 1884, the *Alexander* caught fire in King William Dock in 1850, and there were two serious fires aboard the *Diana* in 1901 and 1906 and another on

11. A whaler in 'difficulties', 1900.

12. A whaler blasting pack ice in Davis Strait. 'Judicious' use of gunpowder was a common means of freeing a ship nipped in ice.

Flenching a Whale, Shetland.

13. Flensing a whale, Shetland, c.1910. Norwegian whalers opened shore stations in the North of Scotland from 1905. Dundee owners were reluctant to become involved, however. In the early days of whaling Scottish whale ships which flensed their catch on shore were not entitled to bounty money.

14. A whale is lashed to the *Eclipse*, ready for the flensers to begin their grisly work.

15. The *Active* beset in ice, 1894. The whaleboats are hung on davits, ready to launch. The crow's nest is prominent on the main mast and a Jacob's ladder hangs from the bowsprit.

16. The *Active*'s football team on Spitzbergen in 1894. Polar bears were keen participants.

17. Dundee whalers negotiate loose ice in Davis Strait.

18. The fleet at work in Davis Strait in 1900 in a photograph illustrating the frozen landscape at high altitudes.

19. One of 100 Polar bears taken by the SS *Active* in 1908. Most bears found new homes in British zoos.

20. Returning across pack ice from a seal hunt.

21. The upper jaw of a Right whale showing its 'curtain' of valuable baleen. It could be sawn, shredded or cut into an endless variety of products. Large jaw bones ended up as gateposts or entrance arches.

22. All hands on deck for skinning walrus at the 'making off' stanchions.

23. Men pose with a large narwhal. Narwhal skins were regarded as 'scraps' but the decorative horns were sold for considerable sums.

24. Shoodlue, the best-remembered Inuit visitor to Dundee, arrived with Captain Milne of the *Eclipse* in 1894.

the *Eclipse* in 1908, all while the ships were in port. No doubt the city's whale men also had a grandstand view of Dundee's most destructive fire, at Watson's spirits warehouse in 1906. The fabled 'rivers of rum' said to have flowed down harbourside streets during the course of the two-day conflagration must have been an inducement for some to jump ship.

Danger was never far away, in the literal sense. Long before the Arctic fishing grounds were reached, crews often spent days braced in their bunks as ships pitched and rolled yet fought on against head-on Atlantic storms and hurricane-strength winds. Mountainous seas left them sodden and cold before the first ice was sighted at Cape Farewell. Sleep on outbound whalers was often impossible. The fog that dogged the north Atlantic was frequently clammy and dispiritingly dense. In 1838 Captain Middleton of Aberdeen noted a breeze springing up and a crewman falling from the heights of the main mast into the sea – 'We jerked him up, but he was so badly hurt that he died within a week'. Middleton also recalled an Arctic gale that blew up suddenly in May 1836: 'The ship was struck by a sea which swept off everything movable abaft the main mast; stern-boat, binnacle, rail staunchings and bulwarks were washed overboard. Fortunately only five men were on deck. One was washed overboard and drowned, another had his leg fractured and shoulder dislocated, a third had his collar-bone broken, the fourth sustained some spinal injuries, while the fifth, though thoroughly drenched, was unhurt'. Such carnage makes the presence of a surgeon on whaling voyages easily understood.

The powerful Dundee steam fleet, built to withstand incredible pack-ice pressure, was not immune to the dangers of the open sea. Student doctor Mathew Campbell on the *Nova Zembla* in March 1884 recorded a 'perfect hurricane' at a latitude no further north than Dundee: 'another wave came and carried away a part of our bulwarks and the sea washed over the deck in torrents. At midnight three boats washed away. Two men missing from the mate's watch must have been washed overboard'. In 1891 the *Polynia* was hit by a huge wave outbound which killed one crewman and injured ten. Two months later the *Polynia* was caught between two ice floes and disappeared altogether. Destructive Atlantic gales also featured in the diary kept by Broughty Ferry ship's steward William Walker in 1919:

> On Monday evening, 6th October, I had a very narrow escape of being killed. It was blowing a heavy gale of wind and I

happened to be going along the deck when an order was given in connection with the sails. Just as I was passing the main mast a heavy block gave way and landed about a foot from me. The ropes coiled around me and I must say it made me a little excited until I got clear . . . the mate, Anton Lindberg, a Swede, was washed overboard and lost; also a water tank, compass and main sail. On going along the deck I found Capt Murray lying on the deck unconscious, with a nasty gash on the head and his right leg broken.

Steam power could be a guarantor of safe passage – or a route into trouble. Auxiliary engine propellers, for example, were frequently damaged through constant abrasion. There was an embarrassing experience for the duo of powerful steamers *Polynia* and *Camperdown* which blazed the trail of the town's sealing activity in Newfoundland in 1862. Both had propellers torn away by ice and faced the ignominy of returning to St John's for repairs – after the frontier townsfolk had gathered to admire the innovative Scottish visitors on their arrival. The Dundee vessels quickly discovered how lucky they had been. No fewer than 35 Newfoundland sealing vessels had been lost – all sailing vessels – in a season that also accounted for the heroic little Dundee whaler *Alexander*, crushed in ice in Melville Bay. Captain Adams recalled for the *Evening Mercury* newspaper of St John's how on one sealing voyage on the SS *Arctic*, 'We had lost or broken three propellers . . . many times all the men were on the ice with prizers, hatchets and blasting powder, and every means available to cut a passage for our magnificent ship'. The theory in 1858 that steam propellers would be effective beneath the level of the ice, and easily hoisted clear of impediments when the vessel was under sail or in ice, was wide of the mark in practice. Mathew Campbell's log of his voyage on the *Nova Zembla* in 1884 recorded a terrible blow from a large mass of ice that struck the rudder and 'threw two men from the wheel and carried away a blade from our screw'. Albert Markham noted in 1873 that pieces of ice 'of considerable magnitude, broken off by our repeated charges, would pass along under the bottom of the ship, and, emerging up the screw aperture, prevent the propeller from performing its revolutions, and therefore bringing the engine to a dead stop'. And when the *Wildfire* damaged her propeller in 1868 she managed to limp 500 miles to Disco Island, only to be abandoned there.

Curiously, it was seldom the cold which brought death to Dundee crews in the early days of whaling. When ships were crushed and abandoned, it rarely happened without warning, and men took to the ice and awaited rescue by the fleet which often sailed in convoy for just such a purpose. 'Casks of bread, beef and other necessities of life are got on deck in readiness for any emergency and other personal property are packed in canvass bags ready for taking the ice,' noted Campbell in 1884. The only major loss of life as far as Dundee was concerned was the near-80 men who perished in the *Thomas-Advice* disaster of 1836 – the year that Halley's Comet was observed for the first time since 1759, a traditional omen of bad luck. More often, it was an accident or carelessness which led to tragedy, leaving the captain with the sad duty of alerting the seamen's missionary in Dundee to break the news to the family concerned. In 1825 the mate of the *Advice* tumbled overboard while harpooning a whale, and was presumed drowned. In 1838 the *Alexander* lost a man and a whaleboat when a harpooned whale lashed out with its tail. Several other men suffered fractured legs. In 1874 the *Camperdown* lost two men, both dying after falling through ice. In 1881 the *Erik* lost a harpooner when a whale's tail crashed down and smashed his boat. And in 1887 James Cumming fell through thin ice to his death while serving with the *Terra Nova*. He was aged 76, had gone to sea at 16 and had made 57 Arctic trips. Guns were an additional hazard and several whaling logs refer to accidental shootings and other near things. The most serious occurred in 1846 when Captain David Sturrock took the *Horn* to Davis Strait. Among her crew was his 18-year-old son. While boat crews were sealing on ice the youth was accidentally, but fatally, shot. The following year the *Horn* lost another boy overboard in the Pentland Firth, and returned from Davis Strait with 15 hands ill with scurvy. Matters did not improve for Captain Sturrock and the second-oldest ship on Dundee's register. Returning from the fishery in 1852 he sailed past the Tay estuary in thick fog, assumed he was five miles offshore, and grounded the 69-year old vessel in poor visibility. She was only 40 yards off Boarhills, near St Andrews, and was quickly dashed to pieces on the rocks.

Undoubtedly the unpredictability of ice posed the greatest danger of all. In 'leads' among the floes, boring and butting through pack ice, anchored by 'nose-hooks' dug into the solid Arctic mass, or protected in comparative safety in an ice dock, ships and men faced the vagaries of the constant, indiscernible movement of ice and the battering-ram icebergs which could easily split a wooden hull.

Driven by polar winds and powerful water currents, ice closed in quickly and without warning, thwarting attempts at navigation because of its unpredictability. And as the Dundee fleet moved ever north in pursuit of diminishing stocks, the most feared words in the whale men's vocabulary – 'nipped,' 'squeezed' and 'beset' – appeared with disturbing regularity in their journals.

The cold became intense as the ships battled to higher latitudes. In temperatures regularly as low as $-22°F$ ($-30°C$) drinking water turned to ice. Temperatures fell so low that ice formed only a few feet from the 'permanent' fire in the galley. By Davis Strait, barely two weeks after leaving Scotland, ropes and rigging had a heavy coat of ice doubling their thickness, 'causing a shower of ice every time we tack'. By Melville Bay, men lay awake in their bunks listening to the cracking ice scraping along the ship's side, dreading the sudden explosion that would cause their downfall by turning their 300-ton vessel to matchwood in minutes. It was an inevitable consequence that some vessels would be wrecked. And, as winter approached and the sun disappeared for weeks over the horizon, exposure to cold tormented whaler crews. One man in the *Dee* in 1836 was able to show the surgeon the bones of his frostbitten toes, which had been frozen off during the winter. He carried them in his vest pocket. 'Now our melancholy situation was in full view,' recorded one seaman as the dreadful suffering led inexorably to death. 'To our own imagination nothing cheerful could present itself. Having nothing before us but darkness, severe cold, hunger and death.' Fresh food, quickly exhausted, was replaced by salt biscuits and beef and seldom prevented the subversive disease scurvy. This creeping affliction had troubled the Admiralty for 100 years, yet the evidence supplied to them on anti-scorbutic remedies by several distinguished scientists and mariners was spectacularly overlooked. The Government did not introduce preventative legislation until the late date of 1859 – even though scurvy had been shown in eighteenth-century conflicts to account for up to 80% of all casualties. Unsurprisingly, the legislation was strictly enforced in the subsequent century and was the subject of a celebrated Lime Juice Trial in Dundee in 1893, which drew the wrath of the local MP and newspaper baron Sir John Leng.

The case concerned the fireman on the *Aurora* who was treated during the return voyage from Davis Strait for the symptoms of 'a slight attack of scurvy'. The master of the *Aurora*, Captain Alexander Fairweather, was duly charged with not serving out one ounce of lime juice daily to each of his crew, as required by the Marine Shipping Act. In court, the ship's doctor agreed that if the man had taken lime juice regularly he very possibly might have escaped the attack of scurvy, 'the ancient curse of the sea'. Captain Fairweather said it was 'impossible' to serve out small quantities to the crew on a daily basis, arguing that the men were often away from the ship for days on end hunting whales, a fact borne out in many journals. A number of the old guard of whaling masters, including Captains Yule, Gray and Milne, testified in court as to the impracticalities of the Act. Besides, the court was told that Fairweather had made no attempt to evade the law. The *Aurora* had a plentiful supply of lime juice, but it was the practice to serve out 40 ounces in a bottle once a month, instead of one ounce daily, and to leave the crew to take it as required.

After hearing evidence, Sheriff Campbell Smith fined Captain Fairweather £1 for breaking the requirement of the law. Although the *Advertiser* sat on the fence – on the one hand referring to 'grandmotherly legislation' while on the other saying that a law that called for the strict and systematic administration of the liquid was not 'a bad one' – the ruling led to an outcry in Dundee. Sir John Leng, with the support of trade leaders such as Captain Phillips of the *Esquimaux*, Captain McKay of the *Terra Nova* and David Bruce, manager of the Dundee Seal and Whale Fishing Company, wrote to the Board of Trade with the city's protest. In his letter of January 23, 1894, Leng reiterated that crews were often absent from their mother ship on whaling or sealing duties. He pointed out that even if space could be found in whaleboats, the lime juice would probably freeze. He said that the men of the *Aurora* were 'superabundantly' supplied with lime juice and that a monthly bottle containing 40 ounces of the liquid was in fact a larger quantity than stipulated by the Act. The efficacy of the Dundee practice in controlling the disease, he argued, was that the city's captains could recall only one case of scurvy in the previous eight years. On a positive note Leng suggested to the Board of Trade that a criminal prosecution should be sought only if a ship sailed without supplies, or if a master failed to serve out allowances or where there was an intention to evade the Act. The reply from Ingram Walker, Secretary to the Marine Department of the Board of Trade, indicated that no leeway would be allowed in keeping the feared disease under control. He pointed out: 'In the case of the *Aurora*, trade practice was allowed not only to modify, but to altogether over-ride the requirements of the law'. The men of the

Aurora, he said, seemed to have been left 'to take it or not, as they pleased'. The conviction stood. Perhaps Sir John should have scrutinised the records of the Tay Whale Fishing Company before delivering his broadside. Inland Revenue returns for surplus provisions for various ships, including the *Active, Victor* and *Intrepid*, show large amounts of lime juice being returned to port unopened, including 10 cases in 1873 and nine in 1874, amounting to 30 gallons and 27 gallons respectively.

Ships caught by ice did not wait for the floes to smash their rudders or squeeze their timbers. They often ran south to the safest anchorage, waited for the ice to surround them and created protective ice docks to shelter the vessels as best they could. This was done by means of long ice saws worked by teams of up to 16 men, encouraged by the usual singing of shanties. The men of the stricken *Dee* adopted the process in October 1836: 'First of all, a triangle had to be raised on the ice, and a block fixed in the junction at the top. Through this block a rope is reeved, to which an ice saw is suspended, and from the other end bell or branch ropes, to allow five or six men to work the saws, which is done in the same way piles are driven for laying foundations for quays or other buildings'. The venerable old whaler *Truelove*, which had been captured by the British in the American Wars of Independence as long before as 1765, benefited from no fewer than 18 ice docks while in Melville Bay in 1856. But James Troup remarks, 'As a winter resource this proved about as useful as crossing one's fingers.'

Ice had a dramatic effect on living and working conditions. Captain William Adams Snr spoke of an occasion when the Dundee whaler *Arctic* had to ram one short stretch for 27 hours: 'That is, letting the ship go as far astern as possible, and then running at the ice full speed, with 300 men on the ice hauling on a strong rope to assist the ship with all available power, and so backwards and forwards until we accomplished our objective'. Moreover, when stalled by ice, whaling captains would often order men to begin 'overing'. This was done by creating a human seesaw, with the ship's company running backwards and forwards across the deck to bring about a rolling motion to break up the ice. Surgeon Mathew Campbell recalled the crew carrying out this process with such a will on the *Nova Zembla* in 1884 that 'her boats almost touched the ice'. Impenetrable ice directly ahead of a ship was sometimes broken by a process called milldolling in which a whaleboat was dropped like a heavy stone from the bowsprit in the hope that its weight would smash the ice below, allowing the vessel to edge forward. More dramatic action was required in 1856 when the crew of the stricken *Princess Charlotte* of Dundee worked for 16 hours manhandling their ice-bound ship into position to give Captain Alan Deuchars the angle to blast the hull with gunpowder to allow the men to salvage their clothes from the wreck. The pressure of being nipped also reached explosive proportions. In a frightening incident in 1882, which Adams described as 'the most trying episode of my life', which is saying something, the SS *Arctic* was heeled over to an angle of 70° first to one side and then to the other, by the severe squeezing of ice alone. 'To give you an idea of the pressure,' wrote the famous master, 'the fore rigging on the starboard side became so slack that it nearly touched the mast; the main hatch had the appearance or shape of a diamond.' Adams had one of his many narrow escapes, but it spoke wonders of the strength of Dundee's wooden whalers 'that on her return to Dundee, after being placed in dry dock by Messrs Stephen & Sons, she was squeezed back into shape by means of hydraulic pressure'.

When there was no wind to move ships, or a frustrating head wind, the crew manned their whaleboat oars 'like galley slaves' and towed the ships by lines attached to the foremast head. This was made easier and enlivened by shanties, and 'when half a dozen were towing against each other, the scene was a very inspiring one, with the roared out choruses echoing back off the cliffs of icebergs'. Tracking was another way of moving a becalmed ship through a lead and towards the fishery. This backbreaking work involved the men towing the ship by using a canvas belt, called a row-raddie, attached to the towing rope, on their pulling shoulder. In his whaling recollections of 1838 Captain Middleton recalled, 'Thirty, forty and even fifty hours at a stretch was not uncommon, and once we were constantly at it for seventy hours'. The Dutch maritime museum in the famous Friesian sailing port of Sneek contains a painting which shows canal boats being 'tracked' by servants wearing similar canvas devices, and the procedure, like many whaling customs, may have originated in northern Holland.

Whaling operations, which included many hours of rowing, towing or tracking, left the men hard-muscled and physically at their peak. Yet men passing through periods of enforced idleness and inactivity when beset in ice, allied to a deteriorating diet, often developed excruciating symptoms of scurvy, rheumatism and frost-bite as stocks of fuel were prudently conserved. The Aberdeen whaling master Captain Parker was noted for insisting on four hours' exercise every afternoon to prevent the men becoming listless and despondent, including a game of follow-my-leader which took his men up and down the rigging like 'monkeys'. Later, Dundee crews played endless games of football on ice with balls made from sealskin, and a surviving photograph of the crew of the *Arctic* 'football team' is a reminder of this activity. Exercise often took unusual forms. When the *Aurora* was nipped between an iceberg and an ice floe in 1886, her 300-strong crew immediately abandoned ship, carrying what they could of their belongings. According to Ingram:

> A current carried the Aurora and the iceberg along at four knots and the hapless 300 had to move over the ice at a smart jog-trot to keep abreast of her. It was a desperate struggle. Most of the men threw away their gear to keep going. One, who hung on to everything lagged behind, fell into a pool and drowned. After two hours the master and mate reboarded the apparently doomed Aurora. The crew's marathon went on for twelve [hours].

The boot was on the other foot, so to speak, in 1869 when seven men from the SS *Arctic* had a narrow escape when they were marooned on an ice floe and carried away at high speed by the current. This time the men were rescued by the pursuing *Arctic* – 'in the nick of time'. Yet seamen were suspicious of any call that removed them from the 'comfort' of their bunks that did not involve the one word that meant big money – 'whale'. The crew of the ill-fated Dundee Seal and Whale Fishing Company vessel *Columbia*, which sank in only four minutes on her maiden voyage in 1868, found themselves stranded 500 miles north of Cape Farewell with meagre provisions. The men were eventually absorbed by an Inuit community but became 'despondent and lethargic'. When the ship's doctor told them that the local water was a source of scurvy and advised them to draw supplies from a spring half-a-mile distant, the men thought it was merely a ruse to get them to take exercise, and ignored him. On their return to port 13 months after setting out, most were immediately admitted to Dundee Royal Infirmary with symptoms of scurvy.

As Dundee emerged as Britain's leading whaling port, a succession of such tragedies and harrowing tales of survival kept it in the headlines for the wrong reasons. Three episodes involving the Dundee fleet in the era of its domination provide examples of the dangers and extremes of human endurance faced by the hardy breed of men who gambled high above the Arctic circle: the *Vega* incident of 1903, a dramatic escape by the crew of the *Snowdrop* in 1909, and the story of the wrecked *Chieftain*, an incident in 1884 which contributed towards the eventual decline of the whaling industry in Dundee.

The Vega – Starvation and Survival

The story of the *Vega* in 1903 is one of uncanny skills and remarkable courage – and yet after she was converted to whaling trim after circumnavigating Europe and Asia with Baron Nordenskiold, one of the classic adventures of Arctic travel and exploration, the start of her career in Scotland was anything but illustrious. A gale prevented her arrival in Dundee in February 1903 and she was left bobbing in the estuary to the amusement of the old salts on the quayside. Adding to their superstitious gossip, her new master, Captain John Cooney, had lost the *Nova Zembla* the previous year.

The *Vega* sailed from Dundee on April 11 with 44 crew under the command of Captain Cooney on her maiden voyage with the Dundee fleet. The early stages of the voyage north were uneventful and soon Cape Farewell, the whalers' familiar landmark on the southern tip of Greenland, was sighted. The *Evening Telegraph*'s account proceeds: 'In a few days they would be in the fishing grounds. The ship bustled with activity as the crew prepared the gear. Everyone was in high spirits'. The happy frame of mind was soon dispelled when the waters proved barren of whales and teeming with dangerous ice floes. The *Vega* proceeded cautiously through ice into Davis Strait and into a narrow lead towards Melville Bay. Massive icebergs drifted towards her. At 74°N the ice hemmed her in, its sharp edges scoring her timbers. Cooney tried an old whaling trick of dropping explosives ahead of the ship to blast his way clear. It was too late. Suddenly, and unexpectedly, a razor-edged block of ice slammed into the *Vega*'s hull, tearing a gaping hole in her port side. Water poured in. It was May 31. Cooney gave the order to abandon ship. The men, with just the clothes they stood in, scampered down rope ladders into rapidly-lowered whaleboats. One of them, Alexander Gray, recalled for the *Evening Telegraph* in 1954 that Captain Cooney had remained in the stern of the sinking ship, grimly determined to go down with her – until he was persuaded by the calling of the crew, at the last minute, to step into one of the boats. Just as Cooney jumped to safety, the *Vega* gave a lurch between converging ice floes and disappeared.

The crew were stranded 40 miles off the west Greenland coast. The nearest civilisation was the Danish settlement of Upernavik, 300 miles south of their position. Cooney ordered the men to distribute themselves among the seven boats saved. But when he took stock of the salvaged provisions, he discovered that there were only one-and-a-half boxes of biscuits and some salted beef. To make matters worse, a blizzard howled around them. Survival seemed impossible. Scantily clothed and equipped, the men moved off on what was to become an epic journey. At first they rowed through the dangerous channels to keep the blood flowing in their veins. It was the only hope of survival in the intense cold. Where the ice-free leads ended, they began a march over jagged ice fields, hauling the boats behind them until open water was reached once again. Snow fell heavily, hampering progress still further. They had no fuel. Only by breaking up the boats' fittings could they make fire to melt ice for drinking water. Rations were almost exhausted. Only two ship's biscuits a day were allowed to each man. Eventually, it was decided that each boat should go its own way, in the hope that at least one would reach the mainland and give news of the others' plight.

On June 5, 1903, after five days and nights of untold hardship, hunger and suffering, often fighting against incessant snow and southerly gales, one of the *Vega*'s boats reached Upernavik. Two days later, after a remarkable feat of navigation and seamanship, the other six boats arrived. 'From the battered, leaking boats, the exhausted crews were carried to the shelter of some huts. There were no medical facilities, and hot salt was used to dress their wounds.' An exploring ship, the *Good Hope*, arrived at the outpost a few weeks after the landing and took off some of the crew. Places had to be balloted for, married men receiving a preference. But some were too ill to be moved. The men of the *Vega* had crossed more than 300 miles of icy desolation in conditions too awful to describe. Many of them were to suffer from the effects of their illness for the rest of their lives. But every one of them would live to tell the tale of their perilous and adventurous journey to the clamouring newspapermen who waited for their story on Dundee's thronged wharves.

The Snowdrop – 'Missing' for 18 Months

On a September morning in 1909 a telegram arrived in Dundee which caused a sensation: 'Indian Harbour, Labrador – *Snowdrop* lost. Crew picked up by vessel . . . all well'. After a full year of hardship, starvation and disease, cast out in remote Arctic wastes, the crew of the ketch *Snowdrop* were apparently safe. Given up for lost, against all odds the smallest ship ever to sail with the Dundee whaling fleet had survived. The scenes of jubilation which the message brought to port can be explained by retelling her dramatic story.

The *Snowdrop* – with obligatory stowaway – sailed from Dundee in April 1908, destination Hudson Bay, to trade with scattered whaling stations and, audaciously, to try her hand at whaling should she come across such a creature. That excitement escaped her, but the tiny ship filled her hold with seals, walrus and bears. On September 18, 1908 *Snowdrop* foundered at Frobisher Bay off Baffin Land after being blown on to rocks. The log of her Dundee master, James Brown, records: 'Ship dragging anchors. Strong S.E. gale. Struck the rocks with her keel. Got all the people ashore'. The little ship was doomed. The crew, now numbering 11 with the emergence mid-voyage of the stowaway John Robertson, clambered ashore with some clothes, a few biscuits and their lives – nothing more. The situation couldn't have been bleaker. They were stranded with hardly any food and only tents for shelter. With the onset of winter, hopes of rescue and survival faded fast. Day by day biscuits were doled out in tiny quantities, but lack of food and the constant fight against the intense cold saw the crew's strength slip slowly away. To eke out their scanty provisions they boiled and devoured seaweed.

News of their non-arrival at Hudson Bay, where the SS *Arctic* had previously tried to diversify from the traditional whaling grounds, eventually reached Dundee. A bottle is said to have been picked up off the coast of Scotland saying that the ship was sinking. *Snowdrop* was presumed lost with all hands. The city mourned, as did the port of Montrose, home of the vessel's owner, Osbert Clare Forsyth-Grant, from Ecclesgreig Castle. But at this perilous point their tale took a dramatic twist. A hunting party of Inuit discovered the pitiful crew and carried them to their settlement, a 65-strong camp of the Singaijaq people. There they were revived with seal meat, fish and warm water. *Snowdrop*'s crew then spent the entire winter with the Eskimos, spread out among the families and eking out a rough, raw existence from the remote and rugged terrain. With scant provisions themselves, the Eskimos were close to starvation. In winter, there was little shelter from the biting cold. To compound their misery, the ship's harpooner John Morrison fell desperately ill. Only the Eskimo women, by roughly amputating a gangrenous limb, saved his life.

Credit for the eventual deliverance of the party was given to one of the crew, Alexander Ritchie from the Kincardineshire fishing village of Gourdon, who painstakingly plotted his way across 500 miles of treacherous water to bring news of the wreck to a remote mission station in northern Labrador. A vessel which had been sent north to relieve the American explorer Robert Peary was diverted to uplift the men. After prolonged suffering and a year of untold hardship, *Snowdrop's* crew, half of it comprising Dundee men, the rest from the north-east of Scotland, and including her owner Osbert Clare Forsyth-Grant, returned safely to Dundee some 18 months after they had set out. Only Morrison was left behind, under the care of Eskimo women for frostbite. Hardly had he recovered than Forsyth-Grant bought the Dunkirk-built *Séduisante* and fitted her out for whaling. In September 1911, in his thirty-second year, he perished in the Hudson Strait. His whaling career had lasted seven years. In that time two of his ships had been lost.

The Chieftain – a Tragedy in the Making

Too many Dundee ships dallied over-long in the polar ice fields. One of them was the whaler *Chieftain*. On May 26, 1884 the *Chieftain*, in her first year in the Dundee fleet, was fishing east of Greenland with her crew of 27, mostly Dundee men, when her master, Captain T. F. Gellatly, alert in the crow's nest as a fledgling skipper would be, saw a school of bottlenose whales quite close to the ship, which he hoped could be added to the four whales and 60 seals already secured. Four boats were lowered carrying five men apiece. The first of them, uncharacteristically crewed by Captain Gellatly himself, made fast to a large whale. John Taylor, the spectioneer, aboard the third boat, secured another. The captain killed his whale swiftly, towed it to the starboard side of the *Chieftain*, secured it and, taking provisions, unaccountably returned to open water to assist his other three boats. A dense fog descended on the ship and her at-work boats, 'as if a heavy curtain had been let down from the skies'. Captain Gellatly shared out the meagre provisions to his exhausted boatmen, who had been engaged in the hunt for nearly 24 hours. Nothing remained but to find the *Chieftain*. This proved impossible in the dense fog, which had also separated the Dundee fleet. With visibility virtually nil, two boats stayed with a dead whale, while the other two searched for the *Chieftain*, working in a circle.

By Wednesday, May 28 the four boat crews were still adrift, their occupants exhausted and suffering from frostbite and exposure, and the provisions almost finished. The following day, Gellatly led the men on to the ice where they drank melted snow and used wooden spars broken off the boats for fuel for a fire. They sheltered from a bitter wind for two hours, despairing of rescue. Suddenly a barque was sighted some miles away. Desperate signals were made and the boat's portable foghorn was sounded, but the ship did not see them. In his exhaustion Gellatly fell into the sea and was helped into a boat, soaked and shivering.

At 5 am on Friday, May 30, with virtually no food remaining, the captain fixed makeshift sails to his boat and decided to try to sail to the north coast of Iceland, 200 miles distant. The only other course open was to remain on the ice in the hope of being picked up by their own or another vessel. And on that day the four boats separated. By the following morning, the men on the captain's boat were all drowsy with exhaustion and hunger and could not row. Captain Gellatly steered continuously for 50 hours as the boat drifted. At 8 am on Sunday June 1, Alexander Allan, a sailmaker, shouted 'land ahead' and a few hours later the tiny boat and her four occupants landed in a bay near a farmhouse in north-east Iceland, where they had to be assisted ashore. There they remained for another three days until one of them, James Allen, a boat-steerer, sighted a passing schooner. This was the Norwegian vessel *Flekkefjord*, which gave up a week's fishing to take the five *Chieftain* men to Seydisfjord, where a doctor was called to dress frostbitten limbs. On June 12 they joined the Danish mail boat *Thyre* and, on June 15, Captain Gellatly of Barnhill, Joseph Ford, Liff Road, George Smith, Gellatly Street, Alexander Allen, Seagate, and Alexander Robertson, Charles Street, all of Dundee, disembarked at Leith, unaware of what had happened to their ship or to the other three whaleboats.

The *Chieftain*'s second boat, under the command of Thomas Elder, second mate, was eventually more fortunate. It had pulled 12 miles to the south-east but had failed to find the *Chieftain*. Then, on May 29, after its crew had endured pangs of hunger and cold for a week, it was sighted by the Norwegian schooner *Schreider* and was plucked to safety. The men, nursed by the Norwegian crew and returned to the *Chieftain* after one week's absence, included one stowaway, Peebles Mowat of Dundee. The third boat, under John Taylor, the spectioneer, was beset by an immediate problem when it had to transfer one of its men, James McIntosh, a line-manager from Dundee, to the *Chieftain*'s fourth boat after it had capsized, drowning a man. Taylor's boat eventually landed in north-east Iceland on June 2. One man had died, the others had frostbitten feet. News of Taylor reached the British Consul in Reykjavik on June 27, and three doctors made a three-day journey on horseback to reach them. Taylor remained in Iceland for eight weeks and finally arrived in Scotland on a Danish mailboat on September 15, still barely able to walk.

The *Chieftain*'s fourth boat, under Alexander Bain, a 37-year-old harpooner, had capsized on May 30, but had righted. Boat-steerer David Buchan drowned during the incident. James McIntosh of Crescent Street, Dundee was transferred from the third boat to join seamen William Christie, James Cairns, Alick Bain and William McGregor. After three days of exhausting rowing without food and water, McIntosh began steering for Iceland, but the men were sodden, half-frozen with cold, faint with hunger and parched with thirst. Their actions became more unreasonable. McIntosh recorded, 'Wully Macgregor swallowing handfuls of salt water . . . then Wully threw the compass overboard and Iceland became problematical'. The next day McGregor 'went mad' and bit the leg of one of his comrades before falling down dead. The next day McIntosh found James Cairns lying with his head on his arms – 'he was cold and dead' – and he too was pushed gently overboard, partly to remove the temptation of cannibalism, recalled McIntosh later. William Christie then died and was committed to the deep. 'Toshie' himself was close to death. His legs had swollen to double their proper size with frostbite, but he had just enough strength to lighten the boat by jettisoning whale rope. That effort exhausted him and he dozed as the boat drifted on. When he awoke, he found Alick Bain dead of the severe cold. McIntosh, who had gone to the whaling when he was 14 and had reached the age of 32 unscathed, wrote that he 'prayed for death'. Alone, he reached safety. He was picked up on June 11 north of Iceland by a Danish fishing vessel. Both of his feet had to be amputated because of frostbite. He reported that the chloroform had no effect on him and that he 'saw his two legs carried away'.

Back in Dundee, Captain William Adams called a meeting in Lamb's Hotel to launch a relief fund for the *Chieftain*'s unfortunate crew. Those who had helped in Iceland were rewarded with £5 each, and the doctor of the Danish ship who amputated McIntosh's legs received a gold medal from his Government. James 'Toshie' McIntosh became a celebrity (and was the subject of a successful local play in the 1990s). Lord Derby sent him £5 to buy a pair of wooden legs.

Dundee's Unitarian minister, the Rev David McRae, bought him a tricycle, with which he set off to London. There the *Bicycling News* launched a successful appeal to raise funds for a pair of proper artificial legs. His story was published by the *Pall Mall Gazette*, which encouraged Londoners to fill the cigar box he carried, with a 'little slit for coppers'. Captain Gellatly, who had not previously commanded a whaling vessel, emigrated to Australia shortly afterwards. The *Chieftain* went the way of most whalers. She was damaged by ice and abandoned off Greenland in 1892, adding to the extensive list of vessels from Dundee that failed to return to port (see Appendix 1).

'Cold Winter was Howlin' ' – the opening line of *The Road and the Miles to Dundee* – might have been written for the strong-hearted, resourceful men who faced icy seas, howling winds, freezing fogs and snow-blizzards with grim cheerfulness before reaching their place of work in the High Arctic. Once there, the ship losses were staggering – on average one every 17 voyages. Steam power did not mean that whaling was all plain sailing. When their ships departed each Spring bank holiday, Dundee crews were ready to endure their lot, 'with smiling spirit till the body gave out, frozen, maimed, snow-blinded, scurvy-ridden, starved – to death'.

SEVEN

Diversification and Decline

'It is now some 30 years since the Arctic whale took offence at the liberty taken with him by visitors, and, being of a retiring disposition, withdrew into private life – a measure dictated by a regard for his health. Great was the dismay when the obese but handy little ships sent yearly to Davis Strait came home "a beggarly account of empty boxes, or, in whaler parlance, "clean".'

Sheffield Telegraph, October 26, 1874

The 1860s were revolutionary years in Dundee whaling, the 1870s were marked by vigorous growth, the early 1880s by an individual yield of 2500 tons of oil and a 100-plus capture of whales, and a record 17 ships left the port in 1885 for the Arctic fishery, Captain Adams confidently returning with a live walrus and telegramming Barnum Circus on his arrival to offer it for £500. The prospects for the new century looked excellent and owners' optimism was as high as the quayside price for corset-making baleen. The hold which whaling had on the mind of the nation through its association with adventure, danger and romance was also firm. But the maps hanging in the whaler offices in Dundee, where 'well-thumbed ledgers recorded the varying fortunes of whaling cruises in the north', showed the fleet venturing ever-higher into the uncompromising northern seas; and 1885, which should have been bookmarked as the record year for Dundee whaling, proved instead to be the start of a wretched depression. Two of the port's 17 ships, the *Intrepid* and *Cornwallis*, were lost, oil fetched only £20–22 per ton, and the total catch was worth just £60,000. 'In this, the year of Dundee's biggest physical effort, some ships broke even but many showed substantial loss.'

If 1885 was disappointing, 1886 was disastrous. Four Dundee ships – the *Star*, *Triune*, *Resolute* and *Jan Mayen* – were squeezed and sunk by ice at 71°N. Five returned 'clean' and others barely met the expenses of their voyage. The total catch for the entire fleet was worth only £6000. It was a turning point. Ships were not replaced and crews who straggled back to Dundee aboard rescue vessels were told not to return for work the following spring. The talk in dockside hostelries was of depression and decline. Masters interviewed by the Dundee dailies were pessimistic. Only 10 vessels sailed in 1887, and confidence was further dented with the loss in Cumberland Gulf of the majestic *Arctic*, the second of that name and for some the finest of all Dundee whalers. Moreover, only one Right whale was caught and one of the town's most respected whale men, James Cummings of the *Terra Nova*, died on the ice, aged 76, on his 57th trip to the Arctic. Further sad news followed in 1890. Captain William Adams, after 20 seasons in command, took ill on his beloved *Maud* and died on his return to Scotland. He was, said the *Dundee Advertiser*, 'the most famous whaling captain in the world'. Doubtless he was, but the ships in Dundee harbour which lowered their flags to half-mast on receiving this news might well have been signalling a wider sense of bereavement in the industry. It was the end of an era in more ways than one. Within 20 years of its peak, the whaling trade was fatally wounded by its own short-termism and indiscriminate efficiency.

Ironically, the 1880s had been launched promisingly with the 15 Dundee whalers in Newfoundland and Greenland in 1881 accounting for 152,706 seals. But by 1889 the catch was only 82,367 seals. The number of whalers in Davis Strait waters halved over the same period, from 12 to 6, with over 1000 tons of whale oil returned to port in 1880 but only 188 tons in 1889. The trend was inexorably downwards, the financial drift south, not north. Masters later acknowledged that they were forced to take smaller whales, females and calves, 'or suckers' as they were known, after the slaughter of previous decades. Arthur Conan Doyle, sailing as whaling surgeon on the SS *Hope*'s voyage to Davis Strait in 1880, suggested that remaining whales had sought sanctuary in inaccessible waters and that 'one's sympathies lie with the poor hunted creature':

'What could it guess, poor creature, of laws of supply and demand, or how could it imagine that when nature placed an elastic filter inside its mouth, and when man discovered that the plates of which it was composed were the most pliable and yet durable things in creation, its death-warrant was signed.'

The 26 whales secured in Dundee's record year of 17 ships in 1885 had looked well enough on paper, yet they had offered up only 12 tons of bone. The quayside price had remained buoyant that year at £1500 per ton but the catch represented only a paltry average of £1000 per ship in bone money – about a third of fitting-out costs. It was the skins and oil of the large catches of seals, narwhal, walrus and small white whales which made the 'record year' barely respectable. Cruising in the same fishing grounds half a century earlier, the *Princess Charlotte* had taken 31 whales, the *Thomas* 28, the *Advice* 29, the *Alexander* 26, the *Horn* 12, the *Friendship* 29, the *Eber* 14, the *Heroine* 36 and the *Dorothy* 18, a season's total of 223 Right whales which produced 100 tons of bone. Such catches must have tormented the memories as well as exercised the financial calculations of Dundee's troubled owners.

The 1880s were also a difficult decade for the trade for reasons other than the drain on its profits. Bad feeling between the rival ports of Dundee and Peterhead escalated in 1880 when Captain Adams acted as a witness against four officers of the Peterhead whaler *Xanthus* charged with being criminally responsible for the loss of their vessel in Melville Bay. Called to give evidence to a Board of Trade inquiry, Adams described the ship as 'worthless' and the crew, whom he had seen at Newfoundland, 'a rubbishy lot'. It must have taken a lot to make Adams so forthright – in every description he is described as a jovial and warm-hearted friend to all. In January 1880 simmering concern about the noise of propellers came to a head in Dundee when a meeting of whaling masters, called over the effect of the noise of steam engines on whales in shallow water, agreed to use sail on approach to the fishing grounds. Steam was deemed permissible for passage to Davis Strait and onwards to Lancaster Sound and for towing dead fish into harbour, or at times of emergency in ice. Otherwise, the captains agreed that no ship should steam towards another amongst whales or in calm water within declared parameters. One can imagine the shareholder pressure on captains to do quite the opposite. In 1881 crewmen were killed on the *Thetis, Erik* and *Polynia*, and there was no dividend for shareholders of the Polar Fishing Company. In 1882 the captain of the *Jan Mayen* faced mutiny when his vessel began to leak after a collision with ice and his crew refused to go further. The *Jan Mayen*, curiously one of two vessels of that name in the fleet at that time, was abandoned. In 1883 the Board of Trade successfully sued the Dundee Whale

Fishing Company for the cost of paying for the return to Dundee of three crewmembers of the *Intrepid* who had been abandoned in Iceland. The unpalatable details of the case were published, including the testimony of the captain that the men had got drunk, refused to go back to the ship, and had been threatened with 'irons'. In 1884 the steam pioneer *Narwhal* was nipped and sank. In 1885 the *Intrepid* and *Cornwallis* were lost, the *Chieftain* badly damaged and a crewman from the *Resolute* accidentally shot and killed on the ice. In addition to the painful loss of four ships in 1886, the reputation of the industry was much damaged by a court action that year over the alleged loss of wages and tobacco by one of the crew of the short-lived Dundee whaler *Earl of Mar and Kellie*.

Such incidents – the calamitous losses of ships and men, the vagaries of markets and the airing of the trade's dirty linen in public – dissolved confidence in the industry and made shareholders shrink from investment. Even a comparatively risk-free one-sixty-fourth share in a whaler could prove a drain on resources and there were often demands on owners to share losses rather than to receive dividends. The four ships lost in 1886, though insured, left a £60,000 hole in the value of the fleet as they were not replaced. Significantly, no ship was constructed for whaling in Dundee after the *Terra Nova* in 1884 – ironically a 'symbol of hope' for the industry's future when she was launched.

The recession continued in the 1890s. The *Dundee Year Book* reported an 'unsuccessful' season in 1892, a 'compound of success and failure' in 1893, sealing's 'non success' in 1894, and 'unremunerative' activity in 1895, and 'only in two cases' did the voyages of Dundee whalers 'pay expenses' in 1896. That year Captain Robertson talked publicly of 'decline' and queried whether Government should support the industry in the way it had been boosted by the bounty system in the eighteenth century. There was 'little improvement' in the results for 1897, and by the following year, of Dundee's local industries there was 'none which has within the past few years shown greater decline than the seal and whale fishing'. That is not to say that there were no years of promise, such as 1899 when 29 whales were killed by five vessels, or profitable performances by individual ships – the *Aurora* captured 14 whales in 1893 and the *Active* took nine in 1895, for example. But the statistics from the decade show a diminution in the size of the fleet and in the quantity and quality of returns.

DUNDEE CATCHES, 1890–1899

YEAR	SHIPS (N&DS)	SHIPS (G)	RIGHT WHALES	SEALS	LOST
1890	7	3	18	50,296	–
1891	6	2	9	91,176	*Polynia*
1892*	5	–	3	3790	*Maud & Chieftain*
1893*	4	–	30	22,519	
1894	5	3	19	13,200	–
1895	6	2	14	36,000	–
1896	4	4	9	13,500	–
1897	3	5	9	5751	–
1898	4	2	6	809	–
1899	6	1	26	–	*Polar Star*

N&DS: Newfoundland sealing and Davis Strait whaling.
G: Greenland sealing.
* Four whalers on Antarctic Expedition.
Sources: Dundee Year Books, Ingram.

Whale returns differed from those in former times in size as well as in numbers. A large bowhead was still a great money-spinner, producing one and a half tons of bone at, say, £1500 a ton, and 30 tons of oil at £20 a ton – a near-£3000 haul. But whales secured in the late nineteenth century were generally smaller than in the bountiful days of William Scoresby's 90-ft giants. Only four tons of bone and 105 tons of oil were landed by the fleet in 1891 and just one ton of bone and 75 tons of oil were yielded by the three whales caught in 1892. That year the Newfoundland sealing was the worst on record and, for the first time in the history of the trade, not a ship left Dundee for the Greenland seal and whale fishing. In 1894, the Dundee Seal and Whale Fishing Company was placed in liquidation. One after another the company's ships had been lost. The *Camperdown*, *Narwhal*, *Resolute* and *Polynia* – names that were one-time household words in Dundee – were successively abandoned in the far north, and the return from the trade was insufficient to warrant their being replaced by new ships. In 1894 the company's last vessel to survive the menace of Arctic navigation, the *Esquimaux*, was advertised for sale at a knockdown price.

Not unexpectedly, Stephen's, who had built a succession of mighty vessels, including the *Terra Nova*, at 740 tons the second largest in the town's history, upped and left for the company's yard on the Clyde where ships for other purposes were in demand. The *Terra Nova* herself, destined for greater things in the heroic age of polar exploration, was shrewdly sold to Newfoundland in 1897. Her losses that year under Dundee ownership were put at £6473. Add to that her losses of 1896, and her shareholders faced a debit balance of £12,576. In December 1897 her owners, too, faced voluntary liquidation. As fewer ships broke even, and the average catch fell to about one whale per ship, an article in the *Sheffield Telegraph* written by the brother of *Advertiser* owner John Leng reflected the gloom felt in the port:

> They were expected to return all be-garland and dripping with fatness – so many masted oil casks, each cask full to the bing; and when they returned with no jawbone in the rigging, no oil on deck, and none under the hatches, no oil money for harpooners nor for anybody on board, there was trouble in the whaling ports.

Had it not been for smaller white whales, seals, walrus, bears and foxes, Dundee companies might have been wound up far sooner. The toll on ships and men chasing diminishing stocks in unrelenting northern regions, where ice and wind conditions were generally the most severe experienced, served to raise the stakes and to make further risk-taking unwise. The heavy losses continued. In 1891 the *Polynia* was hit by a huge wave which killed one crewman and injured 10 others. She reached Davis Strait where she was caught between two floes and disappeared to the bottom, leaving her crew on broken ice 12 miles from shore. The following year the *Chieftain* and *Maud* went down. A leading article in the *Dundee Advertiser* confirmed what experienced skippers already knew, that the downturn in the industry was due to 'climatic disadvantages and the difficulty of getting to the haunts of the whale . . . they have, so to speak, been constantly retreating before their enemy'. In fact, stocks had been squeezed through the industry's indiscriminate practices. In 1873, for example, Captain Adams's *Arctic* took 13 females and two young in her haul of 28 whales. In 1884, in particular, the 100 whales captured included 'many mothers and suckers' and, with the quarry capable of rearing only one young per year, such slaughters gave fishing grounds little opportunity to recover. Another factor in the trade's depression was the falling price of oil, as mineral oil broke its monopoly. By the mid-1890s whale and seal oil was selling at £18 a ton, 'only a third of its price a generation before'.

The ebbing of catches in the 1890s had one extraordinary effect. The price for whalebone, the stalactitic filter plates from the jaw of the Arctic Right whale, remained very high. By 1895 it was £2300 per ton and 10 years later hovered around £3000 as demand for a flexible support for a range of undergarments reached its peak. The monopoly of the jute industry on the banks of the Tay also helped to provide markets for any oil returned, but when a good season came along, such as in 1899 when the *Diana* was first home 'almost full' with 10 whales, it was wisely recognised only as a 'lucky hit' and an adventure belonging to 'very old times'. It also, however, encouraged shareholders to crave the prosperity of the past. Partly because of the scarcity of Arctic whales, and the realisation that for the 150 years the ships had frequented the same waters, owners and masters turned their thoughts to other fisheries. 'If he should strike out and seek fields and floes new and bring off a coup he would be acclaimed a hero by his owners,' encouraged the *Dundee Year Book* as the town's whaling masters pondered on the treasures that might lie at the other end of the world.

In his report from the Royal Navy's historic expedition to the Antarctic in 1842–43, Captain James Clark Ross referred to sighting 'great numbers of the largest-sized black whales lying upon the water in all directions' and that 'any number of ships might procure a cargo of oil in a short time.' If Ross was right, lucrative fishing was to be found in the Antarctic. 'All that was necessary to make a "full ship" was just to sail down south and haul the bone out of the whales' jaws.' Although the explorer's report had long lain on the dusty shelves of the whaling companies while fishing was profitable in the north, by the late nineteenth century Ross's journal had become a fresh source of hope.

The port of Peterhead instigated whaling exploration of Antarctica. The famous Gray brothers pursued the idea and, in 1874, David Gray published a report, *On The New Whaling Grounds in the Southern Seas*, in an attempt to raise the capital required for a pioneering voyage. Later, the brothers created a company for the purpose, but still financial backing was not forthcoming and the notion was dropped. By 1886 the proposal of opening up a new fishery in Antarctica was also under debate in Dundee. The *Dundee Advertiser*, which reprinted the text of David Gray's pamphlet, raised the issue by revealing that the Melbourne Geographical Society (which had also published a copy of the Grays' report) 'are anxious that the Southern Polar Sea should be exploited by our whaling captains'. The *Advertiser* added:

The Melbourne geographers are right in supposing that Dundee whalers are the proper vessels to send thither. If they were dispatched on voyages for commercial purposes they would no doubt bring home much information respecting a territory of which as yet comparatively little is known.

Several years passed before the conditions were properly in place for such an endeavour – the principal one being the growing losses of the Arctic whaling fleet. As the recession in the trade continued, the *Advertiser* urged the whaling masters to experiment with new fisheries. 'The Greenland and Davis Strait fishing are dying out,' the paper warned in November, 1891. 'With a constant market for oil and whalebone at a ransom, there is much in Captain Gray's proposal to tempt the enterprising.' The Dundee paper cajoled the captains to take the initiative, then revealed that the masters were ready and willing to make the venture, and eventually reported triumphantly that the directors of two steamers (the *Active* and *Balaena*) had 'decided to propose to shareholders that these vessels *should* be sent to the whale fishing in the south'.

The Dundee Antarctic Whaling Expedition of 1892, which pre-dated later British and Scottish exploration expeditions, can legitimately claim a place in polar history. In many ways it is remarkable that four whale ships simply upped and left on a journey to the unknown, when, by comparison, years of preparation were devoted to the proposals by Robert Falcon Scott, Roald Amundsen and Ernest Shackleton to take into account the Antarctic's inhospitable climate and conditions and the prolonged absence from home. Yet, in 1892 Robert Kinnes withdrew his four auxiliary steam barques from the northern fishery and fitted them out to search for whales in the Antarctic, offering volunteer crews 10 shillings extra per month over the rate for the Arctic. Equipping the ships, the *Balaena* (Captain Alexander Fairweather), the *Polar Star* (James Davidson), the *Active* (Thomas Robertson) and *Diana* (Robert Davidson), cost £28,000, or an average of £7000 each. The cost, by comparison, of the RRS *Discovery* for the British National Antarctic Expedition of 1901–04 was put at £100,000, while the cost of the *Scotia* for the Scottish National Antarctic Expedition of 1902–04 was £36,000. Perhaps this is why some newspapers questioned the seaworthiness of the four ships. Douglas Liversidge (1963) paraphrased William Burn Murdoch's 1894 account of the voyage: 'Rumour gathered currency in offices and docks. Perhaps the *Balaena* would return; a shrug of the shoulder implied the fate of the rest'.

In spite of public pessimism, and boosted by nautical instruments gifted by an old friend to the city, the London explorer Benjamin Leigh Smith, and zoological materials from Sir D'Arcy Thomson, professor of natural history at University College, Dundee who had acted as surgeon on a whaling voyage, the quartet of ships left Dundee on September 6, 1892 and had a 'long and tedious voyage' to the Falkland Islands, which were reached on December 8. It was soon reported that Dundee crews more used to the permanent chill of Davis Strait suffered from 'great discomfort' as they proceeded southwards and temperatures rose.

The vessels had sailing orders to meet at a given latitude and longitude and came in sight of each other on December 23, 1892. Only six months had elapsed since the same ships were cruising at 80°N near Spitzbergen. The *Balaena's* iron-wood hull still bore the scars of her tussles with Arctic ice, 'and now at the other end of the earth they are seeking pastures new in water never before disturbed by the throb of the screw propeller'. On Christmas Eve the masters boarded the *Balaena's* stout timbers for a riproaring mollie to discuss the prospects for the fishing. On Boxing Day the Dundee vessels were joined by the Norwegian whaler *Jason*, under Captain Carl Anton Larsen, and the five ships began working together, cruising under sail, searching for their quarry over the same 'whale-rich' ground Ross had passed half a century earlier. In the days that followed, many large blue and smaller finer whales were sighted from the decks of the ships, but none of the Right species, or Black whales as they were called by the men, with the jawbone which had become the money-spinner for Arctic ships operating out of Scotland. The quest was fruitless. The *Balaena* recorded, 'The search for the "right" whale was carried out with the greatest avidity, but although the vessel steamed over a large area the only cetaceans that could be seen were finers, bottle-noses and hunchbacks (humpbacks)'.

During the expedition teetotal Captain Thomas Robertson of the *Active* – known as 'Coffee Tam' for his refusal to allow alcohol on board – got fast to a giant blue whale. A second boat also secured a harpoon to it, but the whale made off at speed, trailing both boats and 1440 yards of tarred two-inch rope. A third harpooner struck home and this time the line was passed to the *Active*. Two more lines were taken aboard 'and off went the odd procession', the whale towing the ship for an astonishing 14 hours. With the leviathan showing no sign of weakness, Robertson ordered the *Active*'s engines to be reversed. The lines snapped and the whale got away with what was described as 'half of John Jack's smithy in its tail' (harpoons, lines and rockets). This was the only whale struck by the expedition ships, but it served the critical purpose of making it perfectly clear to the men that unmechanised wooden ships and flimsy rowing boats were no match for the giants of the whale world found in Antarctica.

When 'grave doubts' began to rise over the accuracy of Ross's report and the old whaling hands began shaking their heads, the masters 'reluctantly' followed their sponsors' wishes and began a cull of the region's plentiful seals to cover the cost of the expedition. In Dundee, meantime, hopes remained buoyant that the ships would return whale-rich. Expectations did not subside when a telegram arrived from the master of the *Polar Star* in 'Monte Video' in March 1893, though it was found to be 'undecipherable and unintelligible'. When the news of the expedition's failure was communicated in a second telegram two weeks later, the anti-climax in the town was almost tangible. Great hopes had been raised but scattered to the polar winds. 'No mention is made of whalebone,' *The Courier* reported, and repeated again, almost in disbelief.

The four Dundee sisters returned to port nine months after departure with holds bulging with sealskins and oil, but knowing that not only had their journey been a frustrating failure, but that the future of the industry looked bleaker than before. They had found no Right whales in the southern oceans as Sir James Ross had promised in his journal. On the quaysides despondent men talked of the 'reverse' to what the explorer had seen 60 years earlier, and the unanimous opinion of the four Dundee masters was that Ross had erred in the report of his voyage. Ross, of course, was not a whaler.

Interviewed on his return, Captain Fairweather of the *Balaena*, which had the honour of being the first 'full' whaling ship from the Antarctic, put a brave face on events: 'Although unsuccessful in finding the object we had set our hearts upon, we have had the good fortune to return with a full ship, containing the produce of some 6000 seals, with more oil than our tanks can contain, and with very valuable and large skins filling every spare corner of the ship'. Robert Kinnes also remained upbeat, saying, 'We may not take our money out of it, but I don't think there will be any great loss'. While, in fact, the *Balaena*'s main hatch did cave in under the weight of skins, the irony was that all reports – including those in modern histories – that the 1892 Dundee Antarctic Expedition made ends meet through its seal catches is more myth than fact. The sealskins did not sell. And a substantial loss duly materialised. The skins were heaped in a Dundee warehouse and in August 1893 a meeting of shareholders of the four vessels was told that there had been 'no sales' of the skins brought back by the vessels, 'cause unknown'. (In fact, they were disfigured by tusk marks). It goes without saying that there was little interest in a repeat venture. 'The Antarctic Whaling – The Project Abandoned,' the *Advertiser*'s report of proceedings began, full in the knowledge that the creation of a profitable outlet in the southern oceans remained unaccomplished. Kinnes deserves credit for entrepreneurial cleverness, however. With the hoard still on his hands as 1894 came to a close, he opened a factory in the Overgate to turn the seven to 10-feet long Antarctic skins into a range of boot interiors, gloves and waistcoats. In February 1899, nearly seven years after the quartet of ships explored Antarctica, the unhappy story of the 1892 expedition was brought to a close when shareholders were informed that the total call on their £100 shares would be £57.10s – a massive loss on the enterprise.

There was further disappointment on the scientific front. The expedition personnel included William Speirs Bruce as naturalist and surgeon on the *Balaena*. Bruce, whose grandfather was a minister in Dundee, later led the 1902–04 Scottish National Antarctic Expedition. Also aboard the *Balaena* as assistant surgeon, though neither of them was a doctor, was the artist William Burn Murdoch. The latter wrote extensively about the expedition in his book *From Edinburgh to the Antarctic* (1894), while Bruce referred to it at length in his *Arctic Exploration* (1912) and in various articles for newspapers and scientific journals. Burn Murdoch also penned a lengthy and colourful article for the *Advertiser* which effortlessly destroyed any pretence that he was a scientist: 'The Balaena mysticetus, whalebone whale, right whale, Bowhead whale, or Greenland whale, or whatever the reader may choose to call it, is as perhaps he already knows, of great value. This is owing to its peculiar adaptability for making umbrellas and destroying women's waists'. As for introducing his readers to a scientific description of the Antarctic penguin: 'If you were to put a small boy in a sack, black behind, white in front, and let his toes out at the corners, and make him run a race, you would get an idea of the penguin's motions'.

On the Dundee fleet's return to Scotland, William Speirs Bruce expressed his frustration that he had never been given the opportunity by the commercial nature of the expedition to carry out detailed observations and collections. Bruce told *The Times* that, 'on account of the overwhelming commercialism of the expedition, opportunities [for scientific research] which might have been taken advantage of, have been allowed to pass'. Bruce, however, did produce a substantial paper on his experiences and was able to make continuous scientific observations both on the passage out and homewards. The Dundee fleet sailed into Antarctica to a point further south than that reached by anyone except Sir James Ross and added considerably to knowledge of its meteorology and oceanography. Besides, Dr Charles Donald, who sailed with the *Active*, subsequently reported that the scientific results of the voyage had been 'highly satisfactory' and that the new land discovered was the most important discovery of all. There is little doubt, also, that the Scottish National Antarctic Expedition a decade later was inspired by Dr Bruce's experiences on the Dundee whaling peregrination. He chose the *Active*'s master Thomas Robertson of Newport to captain the *Scotia*, and 15 members of her 29-strong crew were from Dundee. Moreover, it was during a visit to University College, Dundee that he met his lifelong friend Robert Rudmose Brown, with whom he was later to make several important journeys to the Arctic and Antarctic.

Returning to his first instinct, to look for whales in the northern fishery, the owner-manager Robert Kinnes began an experiment in 1899 to examine Hudson Bay for the bone-yielding whale. Two of his ships, the *Polar Star* and the *Active*, which had made losses on the previous year's voyage, sailed in May of that year to the practically unknown waters of the huge basin, entered and explored by Henry Hudson in 1610–11. The *Active* established a shore station at Southampton Island, leaving three Peterhead men to live in a hut and to hunt for whales with the local Inuit population, but the initiative proved 'a complete blank' in terms of bowheads, although many walrus were taken. To make matters worse, the *Polar Star* foundered and was lost, the crew clambering to safety aboard her companion vessel. On return Captain Murray of the *Active* reported the Hudson Bay waters too shallow (whales were highly susceptible to disturbance). Undeterred, the *Active*'s shareholders decided to follow the American practice where, instead of using normal rowing boats, men used sailing boats of a size large enough to enable them to stand up and work under canvas, thereby avoiding the disturbing effect of oars. Three such boats were built in Dundee for the *Active* – marking a departure from the traditions of the trade in the town. Captain Murray steamed once more to Hudson Bay in 1900, with Kinnes as a passenger, but Right whales again were conspicuous by their absence. The *Active* found no quarry and the shore settlement, established to conduct whaling operations over the winter months and to have the produce ready for shipment when the *Active* put in an appearance in the summer, had harpooned only one small whale and shot 103 walrus. When, in 1903, the *Active* returned to port with five whales, 260 walrus and 22 bears, it looked as if the Hudson Bay diversification was finally paying dividends. Alas, the shore station crew had secured only three of the whales, the other two being obtained by 'bartering with natives'. The *Active* had again failed to harpoon a single fish.

The disappointment felt at the failure of the Hudson Bay experiment was tempered by the feeling that should whales be found, the astronomical value of whalebone would repay any outlay. Come 1902, there was talk in Dundee of opening another station, on the west side of Davis Strait, and £5000 was raised for it. But how long these inducements, eked out by occasional lucky hits in runs of whales, would be sufficient to keep alive an industry dying from self-inflicted wounds was difficult to predict, and no major developments took place in terms of ship building or buying. Furthermore, as the migration of her fleet to increasingly dangerous waters continued, the alternative of mineral products caused the harbourside price of whale and seal oil to fall from £30 to under £20, squeezing profits even more. It was a grim period for the industry.

The new century accelerated the decline and brought an end to Dundee's pre-eminence as a whaling port. The *Dundee Year Book*'s annual statistics for 1900 reflected the depression, recording fractions of tons of bone and amounts in hundredweights as fewer whales were taken, where once multiples of tons were common. To make matters worse, it was a gamble where a manager sent his ships. In 1900, for example, the *Esquimaux* was the only Scottish vessel at Newfoundland sealing. Had other owners known that her voyage would be so productive – a 'kill' of 18,000 seals – the entire fleet would have been ordered to fall in line astern. As it happened, the Greenland fishing that year 'failed' for a variety of reasons, including machinery problems and a search for a Yarmouth trawler, and the six Dundee ships sent there returned with only 3500 sealskins. The

Yearbook duly reported 'a considerable falling off in every department except seals, walrus and bears, compared with 1899'.

A triple irony helps to explain the industry's 'bad luck'. Firstly,
there were more whales off the northern fringes of Scotland than
there were off Greenland, but the Dundee whalers ignored them. In
fact, Dundee owners in 1903 were offered a share in this fledgling
coastal industry by Norwegian whaling companies, but turned it
down: 'Local capitalists do not view the venture with that favour
which the founders expected'. The Norwegians capitalised on it,
building five shore stations on the Scottish islands – the remnants of
Bunaveneader can be seen on Harris – and making profits that were
huffily described by the *Advertiser* as 'enormous'. A further irony is
that the Norwegians, in the same year, proposed legislation to take
effect in 1904 to establish a 10-year ban making it illegal 'to pursue,
shoot, or kill' whales in their own territorial waters, thereby limiting
ecological damage off Norway. Finally, it was to the Norwegian
Captain C. A. Larsen, who had prospected with the Dundee Antarctic Expedition, that the greatest honour fell. Larsen had witnessed
the whales of other species in Antarctica and worked out a means to
hunt them, establishing a whaling station on South Georgia in 1904.
Eventually, largely to evade the British administration's taxes on the
remote island, he founded the huge Antarctic factory ships which
would lead to the 'mightiest' phase – and earn his place – in
whaling's history. Returning with the Dundee expedition in 1893,
both Dr William Speirs Bruce and William Burn Murdoch tried to
interest Scots businessmen in a similar venture. No funds were
forthcoming.

Dundee's distant-water fleet continued to melt away. In 1902 the
Nova Zembla was wrecked in Dexterity Fiord when she struck a reef
in a snowstorm in which the *Eclipse* was damaged and required
extensive repairs after striking a rock. The following year four
Dundee vessels proceeded to Davis Strait where they encountered
weather and ice conditions so adverse as to cause the total destruction of the *Vega*, the imprisonment in Melville Bay of the *Balaena* for a
remarkable 90 days and damage to every vessel in the fleet. The
suffering and hardship experienced in such circumstances is difficult
to imagine. On June 14, 1902, for example, the crew of the *Balaena*
used ice saws to begin constructing a canal through solid ice, some
20 metres wide and nearly a kilometre in distance, from the open
water to the imprisoned ship. The sawing was carried out day and
night by the various watches. In some places the men had to saw

through blocks of ice between three and four metres thick, while the average was about two metres thick. On June 19 the canal had been cut up to the boat's prow, a feat of Arctic engineering equivalent in size to almost the width and half the length of the Tay Road Bridge. That day a gale-force wind drove a mountain of ice into the canal. By morning no water was to be seen for miles. The men's incredible effort was for nothing. The historic *Vega*, crushed between two converging floes, left her starving crew facing a 150-mile journey to safety, and even on reaching a Danish settlement, emaciated and frostbitten, they had to draw lots to see which of them could win a place on a tiny mail boat sailing to Denmark. The *Vega*, the first ship to sail over the roof of the world, was replaced in the Dundee fleet by the *Windward*, a ship that had entered the pages of exploration history by carrying the greatest Arctic explorer of them all, Robert Edwin Peary, towards the North Pole. Ironically, the *Windward* lasted only one season whaling with the Dundee fleet, her men being left at their oars in whale boats for 12 days, and two dying, after she was wrecked in Davis Strait. And in the 'disastrous year' of 1909 two vessels, the *Snowdrop* and the shore station ketch *Juantina Agatha*, failed to return and their crews suffered untold privations before they reached safety.

One of the more sinister aspects of so many sinkings during the industry's decline was the suspicion that some losses were caused deliberately to allow shareholders to recoup their outlay from insurance underwriters. As early as 1787 the *Betsy* of London was suspected of being wilfully wrecked and a notice was posted at whaling ports offering a reward for evidence that she had been deliberately scuttled for her insurance value. A court case involving the whaler *Columbia*, lost in Davis Strait in July 1868, in which her boat-steerer Alexander Walker sued the Dundee Seal and Whale Fishing Company for lost wages, raised the issue of intentional loss locally. At Dundee Sheriff Small Debt Court, Walker was asked by the prosecuting counsel, 'Did you ever hear the captain say he had been offered money to lose a ship?' The witness replied, 'Yes, he said he had been offered money by some owners to lose a ship'.

Other fleet reductions were due more to Dundee ship deployment than destruction, however. Nowhere did the golden age of exploration have more impact on a port's crews than in Dundee. In 1901 the *Esquimaux* was purchased for the Baldwin-Ziegler polar expedition (renamed the *America* and soon lost). In 1902 one of Dundee's leading captains, Thomas Robertson, described as 'one of the best ice masters alive', temporarily left the trade to command the *Scotia* for the Scottish National Antarctic Expedition. No fewer than 15 of its 29-strong crew were subsequently hired from Dundee. In 1903 the *Eclipse* and *Diana* left Dundee with Amundsen's stores. In 1904 the *Terra Nova* was purchased by Government for the RRS *Discovery* relief expedition, undergoing a refit in Dundee that entered the pages of shipbuilding history for its speed and efficiency. The *Eclipse* was sold to Norway and the Stephen's-built sealer *Nimrod* to Sir Ernest Shackleton. There was traffic in the other direction in 1905 with the purchase of *Morning* for Robert Kinnes, and she met another newcomer to the fleet, the *Scotia*, in Victoria Dock, fresh from her Antarctic adventure. The two-masted ketch *Seduisante* was purchased to replace the *Snowdrop* and the *Windward* to replace the doomed *Vega*. One turn-of-the-century curiosity was the total of 14½ Right whales returned in 1901. The crew of the *Eclipse* lost half of one while flensing, the carcass becoming separated from the ship during a gale. And in 1905 the *Balaena*'s crew had a bizarre experience when she was so closely nipped by ice that she could not lower her boats. One whale came close enough to the ship to be harpooned from the deck, 'and was secured without a man leaving the ship'.

The 1907 season began in some cases with the burden of the loss incurred by the comparative failure of the previous season remaining to be cleared. The year then deteriorated into one of the worst in whaling history – one which cost Dundee shareholders an estimated £50,000. The fleet's eight ships captured only three Right whales. The cost of fitting out the *Diana* for the season was put at £2285. Her proceeds were £194. The cost of the *Morning* was £4177. Her loss for 1907 was £1914. On the *Diana*'s return to Dundee in November, after a 1400-mile round-trip to Davis Strait, the *Advertiser* commented ruefully: 'Seven months and a day she has been absent, and for that long period of unremitting toil, of ceaseless hardship, and of never-distant danger, what was the result? One small whale'. The occasional success was also recorded. The famous *Scotia*, which was built as the *Heckla* and renamed by the patriotic William Speirs Bruce for his Antarctic expedition of 1902–04, proved to be an extremely able whale ship under Thomas Robertson, her master during the southern expedition. Even in difficult times, the *Scotia*, from 1905 inclusive, took one, four, two, six, eight and three whales, before being earmarked as the first vessel to take part in the North Atlantic Patrol after the sinking of the *Titanic*. As late in the Arctic whaling era as 1910, the crew of the *Morning* were astonished to come across a

plentiful supply of Right whales in Lancaster Sound. William
Anderson, a crewman, recalled for *The Courier* in 1965:

> Jimmy Vannet yelled excitedly from the crow's nest. His words
> were lost in the high winds. Not taking time to use the ladder,
> Jimmy slid down the rigging. Breathlessly he told us, 'Whales
> ahead, and they're big ones.' Five boats were put out, and
> within minutes one whale was floundering at the end of a well-
> aimed harpoon. They were all the real thing, monsters around
> 200 feet long.

If Anderson's memory of measurements was askew, his surprise was
understandable. Right whales in numbers were a thing of the past
and the school had been trapped in a bay by a gathering of predator
swordfish and shark. The *Morning* was soon just one short of its
maximum load of eight whales: 'We could have done it but for an
explorer's ship which began ploughing through the ice where we'd
trapped the whales'. The exploring ship was apparently American
and continued on its bearing despite Captain William Adams Jnr's
protests. News of the great catch spread back to Dundee, and when
the *Morning* sailed up the estuary, thousands lined the docks to give
the crew a welcome they would never forget. And the *Morning*
provided a sight they would always remember. On her deck she
carried the giant jawbones of seven large whales – the best catch seen
in the town for years.

Despite the downturn and decline, the industry survived the
perilous years of the Edwardian era. Jute manufacturing continued
to use whale oil mixed with water for its batching, or softening,
process and whalers had little difficulty selling cargoes locally.
Moreover, whalebone was still greatly in demand from would-be
tight-waisted women, notably at the peak of corset construction
around 1905. Records show that owners such as Robert Kinnes took
advantage of fluctuating prices to hold back supplies until they
received the selling price desired. A report from Hamburg which
caused considerable consternation in Dundee that year revealed that
when the price of Dundee whalebone reached £1500 a ton, German
buyers would be 'impelled' to purchase Norwegian whalebone. This
was the much shorter, inferior baleen secured from large numbers of
finer whales returned to Norwegian-operated shore stations in the
north of Scotland. It fetched, at the time, around £35. The *Advertiser*,
however, calmed concerns by reporting that an offer of £2300 per ton
had just been made to 'a local holder of bone' and had been 'refused'.

25. An Inuit woman and child on the deck of the *Eclipse*. Journals record the women's expertise at dancing and needlework.

26. An umiak, or women's boat, approaches a visiting whaler, Pond's Inlet.

27. Captain John Murray with Eskimos, Hudson Bay, 1909.

28. The *Scotia* and members of the Scottish National Antarctic Expedition, 1902–04. Fifteen of the crew were drawn from Dundee.

7199 B
THE SOUTH POLAR EXPEDITION: CAPTAIN SCOTT AND HIS EXPLORATION SHIP "TERRA NOVA."
ROTARY PHOTO. E.C.

29. A postcard showing Captain Scott and his exploration vessel *Terra Nova* before his ill-fated journey to the South Pole in 1911. The same Dundee ship had rescued him on his 1901 expedition.

30. The *Scotia* led out by the tidal basin by the Tay pilot boat, c.1908.

31. Dundee's Victoria Dock, c.1895.

32. A whaler in Earl Grey Dock. The Royal Arch, commemorating Queen Victoria's visit in 1844, was demolished in 1964 to make way for the Tay Bridge approach road.

33. Waistcoated workers load a cart, Dundee harbour, c.1895. Dundee Customs allowed whalers duty-free coal and some items for the comfort of the crews. There was a temptation to smuggle back the remains of the ship's duty-free stores, and Customs officers carried out searches on the fleet's return to port.

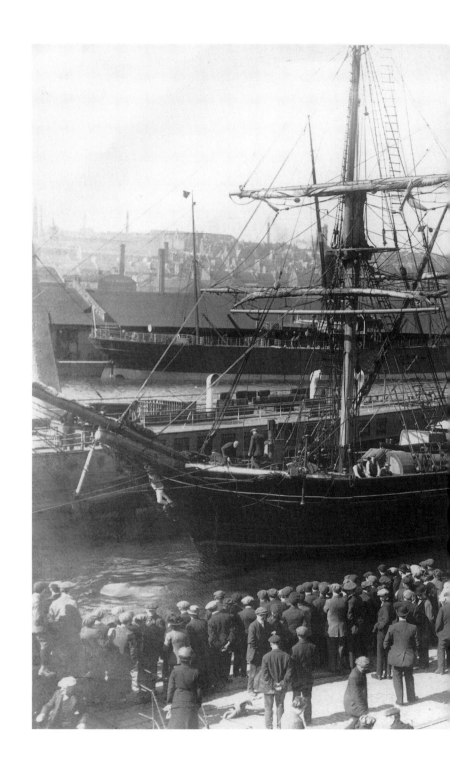

34. The SS *Active* entering Dundee harbour, with the *Slieve Bearnach* paddle steamer seen behind its bow.

35. The whaler *Balaena* in pack ice at Disco Island. By 1918 she was the only survivor of the pre-war whaling fleet.

Importantly, Edwardian Britain was keen on furs, and there was a huge demand for skins. The fleet increasingly benefited from rising prices for animals which, in the past, had been hunted primarily for sport. This trend can be gauged from the mixed catch reported for the 1905 season:

DUNDEE FLEET AND CATCHES, 1905

SHIP	RIGHT WHALES	WHITE WHALES	WALRUS	SEALS	BEARS	FOXES
Eclipse	7	4	8	–	7	–
Balaena	4	2	–	–	14	–
Morning	3	9	42	12	24	–
Scotia	1	–	2	17	13	–
Windward	2	–	3	–	38	40
Diana	2	–	–	–	9	–
Snowdrop	1	–	2	–	17	15
Active	3	20	52	146	31	104

Fox skins, bearskins, narwhal ivory, walrus hides and other commodities, which went to make up what in the trade was known as 'scraps', became increasingly important. By 1905 they were earning each ship £300 on average and, in 1908, the *Paradox* was added to the fleet specifically to be used for 'scraphunting'. The *Courier* noted, 'The demand for furs is great. Fox skins, both blue, good specimens of which are very scarce, and white, are fetching unexampled prices'. Yet the mixed bag of smaller game that was helping to pay the expenses of the voyage was further evidence that bowheads were becoming scarce everywhere. The northern whale fishery was on the brink of extinction.

As one fishery declined, another prospered. By 1909 the first whale brought ashore in the southern hemisphere by a British company had been landed by a new Scottish firm, the Salvesen Whaling Company of Leith. By then, too, the first UK floating factories were being prepared for Antarctica. The traditional system of whaling with wooden ships, precarious rowing boats and hand harpoons had passed. As many as 170 ships had sailed from the UK in the whaling heyday. The most between 1900 and 1910 was eight. Despite valiant Dundee-led efforts – the development of auxiliary steam, the manning of shore stations, the Antarctic expedition, and the introduction of overwintering ships – the biological inevitability of fewer whales ensured the decline was unstoppable. The whale stock had been destroyed.

The start of the First World War in August 1914 proved to be a significant whaling watershed. The old-style Dundee 'fleet', consisting that year of only the *Active* and *Morning*, returned safely to port in October 1914, having survived the Atlantic crossing and enemy shipping, and was at first laid up. In 1915 the ships were taken over by Government and placed under the management of the Hudson Bay Company, which, in December that year, loaded them with ammunition for northern Russia. Lubbock tells what happened next: 'The result was disastrous, for the vessels were never meant to carry heavy deadweight cargoes, and in the first gale on the voyage to the White Sea, they strained so badly that their seams opened and they gradually filled and sank'. The *Active* was lost with all hands off the Orkneys. The only two saved from the *Morning*, which went down off the Faroes, were the captain and his second mate. Family members later reported that when the *Active*, built in 1852 and a survivor of the Dundee Antarctic Expedition in 1892, had sailed from Leith, whaling 'worthies' on the quayside had warned of the dangers of removing her blubber tanks to make the ship suitable for her war cargo. She was in communication with HMS *Albany* 11 days after leaving Scotland and was never heard of again.

The *Balaena* was the only Dundee vessel to survive the war as a whaling ship. The *Diana* had been sold to Liverpool shortly before the war and the *Ernest William* wrecked in Cumberland Gulf. The *St Hilda*, a former yacht, was sold in 1914 and the *Seduisante*, bought to replace the *Snowdrop* in 1910, was promptly lost. The trading ketch *Tilly*, chartered by Robert Kinnes, was wrecked at Cumberland Gulf in 1915, the year, incidentally, that *Discovery* returned to Dundee for the first and only time on her way to Russia with ammunition. The combination of war and the demise of whaling brought the dispersal of other ships that were once household names in Dundee. The *Erik*, after acting as a supply ship for the American explorer Robert Peary, was sunk by a German U-boat. The *Scotia*, which had seen service as the *Heckla* in the Danish Greenland Expedition of 1891–92, left the Dundee fleet in 1912 to initiate the North Atlantic ice patrol after the sinking of the *Titanic*. She returned to merchant duties during the war and, in January 1916, while en route to France with a cargo of coal, caught fire in the Bristol Channel. Nothing could be done to save her. The *Bear*, built in Dundee and sold to Newfoundland owners for sealing, and later Admiral Byrd's famous exploration ship, spent much of the First World War as a revenue cutter at San Diego, and later as a 'rum chaser' on the lookout for smugglers during the prohibition era. The *Aurora*, the former 'top' ship in the Dundee fleet, was sold to the Newfoundland sealing trade after 18 Arctic voyages out of Dundee. In 1911, she was bought for Dr Douglas Mawson's expedition from Australia and later saw service with Sir Ernest Shackleton's 1914–16 Trans-Antarctic Expedition. She sailed from New South Wales in June 1917 and was never seen again.

The *Eclipse*, which had been commanded by Captain David Gray of Peterhead for 39 years and had her fair share of arguments with bergs and floes before being bought by Dundee, was sold to a Newfoundland sealing company at the start of the First World War. She eventually passed into Russian hands and became an exploring ship in Siberian waters. Renamed the *Lomonosov*, she was reportedly withdrawn from service in 1963. After considerable speculation in the 1980s that she may be – or have been – the last Dundee whaler afloat, the Russian maritime authorities reported no trace of her. The last of the race to survive next to the *Eclipse* was the *Terra Nova*, which took Scott and his party on their ill-fated South Pole voyage in 1912. The *Terra Nova* had joined the Newfoundland sealing fleet in 1898 and performed stoutly with other Dundee-built ships, such as *Wolf* and *Neptune*, before being commissioned as the widely publicised relief and exploration ship. She was sent to the bottom by Canadian naval forces in 1943 after her captain could no longer contain a leak. Her figurehead was donated to the Welsh National Museum in Cardiff, where a society dedicated to her memory was formed.

If Dundee had failed to capitalise on its early presence in the unexplored waters of the Antarctic, the shore station established by Carl Larsen in South Georgia to hunt the largest species of whales – the rorquals, which included the giant Blue Whale – went from strength to strength as Argentina and Norway (supported by Svend Foyn's latest explosive harpoon) grasped the initiative from Dundee. By the 1912–13 season the Antarctic industry's 'kill' was, astonishingly, 11,000 whales. Whaling's new era, which included Salvesen's operation at Leith Harbour in South Georgia, was described by Henderson:

> The modern whaling fleet would normally consist of one float-ing factory serviced at sea by a tanker, ten or twelve catchers

and perhaps two tow or 'buoy' boats which were used to pick up dead whales and return them to the floating factory, leaving the catchers free to carry on the hunt. Catches reached a peak in 1930–31 when 41 fleets operating 232 catchers killed 40,201 whales.

Many former Dundee Arctic whale men signed on with Christian Salvesen and sailed out of Leith and other ports for the new fishery which, thankfully, the International Whaling Commission was able to regulate within six years of the 1931 slaughter. However, this history does not concern these ports, that period, the Antarctic region, or the men's anecdotes. The industries were very different in any case. Antarctic whales were pursued by catchers at full speed and killed with exploding harpoons. They were marked by radio transmitters to be picked up and hauled back to factory ships by tow ships. Their stomach cavities were blown up with compressed air to keep them afloat, and strips of blubber removed by steam winch after the whales had been hauled up the sloping ramp to the factory deck. Bones were cut up by steam saw and whale waste was discarded indiscriminately. Robert Smith said: 'The Norwegian station at Grytviken in South Georgia, set up by Captain C. A. Larsen in 1904, had miles of shoreline on Cumberland Bay choked with the bones of whales, spinal columns, loose vertebrae, ribs and jaws and "a hundred skulls within a stone's throw" '. Suffice to comment that the *Balaena*, at 260 tons, was the largest ship of the Dundee Antarctic Expedition of 1892. When her namesake floating factory *Balaena* was launched in 1946, she was a vessel of 15,000 tons; she carried several aeroplanes to spot whales; she controlled a fleet of 10 diesel-powered vessels with ship-to-ship radio and she had an oil capacity of 19,000 tons. Instead of a ship's surgeon she had a fully equipped hospital.

Dundee's last link with Arctic whaling was severed in 1922 when the trading ketch *Easonian* burst into flames and sank at the Eskimo settlement of Kekerten. The *Easonian*, captained by John Taylor, had gone to Cumberland Gulf at the behest of Robert Kinnes & Sons. Although whale 'fishing' had ended in 1914, trading stations were still functioning and their catches had to be brought home. The fire began in the *Easonian*'s engine room while anchored and her typically tough construction prevented her crew breaking through the hull to get at the blaze from the outside. As she slipped beneath the ice her crew found themselves marooned, most of their possessions lost. Eskimos gave the men shelter for two days, until eventually they were taken aboard a Peterhead schooner and returned safely to Scotland. It was not the first Dundee crew sunk, stranded and saved in this way – but it was to be the last. With the loss of the *Easonian*, Dundee whaling came to an end. No longer were the town's whalers to be cheered out of port and welcomed home with 'an appropriate degree of euphoria, dejection or sorrow'.

It was the end of an era which had seen sons follow fathers into the industry, regardless of all the dangers. Masters, especially, had spent entire careers in the trade. Statistics show that life expectancy among whaling captains was not good and that the master of a vessel could expect to be wrecked at least once in his career. Yet Dundee had several who became household names in the whaling trade and in the world of polar exploration and who literally lived and died in the industry. Among them was the famous Dundee mariner Captain William Adams, who went to sea in 1847, commanded whaling ships for 20 years, and died on his return voyage from Davis Strait in 1890. Alexander Fairweather went to sea as a boy on the SS *Tay* in 1863, was harpooner on the SS *Camperdown* in 1866 and, in 1870, became mate of the whaler *Victor*. At 26 he was appointed captain of Leigh Smith's exploration yacht *Diana*, and on his return in 1874 commanded the *Active*. When Fairweather died in May 1896, he had been 'looking forward to a good season's fishing' on the *Balaena*. Captain Charles Yule commanded a timber ship whose cargo was used to build the SS *Esquimaux*, which he took over on completion. He later captained the *Resolute* and *Polynia*, became harbourmaster at Dundee for 37 years and died shortly after his 100th birthday. Captain Harry MacKay, born in Dundee in 1857, became the young-est-ever captain of a whaling ship when he took over the *Aurora* in 1891. He had previously served on the *Resolute* and *Terra Nova* and later became an integral figure in the operation to relieve the *Discovery*. McKay's lifetime at sea ended in 1925 when the *Advertiser* was almost alone in crediting him with the rescue of Captain Scott. Another captain engaged in the trade since boyhood who worked his way up to the position of command was William Guy. After an apprenticeship in the coastal trade, Guy made his first voyage to the Arctic in 1866 in the *Camperdown*. He was appointed first mate on the *Jan Mayen* in 1875, captained the *Nova Zembla* in 1874, and became captain of the *Jan Mayen* in 1883 and then of the *Arctic* in 1884, a vessel he lost in Cumberland Gulf in 1887. He next transferred to the *Our Queen* and the *Aurora* before taking the *Balaena* to the Antarctic.

He retired as the senior captain of the fleet in 1901, after 50 years at sea, nearly 35 years at whaling, 23 as master.

Such men and their crews experienced to the full the vicissitudes of the whaler's calling, returning in triumph, meeting with disaster, drawing both winning numbers and blanks in the lottery of the Arctic fishery. Their legacy survives in the anecdotes which continue to enrich the modern city – but as the next chapter explains, the undiscovered greatness of the Dundee whalers is their lasting contribution to the discovery of hitherto unknown regions of the world.

EIGHT

The Lasting Legacy

'If the philosophers are right in assuming that a Scotchman will be found already in possession of the North Pole, it is ten chances to one that that Scotchman will turn out to be a Dundonian.'

The Piper o'Dundee, September 1, 1897

If the whaling trade 'owed its foundation' to the Arctic voyages of discovery, as one explorer wrote, the industry in Dundee certainly repaid the compliment to those seeking to satisfy their polar curiosity. Dundee whaling ships saw service beyond their purpose. They were the choice of the world's greatest polar explorers – Scott, Shackleton, Nansen, Amundsen, Peary, Mawson and Byrd – yet today, as polar exploration enjoys renewed attention in the form of repeat expeditions, academic research, films, documentaries and shelves of new books, Dundee's impressive contribution remains neglected.

The sturdy veterans of the Dundee fleet – men and ships, and sometimes unwittingly – led the world in Arctic exploration through reaching Farthest North and Farthest South, by charting unknown seas and mapping unexplored coastlines, by observing weather systems and changing topography, and by venturing from the known to the unknown as they plied their trade. It was therefore inevitable that Dundee's whalers became the ships of conveyance for the world's explorers seeking the highest latitudes and the acclaim of the public. A striking example occurred 20 years before the era of Captain Scott's expeditions on the Dundee-built *Discovery* and *Terra Nova*, Shackleton's Antarctic adventures on the Stephen-built *Nimrod* in 1908 and his heroic Trans-Antarctic Expedition of 1914–16 which battered Dundee's *Aurora* to the verge of oblivion.

In 1881 the American Army explorer Lieutenant Adolphus Greely and a party of 25 men decided on an audacious attempt to reach the then completely unknown ice-mass of the North Pole by a sledge journey across the polar ice cap. To take him to his landing point at the high latitude of 78°N on Smith Sound, Greely chose the Dundee-built whaler *Proteus*. Although he was safely delivered by the *Proteus* with stores to last for three years, it was decided to re-supply his party with provisions annually. In 1882 the expedition organisers sent for the Dundee-built sealer *Neptune*, but under her US Navy captain she was unable to reach the Sound because of ice. Next to try was the *Proteus*, which had routinely dropped off the team, but she was nipped in ice and destroyed on her return in 1883, again under US command. Alarmed and concerned for Greely, the American Government decided to launch a major relief expedition, for which its Navy chartered three vessels, the Dundee whaler *Thetis*, the Dundee-built sealer *Bear*, and a merchant ship to carry provisions, the Dundee steamer *Loch Garry*. Yet again the most experienced captains in the American Navy commanded the trio of Dundee ships. This time, though, the Americans effected a rescue which brought them a heroes' welcome on their return. And they did so by prudently attaching themselves to the Dundee whaling fleet as it steamed northwards!

Not only her ships, but Dundee's masters and crews are unsung heroes of polar exploration. They sailed to uncharted seas, discovered new lands, followed new coastlines, noted new wildlife and encountered unknown peoples as they added to seafaring knowledge and contributed to the surveying of remote regions. Several bays and inlets on the shores of Davis Strait, Baffin Bay and West Greenland were discovered and named by them. Governments of circumpolar nations plied them with honours. The Dundee veteran Captain Adams took the SS *Arctic* 'to higher latitudes than the most indefatigable explorers were able to reach', and the *Dundee Advertiser* had 'no doubt' that Adams and the *Arctic* 'properly provided, would settle the question' of the North Pole – 30 years before Robert Peary stood on it. But in the intense industry of each whaling operation, there was never time for headline-grabbing assaults on the roof of the world or thoughts of dramatic acts of personal achievement, and while Robert Falcon Scott and increasingly Ernest Shackleton epitomised the ideal heroic figure of the Edwardian age, the part Dundee captains played in the story of polar discovery remains worthy of exploration itself.

Local Inuit communities had explored northern Greenland and the Arctic islands north of the main Canadian coastline for many centuries, but Western polar exploration is a relatively recent phenomenon. From the 1500s to the 1700s, Arctic discovery was viewed in economic terms: to find a sea route from the Atlantic to the Pacific, the fabled North-West Passage across North America to the Orient, or a North-East Passage from the Greenland seas across the 'roof' of Siberia to shorten the trade route that way. The names of the pioneers of this period, Martin Frobisher, Henry Hudson, William Baffin, Jan Mayen, Willem Barentz and John Davis – the Englishman who gave his name to the Strait so familiar to and feared by whalers – live on in the maps of the regions they reached in search of navigable merchant routes. But the founder of geographical exploration in the modern era was Captain John Phipps, who sailed to Spitzbergen in 1773 with the 14-year-old midshipman Horatio Nelson among his crew. Phipps's pioneering voyage was the first major scientific exploration, and it was followed by Captain James Cook's daring voyage in 1778 when he established the separateness of the Asian and American continents.

It was during these searches for geographical information that explorers also 'discovered' the treacherous ice that would eventually crush so many whalers and strand their crews in unknown regions. Many early explorers, like the whale men who came after them, were poorly equipped, unprepared for the onslaught of scurvy and frostbite, ignorant of the severity of the cold climate, and possessed of few skills essential for survival. Faced by pack ice in their channels northwards, unsuspecting vessels were quickly imprisoned and many men perished.

The Napoleonic Wars, in which seamen were absorbed for naval service and whaling ships were threatened by enemy privateers, brought a suspension of the first burst of exploration. At the conclusion of the conflict in 1815 the discovery of remote regions was viewed by the Admiralty as a satisfactory means of using surplus men and ships. Through the enthusiastic support of Second Secretary to the Admiralty John Barrow, Captain John Ross sailed to Davis Strait in the whaling brig *Isabella* in the pioneering voyage of the second phase of exploration. This voyage 'rediscovered' Smith, Jones and Lancaster Sounds and set in train a series of some 30 naval expeditions during the next 30 years which explored and charted extensive coastal areas of east and west Greenland and significant areas of the Arctic Archipelago. But some 3300 whaling voyages are also recorded as having visited the Arctic between Phipps's voyage in 1773 and that undertaken by Ross in 1818. Mile by mile, degree by degree, whaling masters had pushed north following the migratory routes of the bowhead whale. In fact, the 'rediscovery' of exploration after the wars in Europe was due in large part to the Hull whaling master William Scoresby Snr, who had reached beyond 81°N in 1801. Scoresby, regarded as Britain's Arctic expert of his day, informed the Royal Society that the conditions of thaw he had experienced at high latitude would permit a resumption of Arctic exploration. Ross, in turn, acknowledged in 1819 the information he received from the Davis Strait whale men and, in the first recorded incidence of practical participation in exploration, the Dundee whaler *Alexander* accompanied Ross to 72°N on his historic journey to the North Magnetic Pole in 1831.

The second significant phase of geographical exploration ended with Sir John Franklin's expedition to find the North-West Passage in 1845. Franklin had searched for the route in 1819–1822, an overland expedition which ended disastrously with 11 men losing their lives. He attempted another overland/canoe journey to the Arctic coast-line of mainland Canada in 1825, in which his party successfully mapped more than 1000 miles of territory. Then, in the summer of 1845, he was sent out by the Admiralty to find the fabled passage with two expedition ships, *Erebus* and *Terror*, the names of which were to become associated with death and destruction in the Victor-ian era.

The disappearance of both ships and 129 men – including four from Dundee – among the ice floes of Lancaster Sound gave rise to 30 search expeditions from 1847 to 1859. The huge relief effort included some of the greatest names in exploration. James Clark Ross sailed with the *Investigator* and *Enterprise* in 1848, Robert McClure's search took him through the Bering Strait in 1850–54, and William Penny's Scottish search party left in 1850, as did Horatio Austin's official four-ship Admiralty rescue party. Sir John 'Polar' Ross, aged 73, came out of retirement to lead a private search expedition in 1850–51. In 1852 Sir Edward Belcher led a five-ship Admiralty expedition to the region. American explorers also contributed. In 1850–1851 Edwin J. DeHaven led the first US search for Franklin, to be followed, two years later, by Elisha Kent Kane's second American expedition. When the fate of Franklin and his men was eventually discovered in 1857 by the Scot, Dr John Rae – when he recovered the explorer's personal relics from Eskimos who reported seeing corpses at King William Island – further expeditions, sponsored by his wife Lady Franklin and involving famous explorers such as Francis Leopold McClintock and Charles Hall, sailed to the region to confirm Rae's evidence and to search for survivors. They found remains scattered all along the western coast of King William Island, and at last the expedition's long-lost written record was discovered in a cairn. The *Erebus* and *Terror* had been beset by ice in 1846. Franklin had died in June 1847. The ships had been deserted in April 1848 to attempt a journey south. None of the crew survived and they were assumed to have died from scurvy and exposure.

The Franklin search ships explored vast tracts of uncharted coastlines and pushed further north than ever before as they tried to find an answer to the mystery of the expedition's disappearance – although no contact was ever made with the two vessels. Dundee's Arctic expertise was brought to the fore by the rescue attempts. In 1849 the *Advice* of Dundee battled up Lancaster Sound as far as she could go to help in the search, and was awarded £1000 and a nation's thanks for her efforts. The *Sophia*, a 113-ton brig, was built in Dundee the following year specifically to search for Franklin. The *Resolute* and *Heroine* landed sledging search parties and the *Heroine* aided in the discovery of Eclipse Sound by Captain John Gray of the Peterhead whaler *Eclipse*, as whalers pushed north on the lookout for Franklin. The permanent collection at Broughty Castle Museum includes a letter written by Lady Franklin to Captain Simpson of the *Heroine* thanking him for the help he gave to ships taking part in the relief effort after they had been damaged in a storm. But the loss of Franklin's expedition, and the fruitless search that followed, put an end to the second phase of Arctic exploration. The Government could not afford to maintain such an effort. And as there appeared to be no practical benefit to the nation from the discoveries made in the Arctic Archipelago or, indeed, from finding a potential route to the North Pole, politicians were not alone in losing interest. The public's appetite for exploration had also ebbed away.

A quarter-of-a century passed before the British Government was disposed to initiate the third major phase of polar exploration – with Dundee's whaling industry central to its decision. The Government was inspired to act in 1874 in response to Albert Markham's thrilling journey under Captain Adams on the Dundee whaler *Arctic* the previous year. Markham wrote directly to Government ministers, expanding on his belief in the North Pole regions being explored for Britain's good. Markham told the Admiralty that the fortified Dundee steam ships had superseded the sailing ships of Franklin's day, and that he had not heard of any fatal accidents since ice navigation with steam power had been introduced. He assured officials that the port's ships could reach high latitudes, 'and return with ease and safety', and the significance of this, he told them, 'cannot be over-stated':

> It will be seen, on reference to a circum-polar chart, that the entire area within the 80th degree of north latitude, except at two points – Parry's furthest in 1827, and the American ex-plorations at Smith Sound – is an entire blank. We only seek that it [an expedition] should consist of two moderate-sized screw steamers, one to be stationed at some distance within Smith Sound, the other to advance northward, from which point sledge parties would start in the early spring, and explore the unknown region.

Markham was supported by Dundee Chamber of Commerce, which argued that an Arctic expedition was desirable in order that new haunts of Right whales might be explored. Whaling was a strategic industry and the Chamber's opinion carried weight far beyond Dundee. The *Advertiser*, one of Britain's most influential Liberal dailies, also took up the call, claiming that there were 'material interests of no mean magnitude' in seeing whether the North Pole could be reached. It continued: 'We in Dundee have a special reason for encouraging Arctic research, and in gaining a better acquaintance with those regions of the Polar season where whales do chiefly congregate'. To Markham, however, who had experienced the ex-citement of exploration as the *Arctic*, in 1873, became the first whaler to enter the Gulf of Boothia, discovery was a matter of personal achievement and national prestige. Besides, he had helped that year with the recovery of part of the crew of the American exploratory ship *Polaris* which served to give him a taste for international acclaim.

The *Polaris*, under Captain Charles Hall and backed by $50,000 from the US Government, had left New York on June 29, 1871 on Hall's third expedition to the North Pole. All went well at first and a new Farthest North of 82.16°N was achieved that September. Hall decided to winter further south and laid up the *Polaris* in Thank God Haven at 81°38'N on September 7. On November 8, however, he succumbed to a mysterious illness and died. Debate over how he died and whether a 'mutinous' crew was involved in foul play would rage for years, but at that point he was buried at Polaris Bay. The crew decided to sail southwards, but on the voyage half of the crew became stranded in open boats and thereafter drifted helplessly on ice for six months. Only the timely intervention of the whaler

Ravenscraig saved the day, rescuing 11 members and passing them over to Captain Adams of the *Arctic* and, later, transferring three others to Captain Walker of the *Erik* of Dundee. On arrival in Dundee, the 11 men conveyed by the *Arctic* were put up in Mathers Hotel in Whitehall Crescent. The survivors brought to the city by the *Erik* were housed in Lamb's Hotel, Reform Street. The Americans left Dundee on September 21, 1873 for Liverpool prior to their embarkation for New York with first-class passage. At the West Station crowds cheered as Captain Adams appeared. Leading citizens, according to the *Advertiser*, turned up in numbers, 'all being anxious to get a glimpse of the Arctic explorers'. The Americans, in turn, presented Captain Adams with a testimonial recording their 'heartfelt thanks'. The crew of the *Polaris* reached New York two years and three months after they had departed. A grateful US Government gave the owners of the *Ravenscraig* $1000, with another $1000 for her master, Captain Allan. To Captain Adams of the *Arctic* and Captain Walker of the *Erik* they gave $300 each, to be invested in gold chronometers. Crewmembers of the *Ravenscraig* received $25 each.

A witness to all of this, Albert Markham, by now promoted to Commander Royal Navy, continued to plead with the Government to re-apply itself to Arctic exploration, and in this he was supported in Parliament by the Dundee MP James Yeaman, a whaling shareholder, who reassured the House that although his constituency had lost six or seven ships in the Arctic, they had, however, 'scarcely ever lost any of the crews belonging to these ships'. When an expedition was settled in principle, Mr Yeaman pointed out in Parliament that its two ships would require a great deal of stores, and suggested that 'it would be better to send a sailing ship out to Melville Bay' with them. No doubt he had an inkling where to find one! At one meeting hosted by the Chancellor of the Exchequer, Gladstone, in London, involving representatives of the Admiralty, the Royal Geographical Society, the British Association and a number of other organisations, the president of the RGS, Sir Henry Rawlinson, was asked by the Chancellor about the scale of the proposed expedition. 'Two whalers would be adequate,' replied Rawlinson. Captain Sherard Osborn of the Admiralty, a famous explorer who had searched for Franklin and who had later induced Markham to go on a whaling voyage and thereafter paid for the publication of his report, added, 'It has been laid down as a base of operation that two Dundee whalers with a crew from the Navy of 60 officers and men each would be amply sufficient for the purpose'. To this Gladstone asked carefully, 'Then you believe two whalers would be enough, that they could be purchased at Dundee, and that a contribution of 120 men from the Admiralty would be sufficient?' Osborn replied, 'Certainly'.

By 1874 the Government was convinced by Osborn, Markham and others that the timing was right for a new British expedition to the region of the North Pole. It was agreed, however, to send two Royal Navy survey ships, HMS *Alert* and HMS *Discovery*, for the purpose. If Britain rejoiced in the news, Dundee's whaling captains could have been forgiven a knowing smile. *Alert* had been built by Stephen's Glasgow yard, while *Discovery* had begun life as the Dundee-built whaler *Bloodhound*. This choice of ship did not entirely satisfy Markham, who had won a leading role on the proposed expedition. In January 1875 he returned to Dundee to negotiate for the use of the new SS *Arctic*, under construction in Stephen's yard for Captain Adams to replace the ship of the same name which both men had used in 1873 and which had been lost in 1874. Markham's plan was to let the crew fish for whales as long as possible, but 'for one month strike out for the Pole'. He offered Stephen's £5000 for the planned 828-ton *Arctic* – a sum probably intended as much for the experience of Adams as it was to borrow his new vessel. Stephen's turned him down and perhaps Adams was as disappointed as Markham. The *Daily Telegraph*, on a visit Dundee to cover the North Pole story, had found 'whaling captains who if directed to go to the Pole would not require a second order'. Notwithstanding, the veteran Adams offered plenty of advice to anyone who cared to listen in the Admiralty Office. As to the important matter of expedition ships, he pointed out, 'The *Alert*, which they say is going, is a good vessel. The new *Arctic*, which is being built, would have been a very superior vessel, as she is properly fortified and planned for resisting the ice'. As to a route to the Pole, Adams gently advised the explorers to follow the Dundee whaling fleet.

As it happened, the 1875 British naval expedition under Captain George Nares intended to follow in the wake of the whalers, which were beginning to sail into northernmost waters. Captains Adams and Walker, of the *Arctic* and *Erik* respectively, had already reached Smith Sound lying above 75°N between west Greenland and Ellesmere Island. On August 25, 1875 *Discovery* found winter quarters high on the coast of the remote island, while *Alert* pushed 50 miles on to an ice-locked channel. The aims of the sledge trips the following spring were to trace as much as possible of the coasts of Ellesmere Island and Greenland to determine how far north land existed and to test the possibilities of reaching the North Pole from a route between them. Markham's whaling experience was of little use to him here. On April 3, 1876 he took command of one of the parties with a sledge appropriately named *Marco Polo* and reached Farthest North at 83°20'N, a new record. With his men exhausted and suffering from scurvy, Markham concluded that it was utterly impossible to reach the Pole over the ice and turned his sledge back for his ship. Before doing so, he planted the British flag nearer the North Pole than it had ever flown and celebrated by opening a magnum of champagne donated to him by Dundee businessmen. This act would have been applauded by the crewmembers drawn from the Dundee whaling community. They included three 'ice masters' – the most important men on voyages to high latitudes – who had each been offered £100 by the Admiralty to give up whale fishing for a year, the equivalent of 'double pay'. The Dundee ice masters accomplished their task in some style. The anchorage at 82°28'N was the highest latitude ever reached by any ship.

By the 1870s the quest for the North and South Poles showed signs of becoming a race between explorers of several nations, fuelled by patriotic pride. Exploration, unlike whaling, could bring fame and immortality, and the exploits of the leading explorers were followed avidly around the world. Yet one could not survive without the other. As attacks on polar regions by other nations increased (which served to galvanise the British Government's return to exploration), successive North Pole attempts relied on Dundee expertise. Her ships, as noted, played an important role in the American *Polaris* expedition of 1872. In May of that year, Alexander Fairweather, later master of the *Balaena*, was selected by the London explorer Benjamin Leigh Smith to command the steam yacht *Diana* to explore Spitzbergen and took with him a Dundee crew. After three years' toil on the island's ice-bound coasts, the *Diana* succeeded in relieving Adolf Nordenskjold's Swedish expedition. On his return to Dundee in 1874 Fairweather was appointed master of the *Active*. The fate of the Swedish geographer and explorer was more remarkable. In July 1878 Nordenskjold sailed from Norway to Alaska, becoming the first man to navigate the North-East Passage – the 'roof of Europe' – a feat which saw him escorted into Stockholm by 200 steamships and later created a baron. The ship Nordenskjold used for the voyage was the *Vega*. When added to the Dundee whaling fleet in 1903, the pride of Sweden survived just three months before being crushed between converging floes in Melville Bay. Benjamin Leigh Smith was clearly smitten by the hardy, wooden-hulled Scottish ships, however. In 1881 he took the Peterhead trawler *Eira* on his second voyage to Franz Josef Land, but supplied her with a Dundee captain, William Lofley, and a dozen of Dundee's ablest men. Leigh Smith had hoped to find a 'bridge' to the North Pole, but the *Eira*, too, was crushed in ice, leaving the men to survive a winter 'on a diet of bear and walrus meat, in a primitive hut of stones and turf, with sailcloth for a roof'.

With the organisation by several countries of so many polar expeditions, there was an unprecedented demand for crewmen with experience of Arctic conditions. Astonishingly, one of the most famous and audacious attempts to strike at the heart of the North Pole resulted in eight Dundee ships being used out of the 10 on the international rescue attempt which followed. In 1881 the American Adolphus Greely volunteered for a scientific expedition being planned by the US Army according to recommendations of the 1879 International Polar Geographical Conference, which had designated 1882–83 as the first International Polar Year. Greely was placed in command of a 25-man party sent to build a meteorological station and sailed in July from Newfoundland aboard the USS *Proteus*, better known on Tayside as Alexander Stephen's sealer *Proteus*. In August 1881 Greely was landed on the eastern shore of Ellesmere Island and the *Proteus* sailed hurriedly south before she was caught in ice. There he established his scientific station, Fort Conger, where meteorological and geophysical observations were carried out and from which an exploratory party pushed Markham's Farthest North to 83°24′N. The following year the Dundee-built sealer *Neptune* was acquired and dispatched under American command to re-supply the explorer, but failed to reach Fort Conger, driven back by heavy ice. *Proteus* made another attempt in 1883 but was crushed and sunk with the loss of all Greely's provisions. The explorer was forced to abandon the station and to make his way south by open boat to Cape Sabine. With dwindling provisions his party wintered there. In 1884 the US Government inquired about the whaler *Thetis*, which was then on the point of departure from Dundee to Davis Strait. From new in 1881, the *Thetis* had lost four men drowned, had broken a propeller, had been beset in ice for two weeks in Newfoundland and had caught no Right whales in three seasons. She was hardly the pride of the fleet. Yet the hefty purchase price of £28,000 duly paid by the Americans for the vessel included 'an allowance' for the estimated 'success' of the voyage which she was just about to make when she changed hands.

The US Government was then in a position to launch a major attempt to rescue Greely by using a trio of Dundee-connected vessels. It backed up the *Thetis* with the Dundee-built, Newfoundland-owned sealer *Bear*, and a merchant collier, the Dundee steamer *Loch Garry*. Under the command of Winfield Scott Schley of the US Navy, this unlikely 'American' fleet was piloted through Davis Strait by the Dundee whalers *Arctic, Aurora* and *Wolf*. In June 1884 the expedition vessels found Greely and only six surviving crewmen. The explorer's party had been three years without adequate shelter or supplies.

The Greely rescue effort attained worldwide prominence and thousands gathered to witness the arrival of the survivors in the United States. Americans, however, were astonished to learn that virtually all of the rescue ships had been built in far-off Dundee. Greely himself visited the city to express his gratitude. One wonders what the Scottish crews made of him. One of America's heroic sons, he was a survivor of some of the American Civil War's bloodiest battles, and was the first volunteer private in the United States Army to rise to the rank of Major-General. In subsequent years, Greely's innovations led to the military use of wireless telegraphy, the airplane and the automobile. Later he directed the relief operation after the 1906 San Francisco earthquake. One may also wonder what the Americans thought of the Scots. When the *Bear* struck a rock and developed a bad leak on her way north in 1884, Alexander Fairweather of the *Aurora* mended the leak by the tried and trusted whaling method of inserting a 'feed' of hemp into the breach. The Americans, who were on the point of abandoning ship, were astonished.

Eighteen of Greely's party of 25 had died from the cold, starvation and scurvy and the skeletal survivors were said to have resorted to cannibalism. This much-publicised disaster cast a chill shadow over American exploration of the High Arctic in the concluding decades of the nineteenth century. Conversely, it served only to inspire a new generation of European polar adventurers, including Fridtjof Nansen, Roald Amundsen, Adolf Erik Nordenskjold, Robert Falcon Scott and Ernest Shackleton – all of whom would come to rely for survival on Dundee's whalers.

By this time, Dundee masters like Captains Thomas Robertson, William Guy, William Adams, Alexander Fairweather and Charles Yule were not only household names in Dundee – 'stout weather-beaten men who rolled along the pavements of the Nethergate and

Reform Street followed by little boys' – they were famous names among anyone venturing beyond the 6oth parallel north. They were said to know polar regions as well as the gateway of Earl Grey Dock. They were Arctic navigators and explorers in their own right with an impressive practical knowledge of the frozen regions. In the course of a single season in 1875, Captain Adams' brand-new *Arctic* dashed 'boldly past John Ross's farthest in 1818; Sir Edward Parry's farthest in Prince Regent Inlet in 1825; Franklin's winter quarters at Beechey Island in 1845; Sir James Ross's farthest at Leopold Island in 1848; and many another bay and headland in those remote regions'. And wherever Dundee masters and ships sailed, they left their mark – Adams Sound and Cape Milne, Eclipse Sound and Arctic Bay. The maps of polar regions bear witness to their pioneering activity.

Captain William Adams Snr, whose portrait hangs in Broughty Castle Museum, was recognised as the most astute and experienced of polar navigators. In 1868, the year he took over command of the SS *Arctic*, he made whaling history by sailing up Lancaster Sound and becoming the first master to explore Prince Regent's Inlet, which was much farther west than the traditional whaling grounds of Davis Strait and Lancaster Sound. In 1872 he was the first non-Inuit to see Arctic Bay, named after the Dundee vessel, at 73°N on Baffin Island, and a stretch of water was christened Adams Sound in his honour. In the same year he received a signed address from the survivors of the American exploration ship *Polaris* after he had returned part of their 'castaway' crew to Dundee. His *Arctic* in 1873 was also the first whaler to find its way to the Gulf of Boothia – the journey that had inspired Albert Markham's enthusiasm for polar exploration. Adams was frequently consulted by the Admiralty and by the Royal Geographical Society. He was invited by the Lord Mayor of London to a dinner of Britain's explorers hosted by the Prince of Wales, 'where he was openly spoken about as the fittest man to lead the American exploration in search of the [lost] Greely explorers'. He was later consulted by the US Government about the best way to relieve the explorers who were marooned in Northern Greenland and, in 1885, by the Canadian Government over shipping routes from Hudson Bay. Closer to home, Adams led out the whalers in search of survivors from the Tay Bridge disaster in December 1879.

As would-be North Pole adventurers put various theories forward, William Adams was sought out for his opinion, and as often as it was positive, it was diametrically opposed to contemporary thinking. As to the presence of a Polar Sea north of the ice, which most explorers believed they had to cross to make navigation to the Pole a reality, Captain Adams told a large audience in Newport, Fife in 1883: 'In my opinion no such sea exists. It is plain to any observer that the outlets for the unknown polar area are so limited in extent that the ice cannot get away to the south to enable such a sea to form. The sun, too, is not powerful enough in these high latitudes to melt the ice . . . Therefore I hold that the unknown Polar area is covered by Number 1 ice – that is ice which has accumulated or grown for ages – and that no open water does or can exist'. A quarter-of-a century later Peary discovered for himself the accuracy of the Dundee captain's opinion as he stood on the 13,000 ft-thick polar cap.

There is evidence to suggest that Dundee newspapers, certainly, the whaling owners, possibly, and their masters, perhaps, were unimpressed by the flag-flying race to bag the North Pole. When, for example, the American Government-sponsored expedition ship *Polaris* reached a Farthest North of 82°N, just 400 miles from the Pole in 1872, before its crew were rescued and returned to the safety of Dundee's best hotels, the *Advertiser* drew attention to the fact that their achievement was routine for the home fleet: 'The experience of the *Polaris* shows that beyond the danger which our whalers encounter every year, there is nothing very formidable in the undertaking'. Moreover, there was an attitude, bordering on arrogance, that exploration was much ado about nothing, and an inherent confidence that the Pole was attainable should the town's mariners set their minds to it. The *Advertiser* in 1873 felt that 'Captain Adams with the *Arctic*, properly provided, would settle the question'. Adams himself was ambivalent on the subject, once saying that finding the North Pole would solve a scientific problem, but adding, 'I don't think, however, that the result will be worth the risk and expense involved; not worth the powder and shot, as the saying is'.

As more and more expeditions were beaten back by the ice clogging north-leading channels, the exasperated *Advertiser* commented, 'There is every reason to believe that with two well-appointed Dundee whalers, the region around the North Pole might be thoroughly explored in a couple of seasons at least'. One master willing to try was Charles Yule of the *Esquimaux*. Yule commented, 'All I know is that I should not hesitate to take the *Esquimaux* up Smith's Sound and try to go to the Pole in her; she's quite strong enough for that, and the ice would certainly not stop her'. The *Piper o' Dundee* was also adamant that the Dundonian who, in its opinion, probably lived at the Pole anyway, could easily have his neighbours along for a mollie. It pointed out in 1897, 'If Dundee cared to organise an expedition to the North Pole to bring home her long lost citizen, talent and energy would not be wanting in the ranks of her own local navigators to carry out the task'. This was over 20 years before the North Pole was attained.

While it would be untrue to imply that the captains did not pragmatically accept the presence of party after party of explorers criss-crossing their fishing grounds, there was certainly a belief that it was questionable whether explorers could tell them much they didn't already know. Captain Thomas Robertson, for example, frequently questioned their claims. In 1896 he dismissed the notion that Fridtjof Nansen had been stuck in ice at a 'mere' 77°N. He told how, in the previous season, he had cruised at 81°N and 'much further in some seasons' when ice conditions permitted. Robertson also pinpointed the telling difference between the two sets of adventurers: 'It is whales we are after, not geographical mysteries, and we cannot allow curiosity to run away with valuable time'. Nor was Coffee Tam impressed with Nansen's effort in reaching 86°N in a three-year expedition which was loaded with five years' provisions. It was, he said, 'what appeared to me to have been only one good season's work'. And Salomon Andree's proposed ballooning venture over the North Pole, which had faced sustained criticism from the by-then Admiral Albert Markham, elicited only 'a smile of pity from the captain who has more faith in the keel of a stout ship than in all the balloons that science has ever produced'. Besides, had not Nansen, who had described his famous 1888 crossing of Greenland in a lecture in the Kinnaird Hall, Dundee, been found wandering in that same Greenland in 1894, close to death, and been rescued and evacuated by the town's whaler *Windward*?

Dundee's attraction for would-be explorers was generated not only by its long record of Arctic know-how and survival, but by shipbuilding traditions which leaned heavily on its instinct to continue to build magnetic-impervious wooden ships, ignoring the temptation to turn to iron after its prototype iron steamer – the 'unsinkable' *River Tay* – did exactly that before getting far beyond its namesake estuary. Peterhead and Hull losses suggested that iron was not ideal for polar work, and it was believed that extreme frost made the metal brittle and easily broken. Moreover, at high latitudes explorers' compasses behaved strangely, and when ghostly fogs descended for weeks, navigators felt on surer ground, in a manner of speaking, with timbers below their feet. Wooden hulls had stood the test of time – and Dundee owners and masters were happy to remain faithful to ships strongly built and fortified, both inside and out, to withstand the awesome pressures to which they were at times subjected.

The Stephen's whaler *Bloodhound*, renamed *Discovery* for Nares's expedition of 1875, was of such quality that it was described by the Admiralty as the best exploration vessel ever built. Remarkably, her quarter-century-old plans were dusted down and used as the blueprint for Captain Scott's historic ship of the same name in 1901. And when Scott's National Antarctic Expedition of 1901–04 elected to have its research ship built in Dundee, it was for good reason. The port's whaling shipwrights and carpenters uniquely possessed the skills required to construct the finest wooden vessels. As the *Discovery* adventure began, the veteran shipwrights of Dundee came out of retirement to show the new century's steel riveters that the passing era of whaling could still have its triumphs. Such skills were demonstrated more forcibly two years later when the *Terra Nova* was purchased as a *Discovery* relief vessel and underwent a remarkable refit in Dundee under the direction of Ernest Shackleton. Three hundred workmen gave up the 'Dundee Fortnight' holiday to completely reconstruct the ship, removing and cleaning engines, refurbishing boilers, winches and steering gear, overhauling propeller gear and replacing and reinforcing every seam of her hull. With the nation watching, the entire task took them under three weeks – 'a noteworthy shipbuilding record'. When ready, the *Terra Nova* left Dundee to a crescendo of good-luck foghorns and was towed south towards Antarctica by a succession of fast Admiralty cruisers.

That ships built for strength, rather than speed or size, were ultimately the best choice for experienced explorers was demonstrated, for example, by the flimsy 'unfortified' *Ripple*, which carried the doomed Swedish explorers Bjorling and Karastennius to a watery grave in 1893. It was further demonstrated by an expedition to the Arctic which took place as late as 1913. The *Karluk*, the vessel chosen to voyage north with the Canadian Arctic Expedition that year, was certainly a wooden-hulled whaling ship, but she was nearly 30 years old, had been retired for years, and had been built for the industry in the warm waters of California. She had no ice-breaking equipment or protection, and no experience of surviving in polar seas. But she was a bargain! Jennifer Niven's study of this voyage concluded that the *Karluk* was an old, weak ship and that 'she should never have been made to do the work she was doing'. And even though the *Karluk* was skippered by the 'ice-master' Captain Bob Bartlett, who had been at the helm of the *Roosevelt* from which Peary launched his successful expedition to the North Pole four years earlier, the ship's bow was actually 'too thin to forge through the ice'. Expeditions which did not look to the lessons learned in whaling were clearly vulnerable.

The zenith of Arctic polar discovery was packed into the two decades between 1890 and 1910 when exploration was about achieving Farthest North and, ultimately, reaching the North Pole, some 400 miles distant from the northern tip of Greenland. In the near-two decades from 1900 to 1916 serious attempts were also made to explore the hitherto unknown continent of Antarctica and to reach the South Pole.

As we saw in the previous chapter, Dundee found itself in the vanguard of Antarctic exploration with its pioneering whaling expedition in the summer of 1892. Although this initiative was commercial in nature, the city deserves a place in the story of exploration as the quartet of whaling ships did in fact sail into the southern seas to a point further south than that reached by anyone except Sir James Ross 65 years earlier. The Antarctic did not, as it was hoped, provide a new source of lucrative whalebone, but the expedition's contribution to science and discovery should not be underestimated. The expedition also left its mark in areas previously unexplored. In the Ross Sea it was discovered that Joinville Island was two islands. The smaller is known today as Dundee Island. An inlet discovered by the SS *Active* became the Firth of Tay, a sound Active Sound, a cape was named Cape Scrymgeour and a landfall Kinnes Point after the managing owner of the fleet. Gibson Bay and Cape Alexander bear the names of shareholders in the company which owned the ships.

Two years later, in 1894, the Peterhead whaler *Windward* conveyed the Jackson-Harmsworth expedition on its quest for the North Pole, before continuing its whaling career for a further four years at Dundee. The *Windward*'s role was to carry the expedition to establish a base on the hitherto unexplored north shore of Franz Josef Land, a barren group of islands in the Barents Sea, east of Spitzbergen. There the members of the expedition reached the highest northern latitude ever reached by man. In August 1897 the *Balaena* of Dundee struck out for this remote outpost, ostensibly to hunt for walrus, and soon reached waters that had never before been fished by any whaling vessel, at the high altitude of 81°N. Indeed, the *Balaena* was only the fourth vessel of any type to visit Franz Josef Land, joining the illustrious company of the Austrians who discovered and named the island group in 1873, Benjamin Leigh Smith who sailed on the *Eira* in 1881–1882 and the Jackson-Harmsworth expedition of 1894. While anchored, Captain Robertson of the *Balaena* explored areas of uncharted coastline and also rediscovered the depot of stores left by Leigh Smith 15 years earlier, 'with the explorer's and seamen's empty chests, the lids bearing the names of their respective owners'.

Prior to being wrecked as part of the Dundee whaling fleet in Davis Strait in 1907, the *Windward* had entered the pages of exploration history by carrying the greatest Arctic explorer of them all towards the North Pole. Robert Edwin Peary, a United States Navy civil engineer from Maine before turning to exploring, commissioned the *Windward* in 1898 to make an audacious attempt to be the first to stand at the North Pole. Peary risked a long sledge journey northwards but was forced, suffering from frostbite, into retreat some 300 miles from his objective. Shaken by the news of Peary's condition, the expedition organisers sent the *Windward* again into the icy waters to try to bring him back and secured a second relief ship, the *Erik*, which had been built by Stephen's yard in Dundee in 1865 and sold on to Peterhead owners. As the *Erik* sailed north to relieve Peary, it carried another famous explorer, Dr Frederick Cook. Peary reached the North Pole at his third attempt in April 1909, only to discover on his return that Cook had told an astonished world that he had beaten him to it in 1908 – a claim later proved to be false – which no less an authoritative journal than *The Courier* of Dundee accepted hook, line and sinker!

Like most polar explorers of his generation, the American meteorologist Evelyn Briggs Baldwin chose a Dundee-built whaler from Stephen's yard for his attempt to become the first to reach the North Pole. Baldwin had served as meteorologist with Peary and was an impressive polar pioneer in his own right. A chance meeting between Baldwin and William Ziegler, a multi-millionaire businessmen with interests in real estate and food retailing, led to Baldwin persuading Ziegler that the Pole could be reached from Franz Josef Land. Baldwin turned to the *Esquimaux*, a survivor of many Arctic fishing seasons, for which he paid £5100 in 1900. When she emerged from a money-no-object refitting at Dundee Shipbuilders Company Ltd, as Stephen's had become, she had been patriotically renamed

America. In late summer 1901 Baldwin and his wealthy collaborator made their first attempt on the North Pole by taking the *America* to Franz Josef Land. Thirty men and 400 dogs were landed and set out across ice for the Pole, but were beaten back by bad weather. The *America* by this time was in danger of being imprisoned by ice; Baldwin was accused of running her for Tromsø in northern Norway on the pretext of a shortage of coal. He insisted he was ready to try again in 1903, but Ziegler was so dissatisfied with his conduct that the leadership was taken from him and given instead to the expedition's photographer, Anthony Fiala.

Fiala left for the Franz Josef archipelago in the *America* in June 1903 and managed to force the Dundee ship to 82°N, a record for any vessel in that region. Returning south, the *America* was suddenly nipped in Neplitz Bay. Pressure ridges of ice tore out her stern and raised her hull on to the pack and, on November 21, 1903, the former *Esquimaux* of Dundee was abandoned. When the plight of the men was relayed to Britain, the finest ship available, the Dundee-built *Terra Nova*, which had just returned from rescuing Captain Scott in Antarctica, was chartered for a relief attempt. In the spring of 1905 the *Terra Nova* crashed her way through the ice to recover the explorers and returned them safely to London. In August 1905 Anthony Fiala offered grateful thanks to her officers and crew through the columns of the *Advertiser*, by which time the *Terra Nova* had returned to her old job as a Newfoundland sealer. In 1955 a small cork buoy marked *Baldwin Ziegler Expedition 1901* was found off the Norwegian coast, presumed to have drifted in Arctic waters for over 50 years.

While Baldwin was examining his newly purchased *Esquimaux* in 1900, the hammering of nails from Marine Parade signalled the construction of the best-known ship ever built at Dundee – the Royal Research Ship *Discovery*. Robert Falcon Scott's vessel was built for exploration, of course, and was never intended to be a whaling ship. Yet she was constructed using the plans of a successful whaler and she would not be berthed on Dundee's waterfront today had it not been for the judicious use of dynamite brought by two Dundee whalers, the *Terra Nova* and the *Morning*, which freed her from her icy imprisonment in McMurdo Sound. When the National Antarctic Expedition was being organised in 1900, there was only one yard in the country with craftsmen who had the experience to build a wooden ship strong enough to carry the explorers of the new century through ice-ridden seas. The contract went to Dundee Shipbuilders

Company Ltd, the former Stephen's Yard, whose skilled workforce had led the world in the construction of reinforced, wooden-hulled polar ships. *Discovery* drew on all the lessons learned in half-a-century of whaling in Arctic regions. Her timbered sides were 26 inches thick, as against the normal half-inch plates of a steel ship. The main frames were of oak, reinforced outside and inside by pitch pine, fir, mahogany and elm. Her bow was even thicker and strengthened on the outside with steel plates for battering through ice floes.

It wasn't enough. Two years after her launch in Dundee in March 1901, *Discovery* was frozen in at her winter base in Antarctica and there she remained for 23 months while Captain Scott and Lieutenant Shackleton made daring excursions into the mountains. On learning the news, the expedition's London-based organisers turned again to Dundee for a ship to mount a relief voyage, this time the whaler *Morning*. The German-built vessel was underpowered, however, and could not get to within a mile of the stranded *Discovery*. She beat a retreat, after transferring stores and evacuating Shackleton, whose health was said by Scott to be causing concern. In fact, along with Dr Edward Wilson and Scott, the young lieutenant had completed an arduous 93-day, 1000-mile sledge attempt on the South Pole while suffering from scurvy and exhaustion. Shackleton's biographer Caroline Alexander commented, 'Though mortified by his early return to England, Shackleton arrived home a hero who had gone farther south than anyone before'.

A stronger relief expedition was organised for 1903, and on this occasion the *Morning* was met in the south by the pride of the Dundee whaling fleet, the *Terra Nova*, after her rapid refit in Dundee under Shackleton's direction. Early in January 1904 the *Terra Nova* and *Morning* arrived within 17 miles of *Discovery*, but six weeks passed before Captains Harry McKay and William Colbeck penetrated the ice and freed the *Discovery* by blowing out a channel with gunpowder. Today, *Discovery* is berthed in her home port and is the centrepiece of a visitor centre which tells Captain Scott's heroic story. It is not commonly known that there were instructions from the Admiralty that if *Discovery* was still fast by the end of February 1904, she was to be abandoned to her fate. Fortunately, the city's whale ships – and Captain Harry McKay's expertise with explosives – rescued the only purpose-built exploration vessel constructed in Britain in the modern era. The three ships safely left McMurdo Sound with nine days to spare.

Scott, of course, was to try again for the South Pole in the *Terra*

Nova – only to be beaten to it by the Norwegian giant of exploration, Roald Amundsen, who arrived a month earlier. A decade before that, in March 1903, Amundsen's brother visited Dundee to confer with her whaling captains. Roald Amundsen knew that the only chance he had of reaching his then objective of the North Pole was to be properly supplied for his sledge attempt on the roof of the world. He instructed his brother to negotiate with Captains William Adams and William Milne to convey stores to Smith Sound, at a latitude of 81°N. Amundsen, who was to make his way to the point overland, would then intercept the ships before re-stocking for his polar attempt. By April 1903 the *Eclipse* and *Diana* were ready to leave with Amundsen's stores. Hundreds of people descended on the quayside to watch the two vessels nose through the lockway at Victoria Dock into Camperdown Dock on their way to their historic meeting with the Norwegian explorer, pencilled in for late June. The first news of their mission was disconcerting, however. The *Courier* reported: 'He did not keep the tryst at the appointed place'. In fact, there was no report of Amundsen by any of the Dundee fleet or by the Eskimo communities they encountered. Nor had the crew of the *Vega*, abandoned south of the meeting point, reported any sight of the explorer when they reached Upernavik by open boat. Nonetheless, Adams of the *Diana* and Milne of the *Eclipse* forced a passage north through Melville Bay to keep the appointment. Indeed, while cruising Smith Sound waiting for Amundsen, they came across the Danish Ericksen expedition in 'a pitiful condition' and 'living on eggs'. It had one gun and no boat. The Dundee captains left medical stores, ammunition, food and boat materials and Mylius Ericksen, who had set off into the wilds of Greenland in the summer of 1902, eventually reached the safety of Upernavik in June 1904. Meanwhile, arrangements were made within the Dundee whaling fleet to police Davis Strait in case they could provide assistance.

The reason that the Dundee whalers did not meet Amundsen on June 26, 1903 as arranged was that the Norwegian's expedition did not leave Norway until June 17, instead of at the beginning of May as originally planned. The Dundee ships, as few others could, remained in the perilously dangerous latitude 'as long as possible', indeed for another eight weeks – and on their return the captains reported their feeling that Amundsen's ship, the *Gjoa*, with a crew of just eight, was too small a vessel to penetrate the ice-jam. This time they were wrong. The little fishing vessel made history by being first to successfully navigate the North-West Passage.

Disappointed by his evacuation from the 1901 British expedition, Ernest Shackleton was determined to return to the Antarctic. In 1908 he chose the Stephen-built *Nimrod* for his first expedition under his own leadership. In fairness, the 41-year-old, three-masted sealer was not the explorer's first choice. He had set his heart on a three-year-old Norwegian ship called *Bjørn* but its asking price of £11,000 was beyond his reach. Forced to look for a less expensive ship, he was able to purchase the *Nimrod* for £5000. The *Nimrod* was only half the size of the Norwegian ship and had a maximum speed of barely six knots under steam. Shackleton did not think much of her at first, recalling in *Heart of the Antarctic*, 'I must confess I was disappointed when I first examined the little ship, to which I was about to commit the hopes and aspiration of many years. She was very dilapidated and smelt strongly of seal-oil . . . my first impression hardly did justice to the plucky old ship'. Later, he described her as 'one of the finest I have known', and confided in a letter that *Nimrod* was a far stronger ship constructionally than his famous *Endurance* of 1914.

Irish-born Shackleton, the son of a doctor who moved to London, went to sea at the age of 16. By 24 he had qualified to command a British ship anywhere on the seven seas. His Arctic calling owed its origins to an early battering around Cape Horn: 'I felt strangely drawn towards the mysterious south . . . we rounded Cape Horn in the depth of winter. It was one continuous blizzard all the way . . . Yet many a time, even in the midst of all this discomfort, my thoughts would go out to the southward. But strangely enough, the circumstance which actually determined me to become an explorer was a dream I had when I was twenty-two. We were beating out to New York from Gibraltar, and I dreamt I was standing on the bridge in mid-Atlantic and looking northward. It was a simple dream. I seemed to vow to myself that some day I would go to the region of ice and snow and go on and on till I came to one of the poles of the earth, the end of the axis upon which this great round ball turns'.

The supreme prize of reaching the Pole was never his, but Shackleton came to know and to regard Dundee well. Invalided home from the 1901 National Antarctic Expedition, he returned to the city in 1902, still only 28 years old, to oversee the refit of *Terra Nova* for the *Discovery* relief operation. In January 1904 Shackleton was appointed Secretary of the Royal Scottish Geographical Society which brought his move from London to Edinburgh. He also dabbled in journalism and business. But that November, the *Courier* revealed that Shackleton was to 'uphold the Unionist cause in the next election'. He resigned his position at the RSGS to further his political career and stood for election in 1904 in one of Dundee's two parliamentary seats. In the electoral backlash against the Unionists that year Shackleton finished in a lowly fourth place in a poll won by the Liberal Edmund Robertson, coincidentally the Admiralty Secretary. He made many friends in the city, however, the *Courier* reporting: 'The Lieutenant's breezy personality and his attractive manner has gained him much popularity'. One of the paper's correspondents remarked tellingly that Shackleton had won friends in Dundee whose political opinions were 'as far apart from him as are the Poles'. Shackleton noted that he had got all the cheers, but that 'the other candidates got the votes'. The defeat in Dundee did not unduly worry him and, a year later, he set off again for his greater love, the Antarctic, which he christened 'The birthplace of the clouds and the nesting place of the four winds.' And for this adventure he chose the *Nimrod*.

The *Nimrod* expedition was expected to leave New Zealand at the beginning of 1908 and proceed to winter quarters on the Antarctic continent. Here the men and stores would be landed, followed quickly by the retreat of the ship to New Zealand to prevent her from being frozen in. Thereafter shore parties were to make daring incursions into the unexplored continent. In the event the *Nimrod* was frozen in several times as Shackleton drove her to stopping points around the Ross Sea before sending her northwards to safety. In December 1908 Shackleton's sledge party reached an altitude of 10,200 ft on the Antarctic plateau. The men were making only four miles a day and were weak from lack of food. By January 2, 1909 Shackleton was near breaking point: 'I cannot think of failure yet I must look at the matter sensibly and consider the lives of those who are with me . . . man can only do his best'. Two days later he wrote, 'The end is in sight. We can only go for three more days at the most, for we are weakening rapidly'. They fought through a blizzard on January 4, 5 and 6. On January 7 and 8, just 100 miles from the Pole, ferocious winds kept them in their sleeping bags. On January 9 they struggled out, man-hauling their sledges, and reached Farthest South at 88°23'S – just 97 miles from the South Pole. They planted the Union flag, stayed a few minutes, and then turned round and headed for base camp. On March 4 they were safely back aboard *Nimrod*. Shackleton's sledge-meter recorded their distance travelled as 1755 miles.

In recent times the opinion has grown that had it not been for his selfless action to save the lives of his men, this friend of Dundee would have stood at the South Pole years before the Norwegian Amundsen. As for his Dundee ship, third officer and boatswain Alfred Cheetham described in a manuscript journal from the expedition how well 'Our *Nimrod*' survived 'some very bad bruising' and how 'the good little ship used to shake herself like a dog' after every squeeze. The veteran Cheetham knew a good ship when he saw one. He served on the *Morning* for the relief of the *Discovery* in 1903; also on the *Nimrod*, the *Terra Nova* and the *Endurance*.

The *Terra Nova*, meanwhile, was not done with her Antarctic adventures. After relieving the *Discovery* in 1904, the Stephen's-built vessel had returned to sealing with Bowring Brothers Ltd of Newfoundland, where she proved to be outstanding at her task, taking over 850,000 pelts – the third largest number of any sealer. In November 1909 she was sold to the Admiralty and became the headquarters ship for Captain Scott's epic journey to the South Pole the following summer. The *Terra Nova* performed splendidly throughout the journey – though, en route, in Melbourne, Scott received Amundsen's cable announcing his own trip south; in other words, the race for the South Pole had begun. The Dundee ship's role was not simply to decant Scott at Cape Evans in January 1911. She was used to take the Eastern party to seek a landfall on King Edward VII Land, only to discover Amundsen's *Fram* anchored in the Bay of Whales. The party returned to Cape Evans with the news and the *Terra Nova* then sailed north to Cape Adare on the tip of Victoria Land, and so became host to the Northern Party. She next overwintered in New Zealand before returning once again to Cape Adare to recover the men. History has recorded how Scott's polar party all perished on their return from the South Pole, but their ship soldiered on as expedition conveyance and eventually returned safely. For her exploits in two major polar journeys in the Heroic Age the *Terra Nova* of Dundee is properly ranked among the elite of all expedition ships.

Another Dundee whaler whose career was interrupted by exploration duties was the *Aurora*. After a hugely adventurous phase in which she barely survived her 18 whaling trips from Dundee, the *Aurora* was bought in 1911 for Dr Douglas Mawson's Antarctic expedition from Australia. Said the *Courier*.

There are two Dundee-built ships lying within a 100 yards of each other in the South West India Dock, London, just now. One

is the Tay steamer Shamrock, the other the sealing vessel
Aurora, which is to take Dr Mawson from Australia to the
South Polar regions. The Aurora, a typical Dundee whaler,
which made a fast voyage of nine days from St John's Newfoundland, is now being got into trim for her new expedition.
Captain Davis, who is supervising matters, said that Dr Mawson and himself were quite delighted with the ship, with the
massiveness and soundness of her timbers. They prefer her to
the Terra Nova, itself Dundee built, but which cost Captain
Scott £6000 more. The Aurora was recommended to Dr Mawson
and Captain Davis by Captain Bartlett, Commander Peary's
skipper, who has sailed in her and speaks highly of her qualities.

It says something for Dundee shipbuilding that two of the greatest
exploration captains valued the *Aurora* so highly. Captain Bartlett
commanded the *Roosevelt* which took Robert Peary to the North Pole
in 1909, and Captain John Davis was a member of Ernest Shackleton's 1907–09 expedition, later commanding the *Aurora* for Shackleton during his spectacular Trans-Antarctic Expedition of 1914–16.
The *Aurora* could boast an impressive pedigree. She had not only
struck it rich in whaling and sealing, she had helped in the rescue of
Adolphus Greely, had survived a month in the ice pack in 1895, a
collision in 1908, and rounded off her commercial career in 1910 by
being 'lost' for several weeks. But between 1911 and 1914 she
steamed effortlessly for 30,000 miles in high southern latitudes,
allowing Mawson to chart 1500 miles of unexplored coastline and
Dundee to add another name to the list of home vessels despatched
on historic voyages of discovery.

Shackleton's ambitious plan to cross Antarctica was hatched on
his return from the *Nimrod* expedition – when he had become a
national hero overnight. Although the Norwegian flag had since
fluttered at the South Pole, Shackleton believed that the first crossing
of the Antarctic Continent, from sea to sea via the Pole, a distance of
some 1800 miles over unexplored territory, apart from its historic
value, would be a journey of great scientific importance.

Two ships were required for the expedition. For his principal ship
Shackleton paid £14,000 for the Norwegian-built *Endurance* which he
planned to use to transport the trans-continental party to his dis-
embarkation point on the Weddell Sea coast. The *Aurora*, meanwhile,
was purchased from Douglas Mawson and was to be his welcoming
ship at his old Ross Sea base on the other side of the continent. When

the expedition was announced early in 1914, Shackleton received nearly 5000 applications to join the adventure, from whom 56 men were picked. Yet the proposed expedition was sadly short of funds. Shackleton spent much of 1907 desperately trying to raise sponsorship for his venture. He wrote to the Dundee jute philanthropist Sir James Caird asking for a £50 donation. Caird promised him the staggering sum of £10,000 if he would come to Dundee to discuss the matter. The two men met in Caird's office and, after the project had been explained, the elderly, bearded figure sent him an unconditional cheque for £24,000, almost the entire cost of the venture.

Shackleton's 1914 voyage is now part of polar history. The *Endurance* sailed into the Weddell Sea but was beset by ice on January 20, 1915, just one day's voyage from the new continent. After drifting in her icy prison through the winter months, she was crushed on October 27. Shackleton and his crew of 28 men abandoned ship with their sledges, dogs and three small boats. Stranded 340 miles from the nearest land, with provisions for three months, they marched on ice as far as they could until conditions improved before launching the boats and rowing to Elephant Island, 100 miles distant from their drift. From there Shackleton left most of his men in huts made from two upturned boats and took a crew of five in the 22ft-long *James Caird* open lifeboat across 800 miles of treacherous seas to South Georgia on one of the epic voyages of maritime history. On arrival 14 days later the men force-marched across mountains and glaciers to reach a remote Norwegian whaling station and safety. Shackleton was then loaned a schooner by the Chilean Government and set off to rescue his marooned men on Elephant Island. 'Not a life lost, and we have been through Hell,' he famously recorded.

The *Aurora*, meanwhile, under the command of Æneas Mackintosh, sailed from Hobart, Tasmania for the Ross Sea on December 24, 1914. The ship had been refitted in Sydney and made ready for a possible two-year commitment in Antarctic waters. Shackleton's orders were for the Dundee whaler to make a base at some convenient point in or near McMurdo Sound and to lay depots of fuel and food marked by flags and cairns at 80°S, so that they could be spotted by the sledging teams arriving from the Weddell Sea coast.

The *Aurora* worked her way as far south as she could go, anchored to the sea ice, and Mackintosh left with a party to establish the inland depots. First officer Lieutenant J. R. Stenhouse was left in command of the ship with instructions to select a base for winter quarters. The *Aurora*'s ice anchors would not hold, however, and thereafter began a long and famous drift as the ship became helpless in the grip of the ice. Throughout, Stenhouse kept the vessel barely afloat or nipped, but in one piece, with daring displays of seamanship. Many times the *Aurora*'s anchors would not hold because of the breaking of the pack and Stenhouse learned the Dundee whaling way as she was edged forward through the ice-encumbered waters. Month after month the *Aurora* drifted, Stenhouse recording moments of danger in his personal log:

> July 22.—Ship in bad position in newly frozen lane, with bow and stern jammed against heavy floes; heavy strain with much creaking and groaning. 8 a.m.—Called all hands to stations for sledges, and made final preparations for abandoning ship. Allotted special duties to several hands to facilitate quickness in getting clear should ship be crushed. Am afraid the ship's back will be broken if the pressure continues, but cannot relieve her.

Although sadly battered during 12 months' imprisonment in the ice, during which time she drifted 500 miles, the *Aurora* survived once more and eventually returned safely to New Zealand – leaving behind, among other things, her rudder and anchor in Antarctica.

So long eclipsed by his rival Captain Scott, Shackleton's star is in the ascendant as, increasingly, historians question Scott's leadership qualities and character. There was no rapport between the charismatic Anglo-Irish doctor's son and the disciplined naval commander of *Discovery*. Twice Shackleton had redeemed disaster with glorious failure and, typical of his unselfish nature, he named the 200 miles of previously undiscovered coastline the Caird Coast, after his benefactor and friend in Dundee. Shackleton paid his last visit to Dundee in 1919 to make personal calls on some of the people who had supported him. Three years later he set out for the Antarctic for the last time. He never returned.

By the inter-war years, far fewer vessels of the once-supreme Dundee fleet remained afloat. One of them was the *Bear*, a sealer built in Dundee in 1874, and known as the White Angel of the Arctic during 34 Arctic trips in which she saved about 400 sealers or whalers beset or abandoned in ice. It was the *Bear* that had pushed her way through the ice in 1884 to rescue Adolphus Greely when other relief efforts had failed. She was also used to maintain order at Nome at the time of the Alaskan gold rush in 1899–1900. Shortly before her withdrawal in 1924, the *Bear* relieved Roald Amundsen, who was frozen in north of the Bering Strait after the failure of his polar flight. Due largely to this, she was reprieved, and she was bought by the American explorer Admiral Richard Byrd for $1050 and continued on her remarkable voyages of discovery under his brilliant command.

In 1933–35 and again from 1939–41 the *Bear* sailed south to Antarctica with Byrd and on the second expedition reached a point, some 1500 miles south of New Zealand, which was claimed to be the farthest south for any ship. Byrd wrote that though the *Bear* was a wooden ship, 'She could lower her head and bore through where the iron hulled vessel had to seek a better 'ole'. The brave old *Bear* survived until 1963 when she sank off Nova Scotia. Her bell is displayed in the Explorers' Club in New York, the city she returned to in triumph with Greely's survivors from the north and where she had received a national welcome on Byrd's return from the south.

Dundee was the only whaling port left in Britain during the Heroic Age of polar exploration, and her ships and men were ideally suited to either purpose. When the 1902 Scottish National Antarctic Expedition poached more than a dozen men, including the captain, from the Dundee whaler *Balaena*, the *Advertiser* commented: 'Long experience of Arctic winters and the hardships they involve has eminently fitted these sailors for such navigation. So much is made evident by the strenuous attempts to induce the men to desert the whale fishing industry for the more remunerative task of pole hunting'. And when officials from Captain Scott's National Antarctic Expedition of 1901 arrived in Dundee in 1902 to recruit local men for a *Discovery* relief ship, they offered 'unusually high wages of up to £6 per month'. The rate for able seamen at the time was barely half that. Not every expedition was successful in persuading local men to jump ship, so to speak. The Danish explorers who arrived in Dundee with the Danish Consul to persuade the town's whaler captains to convey their Greenland Expedition of 1902 were 'somewhat astonished' to be informed that the captains had all left for the season's fishing!

Doubtless the primary goal of whaling captains was commercial success, and there was nothing as important as the £1000 of bone on the end of a harpoon line. Yet the cause of science was neither ignored nor forgotten. Even Coffee Tam Robertson, who took a dour view of the egotism surrounding exploration, carried out deep-sea soundings across a vast uncharted breadth of ocean during his command of the *Scotia* in 1902–04 and 'brought back a splendid record of successful exploring'. Despite wry scepticism, the era of exploration which led to the first footsteps on the landless North Pole at 90°N excited Dundee's captains and people as the greatest explorers in the world paid homage to the port's knowledge of polar regions. The Dundee masters may have been characterised as mere 'blubber hunters', whose minds were occupied with oil and whalebone to the exclusion of all else, but: 'More than one eminent scientist has expressed his indebtedness to them for specimens and observations collected and made at no little inconvenience during a commercial venture, always arduous, and often vexatious in the extreme'.

The immense contribution that Dundee captains had made to the course of exploration was recognised and rewarded. William Adams was honoured by several scientific societies and governments. Captain Harry McKay was another master whose services to exploration were honoured, but this time in sadder circumstances. While sailing on the *Aurora* at 77°N on the eastern side of Davis Strait in the summer of 1893, McKay discovered the wreck of the *Ripple*, a Swedish survey vessel which had been holed and driven on to ice. The crew had perished, but McKay found one body and a quantity of personal possessions, some of which gave clues as to the movement of the scientists. To express its gratitude for the care with which McKay had carried out the safe return of expedition relics, the Swedish Geographical Society presented him with a commemorative medal. In 1900 Captain Milne of the *Eclipse* received an honour from the Meteorological Society and, in 1907, Captain Thomas Robertson of the *Scotia* was presented with a silver trophy by the Norwegian Government.

William Adams was followed into Dundee's whaling fleet by his son of the same name, and it was not long before William Adams Jnr became a respected Arctic expert. He took his ship loaded with Amundsen's expedition supplies to the most northerly regions of Baffin Bay, and for this service he was honoured by King Haakon of Norway with the award of the Distinguished Order of St Olaf. Captain Adams was also the recipient of a medal from the Danish Meteorological Society in recognition of his services in compiling a log on behalf of the Society during his 1899 whaling voyage to Davis Strait. The daily entries and detailed observations he made that year also won him an award in the form of charts and books from its sister British society. In later life, while he worked with the Brocklebank shipping line of Liverpool, Adams was approached by Cambridge

University to lend them his Arctic log books and to help with a geographical survey. Adams explained this demand on his services in an interview with *the Courier* in 1938, four years before his death at the age of 73: 'When I first went whaling 40 and 50 years ago, much of the land in which we traded was unexplored. The result was that the crews had to collect as much information as possible to guide them through these dangerous waters'. Captain Adams, in the article, also paid tribute to his father's adventurous life, and made the claim that he had prepared one of the first charts of the northern regions. The son had one proud achievement that the father never matched, however. In 1892 he sailed with the Dundee whaling expedition to Antarctica.

Dundee was the foundation on which modern polar exploration was established. It built more exploration vessels than any other port and through its ships and men helped to facilitate exploration, investigation and research in polar regions. The town's ships took the most renowned explorers of the day to their goals, helping them on their heroic pathways, and just as often securing their safe return. The port's whale men represented the greatest body of expert Arctic knowledge in the western world, and they lived out that expertise through a series of penetrating voyages which involved ever-present danger and the exhilaration of discovery as they plotted, pushed and progressed to previously inaccessible Arctic latitudes. For this they did not receive fame, wealth and public adulation as the nation's patriotic explorers did. But the one could not have existed without the other.

Appendix 1

THE DUNDEE WHALING FLEET, 1753–1922

SHIP	CONSTRUCTED	REGISTERED AT DUNDEE	DETAILS/FATE
Achilles	North Shields, 1813	1819–1830	Lost Davis Strait, 1830
Active	Peterhead, 1852	1873–1914	Lost off Orkneys, 1915
Advice	Whitby, 1785	1804–1853	Lost Davis Strait, 1859
Albert	Yarmouth, 1889	1903–1908	Sold Peterhead, 1908
Alert	(Peterhead ship)	1900–1901	Used at Dundee shore station
Alexander (1)	Stockton, 1807	1830–1862	Crushed Melville Bay, 1862
Alexander (2)	Dundee, 1864	1864–1869	Lost in Davis Straits, 1869
Apollo		1789	Lost 1789
Arctic (1)	Dundee, 1867	1867–1874	Lost Prince Regent's Inlet, 1874
Arctic (2)	Dundee, 1875	1875–1887	Lost Cumberland Gulf, 1887
Aurora	Dundee, 1876	1876–1893	Sold 1894
Balaena	Norway, 1872	1891–1914	Sold Liverpool, 1916
Calypso	Whitby, 1787	1808–1822	Lost Melville Bay, 1822
Camperdown	Dundee, 1860	1860–1878	Abandoned Davis Strait, 1878
Chieftain	Lossiemouth, 1868	1868–1892	Abandoned Coutt's Inlet, 1892
Columbia	1835	1867–1868	Lost Exeter Sound, 1868
Cornwallis	Maryport, 1862	1883–1885	Lost Davis Strait, 1885

Diana (1)	Norway, 1871	1872–1873	Yacht
Diana (2)	Jarrow, 1812	1892–1913	Sold Liverpool, 1913
Dorothy	Prior to 1753	1827–1840	Abandoned Atlantic, 1840
Dundee (1)	Bristol prior to 1790	1753–1782	Lost Greenland, 1782
Dundee (2)	Dundee, 1859	c.1790–1797	Sold Wm Scoresby, c.1797
Dundee (3)	Alloa, 1856	1859–1863	Lost in ice, 1863
Earl of Mar & Kellie	Spain, 1918	1885–1890	Sold 1890
Easonian	Hull, 1819	1921–1922	Lost by fire, Kekerten, 1922
Ebor	Aberdeen, 1867	1831–1840	Sold Montrose, 1840
Eclipse	Calcutta, 1809	1892–1909	Sold Norway, 1909
Emma	Dundee, 1865	1863–1864	Lost Davis Straits, 1864
Erik	Hull, 1879	1865–1883	Sold Peterhead, 1883
Ernest William	Dundee, 1865	1903–1913	Wrecked Kekerten, 1913
Esquimaux	Shoreham, 1777	1865–1900	Renamed *America* 1900
Estridge	Thorne, 1801	1797–1825	Lost Melville Bay, 1825
Fairy	Hamburg, 1803	1821–1851	Sold Peterhead, 1851
Friendship	London prior to 1757	1809–1835	Sold Newcastle, 1841
Grandtully	(Peterhead ship)	1757–1762	Sold on
Greda	Norway	1903	Used at Dundee shore station
Harold Haartfagre	Dundee, 1831	1875–1878	Returned to Norway
Heroine	Sunderland, 1783	1835–1858	Lost Melville Bay, 1858
Horn	Peterhead, 1851	1806–1852	Lost off St Andrews, 1852
Intrepid		1866–1885	Foundered Greenland, 1885

Ship	Built	Years	Fate
Jan Mayen (1)	Peterhead, 1859	1878–1882	Abandoned Greenland, 1882
Jan Mayen (2)	Germany, 1873	1875–1886	Lost Cape Atholl, 1886
Jane	1783	1807–1809	Wrecked Tay Banks, 1809
Juanta Agatha		1902–1910	Lost Cumberland Gulf, 1910
Jumna	Whitehaven, 1853	1861–1863	Lost Melville Bay, 1863
Kate	(Peterhead ship)	1902	Used at Dundee shore station
Mary Ann	1784	1803–1819	Lost in ice, 1819
Maud	Whitby, 1865	1886–1892	Wrecked Davis Strait, 1892
Mazinthien	Italy, 1850	1878–1883	Wrecked Peterhead, 1883
Morning	Norway, 1871	1905–1914	Wrecked Orkneys, 1914
Narwhal	Dundee, 1859	1859–1884	Lost Cape Searle, 1884
Nova Zembla	Germany, 1873	1876–1901	Wrecked Dexterity Fjord, 1902
Our Queen	Liverpool, 1860	1878–1879	Nipped, Admiralty Inlet, 1879
Paradox		1907–1909	Lost in ice, 1909
Polar Star	Peterhead, 1857	1882–1899	Lost Cumberland Gulf, 1899
Polynia	Dundee, 1861	1861–1891	Lost Lancaster Sound, 1891
Princess Charlotte	Whitehaven, 1810	1820–1856	Lost Melville Bay, 1856
Queen Bess	1886	1901–1908	Sold 1913
Ravenscraig	Kirkcaldy, 1853	1866–1879	Wrecked Davis Strait, 1879
Resolute	Dundee, 1879	1880–1886	Lost off Labrador, 1886
River Tay	Kinghorn, 1868	1868	Lost Davis Strait, 1868
Rodney	1766	c.1788–1810	Lost Greenland, 1810
St Hilda	Woolston, 1875	1908–1911	Sold 1914

Ship	Built	Years	Fate
Scotia	Norway, 1872	1905–1914	Ex-*Heckla*, sold 1913
Sedusante	France, 1878	1909–1911	Lost Nottingham Island, 1911
Snowdrop	Dundee, 1855	1883–1908	Lost Labrador, 1908
Spitzbergen	Germany	1877	Lost delivery voyage, 1877
Star	1855	1883–1886	Wrecked Frobisher Strait, 1886
Success	Prior to 1788	c.1788–1792	Sold 1792
Tay (1)	Prior to 1790	c.1790–1798	Captured by privateer, 1799
Tay (2)	Prior to 1813	1813–1819	Lost Davis Straits, 1819
Tay (3)	Dundee, 1850	1858–1874	Lost Melville Bay, 1874
Terra Nova	Dundee, 1884	1884–1898	Sold Newfoundland, 1898
Thetis	Dundee, 1881	1881–1884	Sold USA, 1884
Thomas	Yorkshire, 1809	1823–1836	Lost Davis Strait, 1836
Three Brothers	Jarrow, 1811	1813–1830	Lost Melville Bay, 1830
Tilly		1915	Lost Cumberland Gulf, 1915
Triune	Sunderland, 1869	1883–1886	Lost Davis Strait, 1886
Vega	Germany, 1872	1903	Lost Melville Bay, 1903
Victor	Peterhead, 1847	1864–1881	Crushed Davis Strait, 1881
Wildfire	Quebec, 1854	1859–1868	Lost in ice, Davis Strait, 1868
Windward	Peterhead, 1860	1903–1907	Wrecked Davis Strait, 1907

Appendix 2

Glossary of Whaling Terms

BALEEN: the flexible, fringed plates in the upper jaw of a bowhead whale's mouth, used to filter out animal food as sea water is expelled with its tongue. The most valuable part of the whale and generally called 'whalebone'.

BAY ICE: 'young', newly formed ice, usually created by a fresh fall of snow in protected bays and inlets.

BESET: trapped in ice.

BLUBBER: the layer of fat beneath a whale's skin.

BOAT-STEERER: the member of crew who steered a whaleboat during the pursuit of a whale. He ranked second to the harpooner, who was in charge of the boat.

BOLLARD: a vertical wooden post at the prow of whaleboats around which the whale line was looped to produce control by friction behind a harpooned whale – a practice which occasionally led to the bollard catching fire!

BORING: forcing a ship through ice by ramming it, usually a feature of the era of steam-powered whalers.

BRAN: 'on the bran' – a term used for ships cruising in clear water on the edge of an ice field waiting for whales to appear.

CANT PURCHASE, also cant tackle and cant fall: an apparatus attached aloft to the mainmast and used to hold and rotate the whale carcass during flensing.

CLEAN: as in returning to port 'clean' – in whaling parlance a whaler that has returned with no whales. In essence, the 'dirtier' the ship from whale residue, the greater the delight of captain and crew.

CLASH: an iron stanchion fixed into a socket on the deck, standing about three feet high, with a row of iron spikes along its top. In 'making off', pieces of blubber were placed on the spikes with clash hooks, in readiness for the skin to be separated from the blubber. The men would hold the clash hook in one hand, and their sharp skinning knives in the other.

DOUBLING, or 'trebling': an expression describing the number of layers of planks applied to the exterior timber frame of a ship.

A FALL!: the most important cry on board a whaler, meaning a successful strike on a whale with a harpoon. At the sound of a 'A Fall! A Fall!' all hands would rush on deck and remaining boats would be launched to assist the 'fast' boat.

FAST BOAT: the whaleboat secured or 'fast' to a whale with a harpoon. All other boats were termed 'loose' boats. Should the line break, the whale became a 'loose' fish and could become the prize of any other ship.

FLENSING or flenching, or flinching: stripping blubber from the carcass of a whale or seal, usually the job of the harpooners while their catch was tied alongside the ship. A skilful operation using razor-sharp knives with long handles. A seal could be flinched in under one minute – a whale could take many hours.

FLOE: an extensive field of ice.

FORE-GANGER: a strong, lightweight and supple untarred rope attached to the harpoon and, at its other end, to the tarred, heavyweight whale line. From the Dutch *voorganger*, 'he who goes before another'.

FLUKES: the tail of a whale.

GAMMING: social conversation or visits involving crews from different ships beset in ice or in open water. Peterhead whale men used the term 'foy' for this.

GROG: alcoholic drink banned from personal lockers, but often distributed by the captain as a reward, and described on an 1838 voyage as 'a compound of Jamaica rum and water in the proportion of two parts of the former to one of the latter'.

HOME LETTERS: personal letters collected by the captain of a home-bound whaler from other captains and crews of the fleet, for posting on in Dundee.

ICE-BLINK: a white-tinged sky denoting the presence of ice.

JACK: or often simply 'the flag' – an ensign displayed by every whaleboat fast to a fish. Also the flags flown from the mother ship.

KRENG: the carcass of a whale allowed to sink into the sea after flensing, or any whale material discarded. 'Krenging' was the task carried out on deck after flinching, in which smaller knives were used to strip off any parts of flesh adhering to the blubber. From the Dutch word *kreng*, meaning carrion.

LEAD: a narrow channel of water between ice floes or fields, through which a whaler was able to pass.

LINE-MANAGER: a senior officer who had the important responsibility of coiling and arranging whale lines in whaleboats.

MAKING OFF: the finishing process on deck when blubber attached to a whale skin was separated for storage. According to Scoresby in 1820, making off derives from the Dutch word *afmaaken*, signifying to finish or complete.

A MOLLIE: having a night of it, a knees-up, often with a number of captains congregating together on board one ship. The Dundee equivalent of the Peterhead word 'foy'. Also the name given to an Arctic bird.

NIPPED: squeezed or crushed by moving pack ice.

OVERING: the ship's practice in ice of creating a human see-saw, with the crew running from one side of the deck to the other, to bring about a rolling movement to break up the holding ice.

PAN: a pile of newly flensed sealskins.

PAYABLE FISH: a whale whose bone was over six feet in length.

PIGGIN: a small wooden bucket carried in whaleboats and used for bailing.

POLYNIA: an area of water remaining ice-free, even in winter. Also the name of one of Dundee's successful auxiliary steam whalers.

ROCKNOSING: a term used for whaleboats cruising close to land to intercept whales, often while their ship was harboured or over-wintering.

SEA HORSE: an early whaling term for a walrus.

SKEEMAN: the senior officer in charge of operations in a ship's hold during making off.

SPANNING OUT: attaching the lines to harpoons, coiling and joining ropes, tasks carried out on outbound voyages.

SPECTIONEER: the chief of harpooners and the member of crew under whose direction the whale was cut up. The word is derived from the Dutch *spek*, meaning blubber. A senior and well-paid position.

SPURS: spikes on the soles of the boots worn by the spectioneer and harpooners during the flensing operation on a tied-up whale, to avoid the possibility of slipping off the oily surface of the fish.

STORE DAY: the day shortly after leaving port when provisions such as tea and tobacco were handed out.

TO KEEP OFF HER EYE: to approach a whale from behind, so as to be unobserved and thus safer.

TROCK, or truck: to barter, a word used by the Inuit to trade.

WATER SKY: a blue-tinged sky that whale men assumed denoted the presence of open water.

WHALEBOAT: an open boat, usually 25 feet long, usually crewed by six men, from which whales were harpooned, lanced, and towed to the whale ship. Ships would carry around six of these boats.

UMIAK, also oomiack: a large, open canoe-style boat used by Eskimos to approach whale ships.

YAK: whaler's term for Eskimos.

Sources and Select Bibliography

DUNDEE WHALING JOURNALS

Anon (Captain Davidson?), A Journal of A Voyage from Dundee towards Davis Straits On Board The Dorothy, Captian (sic) Davidson, 1834, Dundee Central Libraries.

Anon, Log of the Ketch 'Snowdrop' from St John's Newfoundland to Davis Strait, 1907, Montrose Museum.

Campbell, Mathew, Diary of a Voyage to Davis Straits aboard the 'Nova Zembla' of Dundee, 1884, *by Matthew Campbell, Surgeon*, Dundee Museum & Art Galleries.

Hilliard, R. H., Voyage to the Seal Fishing off Greenland on the SS Narwhal of Dundee in 1859, Dundee Museum & Art Galleries.

Kerr, Dr, *The Voyage of the Esquimaux* (1871), reprinted in the *Dundee Advertiser*, October 1871.

Macklin, Thomas, Notes on a Whaling Voyage to Davis Strait, in the SS Narwhal of Dundee, 1874, Dundee Museum & Art Galleries.

Markham, A. H., A Whaling Cruise to Baffin's Bay and the Gulf of Boothia, and An Account of the Rescue of the Crew of the Polaris, London, 1875.

Murray, Captain John, The voyage of the SS Active of Dundee, from Dundee to Hudson's Bay (partly the log of the ketch *Ernest Williams* which overwintered), 1903–1904, private collection.

Rae, Dr G. A., *A Summer's Whale Fishing* (SS Arctic 1871), reprinted in the *Dundee Advertiser*, August 1871.

Smith, Alexander, An Account of a Voyage to Greenland aboard the whaler 'Camperdown,' 1861, *by Alexander Smith of Dundee, chief engineer*, Dundee Central Libraries.

Walker, William, Narrative of a Voyage to the Arctic, etc, 1919, private collection.

Wanless, John, The Log of the Thomas, 1833, Dundee Museum & Art Galleries.

Wanless, John, The Journal of a voyage to Baffin Bay, ship Thomas, commanded by Alex Cook, 1834, Dundee Museum & Art Galleries.

OTHER PRIMARY SOURCES

Anon., Whaling. Manuscript lecture notes by 'KPC', dated 14.10.63 delivered to 'Dundee audience'. Private collection.

Copy Letter Books, Collector of the Board, Customs and Excise, Dundee City Archives.

Correspondence on the capture of the Eliza Swan of Montrose by the US frigate President, July 1813, Montrose Museum.

Dundee and District Jute and Flax Workers' Union, General and Executive Committee minute and letter books, Dundee City Archives.

Dundee Social Union, *The Report on Housing and Industrial Conditions in Dundee*, John Leng, Dundee, 1905.

Dundee Social Union, committee minutes, 1906–1920, Dundee City Archives.

Dundee Town Council Minutes, 1740–1760, Dundee City Archives.

The Labour Commission, *The State of the Jute Industry*, 1890.

Lennox, Dr David, Working Class Life in Dundee, for Twenty-Five Years, 1878–1903, unpublished thesis, University of St Andrews, nd, c.1905.

Minute Book of the Whaling Ship 'Intrepid' – 1865–66, University of Dundee Archives.

Receiver General of HM Customs, Edinburgh, Bounty Payment Records, 1750–1800.

Records of the of Guild Court of Dundee, 1730–1750, Dundee City Archives.

Sanger, Charles W., The Origins of the Scottish Northern Whale Fishery, unpublished PhD thesis, 1985.

Shipping Records, Burgh of Dundee (various dates), Dundee City Archives.

Tay Whale Fishing Company records (R. Kinnes & Sons Ltd), 1845–1920, University of Dundee Archives.

Yeaman, James, *The Seal and Whale Fisheries of Dundee*, Report for the Meeting of the British Association for the Advancement of Science in Dundee, September, 1867.

Newspapers and periodicals (various dates)
The Dundee Advertiser, John Leng & Co, Dundee.
The Dundee Courier, D.C. Thomson & Co Ltd, Dundee.
Dundee Directories, various publishers.
The Dundee Year Book, John Leng & Co, Dundee.
The Courier and Advertiser, D.C. Thomson & Co Ltd, Dundee.

The People's Journal (Dundee edition), John Leng/D.C. Thomson, Dundee.

The Piper o' Dundee.

The Montrose Review.

SELECT BIBLIOGRAPHY

Aldridge, Don, *The Rescue of Captain Scott*, East Linton, 1999.

Alexander, Caroline, *The Endurance, Shackleton's Legendary Antarctic Expedition*, London, 1998.

Amundsen, Roald, *The South Pole, An Account of the Norwegian Antarctic Expedition in the Fram, 1910–1912*, London, 1912.

Anon., *A Shipbuilding History, 1750–1932*, printed for Alexander Stephen & Sons Ltd.

Anon. (David Gibb), *Sufferings of the Ice-Bound Whalers; containing copious extracts from a journal taken on the spot by an officer of the Viewforth of Kirkaldy*, Edinburgh, 1836

Buchan, Alex R., *The Peterhead Whaling Trade*, The Buchan Field Club, Occasional Publication No. 1, Peterhead, 1993

Burn Murdoch, W. G., *From Edinburgh to the Antarctic, An Artist's Notes and Sketches during The Dundee Antarctic Expedition, 1892–93*, London, 1894.

Carstairs, A.M., *The Nature and Diversification of Employment in Dundee in the Twentieth Century*, in S. J. Jones (ed.), *Dundee & District*, British Association, 1968.

Chatterton, E. Keble, *Whalers and Whaling: The story of the Whaling Ships up to the Present Day*, London, 1925.

Conefrey, Mick, and Jordan, Tim, *A History of the Arctic and its Explorers*, London, 1998.

Credland, Arthur, *Whales and Whaling: The Arctic Fishery*, Shire Album Series No. 89, City of Kingston upon Hull Museums and Art Galleries, 1982.

Duncan of Jordanstone College of Art, *Whaling on the Tay, An Historical Account*, n.d., privately printed, c.1960.

Eber, Dorothy Harley, *When the Whalers Were Up North: Inuit Memories from the Eastern Arctic*, Montreal, 1989.

Elliot, Gerald, *A Whaling Experience: Salvesen in the Antarctic*, Norwich, 1998.

Gauldie, Enid (ed.), *The Dundee Textile Industry, 1790–1885*, The Scottish History Society, Edinburgh, 1969.

Gibb, David, *A Narrative of the Sufferings of the Crew of The Dee, Whilst Beset in the Ice at Davis' Straits, during the winter of 1836*, Aberdeen, 1837.

Gillies, Ross W., *Arctic Whalers, Icy Seas: Narratives of the Davis Strait Fishery*, Toronto, 1985.

Henderson, D.S., *Fishing for the Whale; a guide-catalogue to the Collection of Whaling Relics in Dundee Museum*, Dundee Museum, 1972.

Holland, Clive (ed.), *Farthest North: A History of Polar Exploration in Eye-Witness Accounts*, London, 1994.

Idiens, Dale, *Eskimos in Scotland, c.1682–1924*, in Christian Feest (ed.), *Indians and Europe: an introductory collection of essays*, Aachen Edition Herodot, Rader Verlag Forum 11, 1987.

Ingram, John, Shipping Notebooks (various), Dundee Central Libraries, University of Dundee Archives.

Jackson, Gordon, 'The Battle with the Arctic: Montrose Whaling, 1785–1839', in *The Port of Montrose, A History of its harbour, trade and shipping*, Tayport, 1993.

Jackson, Gordon, *The British Whaling Trade*, London, 1978.

Jackson, Gordon, with Kate Kinnear, *The Trade and Shipping of Dundee, 1789–1850*, Abertay Historical Society, Dundee, 1991.

Jackson, J. M. (Ed), *The City of Dundee, The Third Statistical Account of Scotland*, Arbroath, 1979.

King, J.C.H., and Lidchi, Henrietta, eds., *Imaging the Arctic*, London, 1998.

Liversage, Douglas, *The Whale Killers*, London, 1964.

Lubbock, Basil, *The Arctic Whalers*, Glasgow, 1937.

Lythe, S. G. E., 'The Dundee Whale Fishery', *Scottish Journal of Political Economy, Vol XI*, 1964, pages 158–169.

Lythe, S. G. E., *Gourlay's of Dundee, The Rise and Fall of a Shipbuilding Firm*, Abertay Historical Society Publication No. 10, 1964.

McIntosh, James, *The Life and Adventures of James McIntosh, the Legless Cyclist, with an Account of his Adventures in The Arctic Regions*, Dundee, n.d., c.1886.

Macleod, Innes ed., *To the Greeland Whaling: Alexander Trotter's Journal of the Voyage of the Enterprise in 1856* from Fraserburgh and Lerwick, Shetland, 1979.

Mielche, Hakon, *There She Blows*, London, n.d., c.1960.

Middleton, Lewis, *Whaling Recollections, 1818–1838*, privately printed, Aberdeen, 1838.

Niven, Jennifer, *The Ice Master, The Doomed 1913 Voyage of the Karluk*, London, 2000.

Pyper, James, *The History of the Whale and Seal Fisheries of the Port of Aberdeen*, reprinted in *The Scottish Naturalist*, May–June, 1929.

Robertson, R. B., *Of Whales and Men*, London, 1958.

Savours, Ann, *The Voyages of the Discovery*, London, 1992.

Scoresby, William, Junior, *An Account of the Arctic Regions, with a Description of the Northern Whale Fishery*, Edinburgh, 1820.

Shackleton, Sir Ernest, *South*, London, 1918, reprinted London, 1999.

Smith, Robert, *The Whale Hunters*, Edinburgh, 1993.

Speak, Peter, *William Speirs Bruce, Polar Explorer and Scottish Nationalist*, National Museums of Scotland, Edinburgh, 2003.

Speirs Bruce, William, *Arctic Exploration*, London, 1912.

Sutherland, Gavin, *The Whaling Years, Peterhead 1788–1893*, Centre for Scottish Studies, University of Aberdeen, 1993.

Troup, James A., *The Ice-Bound Whalers: the story of the Dee and Grenville Bay, 1836–7*, Orkney, 1987.

Index